Books by J. R. Ackerley

My Dog Tulip
My Father and Myself
We Think the World of You
Hindoo Holiday

HINDOO HOLIDAY

———————— ◇ ————————

An Indian Journal

———————— ◇ ————————

J. R. ACKERLEY

POSEIDON PRESS
NEW YORK   LONDON   TORONTO   SYDNEY
TOKYO   SINGAPORE

POSEIDON PRESS
Simon & Schuster Building
Rockefeller Center
1230 Avenue of the Americas
New York, New York 10020

1   3   5   7   9   10   8   6   4   2

Library of Congress Cataloging in Publication Data

Ackerley, J. R. (Joe Randolph), 1896–1967.
Hindoo holiday: an Indian journal/J. R. Ackerley.
p.   cm.
Reprint. Originally published: London: Chatto & Windus, 1932.
1. Ackerley, J. R. (Joe Randolph), 1896–1967—Journeys—India.
2. Authors, English—20th century—Journeys—India.   3. British-
India—History—20th century.   4. India—Social life and customs.
I. Title.
PR6001.C4Z5   1990
828'.91203—dc20
[B]   89-78113
CIP

ISBN 0-671-70705-1

To My Mother

PRINCIPAL CHARACTERS

His Highness the Maharajah Sahib of Chhokrapur

The Dewan (or Prime Minister) Sahib

Babaji Rao, The Secretary Sahib

Abdul Haq, my Tutor

Narayan, the Guest House Clerk

Sharma, his friend, valet to the Maharajah

Hashim, the Guest House waiter

Habib, my servant

PREFACE
TO THE SECOND EDITION

WHEN this journal was first offered for publication it was thought necessary to make a number of omissions. Nearly twenty years have passed since then, and the State of Chhokrapur, if indeed it ever existed, has dissolved away in the new map of India. I have therefore taken the opportunity afforded me by this new edition to restore most of the omissions and work in a little extra material.

J. R. A.

March 1952

EXPLANATION

HE wanted some one to love him—His Highness, I mean; that was his real need, I think. He alleged other reasons, of course—an English private secretary, a tutor for his son; for he wasn't really a bit like the Roman Emperors, and had to make excuses.

As a matter of fact he had a private secretary already, though an Indian one, and his son was only two years old; but no doubt he felt that the British Raj, in the person of the Political Agent who kept an eye on the State expenditure and other things, would prefer a label—any of the tidy buff labels that the official mind is trained to recognise and understand—to being told, 'I want some one to love me.' But that, I believe, was his real reason nevertheless.

He wanted a friend. He wanted understanding, and sympathy, and philosophic comfort; and he sent to England for them. This will seem strange to many people who have always understood that Wisdom dwells in the East; but he believed that it abode in the West—and perhaps I should add that he had never been there. There are, of course, quite a number of Britishers already living in India; but I don't think he ever entertained any serious expectation of finding what he wanted among them. No—the pure, unsullied fountain-head; he must go to that—and that was how it happened.

Some one who had met him there said to me: 'Why don't *you* go out to him?'

'Are there any qualifications?' I asked.

'Yes, he wants some one like a character named Olaf in *The Wanderer's Necklace* by Rider Haggard.'

So I went.

This isn't a history of India. About all that I knew of that country when I sailed for it was what I was able to recollect from my schooldays—that there had been a mutiny there, for instance, and that it looked rather like an inverted Matterhorn on the map, pink because we governed it. My knowledge, in short, was not exhaustive; it is not exhaustive now. In that muddled land, I am told—for I did not have the opportunity to travel far or much—there is no uniformity; racial, religious, and caste distinctions have severed one man from another, and language, dress, custom, and superstition vary from place to place.

This journal, then, which developed day by day out of almost complete ignorance, and for whose accuracy in fact, since I was depending solely upon my memory, I cannot therefore vouch—this journal, then, concerns itself exclusively with the small Hindoo native state of Chhokrapur (a name for which, since I have just invented it, it will be idle to explore the map)—and it does not pretend to have exhausted even that.

PART I

PART ONE

December 28th

CHHOKRAPUR has no railway station. The nearest is at Dipra thirty-five miles away, and there the Maharajah's car was awaiting me. It was manned by a very fat chauffeur and a small boy. With me was a black-bearded Mohammedan, servant to His Highness, who had met me at an earlier stage in my journey with a letter of instructions.

We drove off, passing about midway through Rajgarh, the nearest British Cantonment to Chhokrapur, and residence of the Political Agent.

A sudden turn from the main road, which seemed to skirt the town, brought us through white gates up a long red-gravel drive on to this small conical hill. The hill is flattened at the top to form a plateau, and is appended, like the full-stop in an exclamation mark, to a long rocky ridge which rises in a gradual incline to the south. There are two houses on the plateau, one big and one small, and I was set down in front of the latter. This was to be my abode for some months, so as soon as I arrived I made a tour of inspection. It did not take long. I found an oblong, one-storeyed building, with thick walls whitewashed inside and out. There were two communicating rooms, two verandahs, one in front and the other behind, and an outhouse bathroom in a corner of the back porch, from which stone steps led down to a small walled courtyard at the foot of the stony ridge. There were no windows, but five doorways, one from each room to each verandah, and one between the two rooms. The house was simply furnished. Canvas carpets, striped blue and red, covered both the floors, and across the thresholds of the open doorways long linen curtains of a rose pattern floated in the breeze. A round table and three chairs completed the sitting-room; in the other was a gigantic iron bedstead and a small table with a mirror on it. The outhouse contained a bath-tub on a wooden platform, some large earthenware water-vessels, a po, a close-stool, and a washstand. The washstand contained a little water and a drowned mouse.

When I had inspected my house I returned through the bedroom to my sitting-room and found the Mohammedan, the chauffeur, and the boy facing me in a grave semicircle behind my luggage, apparently awaiting further instructions.

I glanced at them nervously. They all salaamed with one movement and became erect again. I had already tried English on them and failed; so now I gave a 'That'll do' nod which was also without effect. Feeling quite at a loss I sat down at the table and opened my notebook to write, hoping that they would eventually fade away for lack of attention; but when I looked up again they were still there, gravely watching me, and they began at once to talk and make signals, at first separately and then together.

'Maharajah Sahib,' I said hopefully.

They nodded agreeably.

Through the open doorway I could see the other house about one hundred and fifty yards away—a massive, square, white building, on the farther side of the plateau.

'Palace Maharajah Sahib?' I asked, pointing to it.

They all nodded agreeably again. Then appeared an imposing figure, very old, with a patriarchal grey beard and a network of wrinkles on his handsome brown face. He was barefoot, and clad in airy white draperies, and a bunch of keys dangling from his waist identified him among the Apostles.

He, too, seemed to have something urgent to impart, but was also unable to speak English. After considerable cogitation, however, he produced the word 'Ticket'; I played a

4

visiting-card, and with exclamations of satisfaction St. Peter departed with it, followed by the chauffeur and the boy.

I had already noticed, in the mirror in the bedroom, that my face was spectral with dust, so I introduced the Mohammedan to the drowned mouse, and conveyed by gesture that besides some clean water I would like a cup of tea, for it was now about four o'clock. He went off on these errands, and while I was rolling up my shirt sleeves, an ancient man with bare, skinny legs and a straggling beard crept slowly and soundlessly in, carrying what looked at first like bagpipes, but turned out to be a swollen dripping goatskin of water slung under one arm. The weight of his burden bowed him down, and he did not raise his eyes to me in passing, but sketched a salaam with an unsteady, wandering hand. He looked very like a goat himself. Left to myself, I began to wonder what my first meeting with the Maharajah would be like. I had heard that he possessed a pronounced sense of the theatre, and used to send on ahead of him, to herald his approach, a naked warrior armed with a spear. Something as melodramatic, I hoped, was in store for me; but even as I speculated and slung water over my face and neck, I heard a pattering behind me, and perceived, through soapsuds, St. Peter hurriedly returning.

'Maharajah Sahib! Maharajah Sahib!' he whispered excitedly, pointing behind him to my sitting-room.

This was very upsetting. I had spent several months in corresponding and arranging this meeting with His Highness; I had travelled over six thousand miles to accomplish it; he might at least have managed better than to catch me in this state of unreadiness. He wasn't playing up.

'Ask him wait,' I said, with economy of words and effect; and hurrying into the bedroom, I had just time to dry my face and restore my collar and tie when a shadow fell across the threshold of the sitting-room, and a stout Indian of unpleasing aspect, in a black frock-coat, entered and drew aside the curtains for His Highness to pass.

I had been given a detailed description of the Maharajah,

but found myself unprepared nevertheless for the curious figure which now hobbled into the room. His face with its bridgeless nose, sunken lips, prominent chin and protuberant brown eyes, over which a faint bluish film had formed, bore a strong resemblance to a pekingese dog; halfway down the collapsed bridge of his nose, from the centre of his forehead, trickled some spots of yellow paint; a diamond shone in the lobe of each ear, and from beneath the front of his little round hat, which was made of green velvet

and gold brocade, a wisp of dark grey hair upcurled. He was small and very slight, and his stiff-jointed body was neatly sheathed in a long-skirted coat of violet and grey tweed with a high military collar of grey velveteen and cuffs of the same material; his trousers were of white cotton, wrinkling tightly down the lower half of his leg, but expanding above the knee; his socks were bright purple, and upon his long thin feet he wore a pair of patent-leather dancing-pumps. I took in these details slowly.

'His Highness the Maharajah Sahib!' announced the stout person pompously.

Carrying my coat with me, I hastened forward and shook

hands, apologising for my condition; but he took no notice of this.

'But you are so early!' he said. 'I did not expect you for another hour, for I intended to come part of the way to meet you; but just as I was thinking of starting they brought me your card!'

He seemed quite vexed about it, and, turning to his companion, uttered some brief remarks in Hindi which caused the other to pass a nervous hand over his jaw and mouth; but immediately he returned to me with—

'Welcome to India!'

—and introduced his companion as Mr. Babaji Rao, his private secretary.

I placed a chair for him, and, leaning on his stick, he hobbled round the table and sat down.

'Have you had your tea?' he asked. I said I had ordered it, and he told his Secretary to hurry it up; but at that moment it arrived, borne by a tall, handsome waiter in a long, blue uniform coat with a sash round his waist.

He shuffled off his shoes outside the door, and entered with bare feet.

'Won't you join me?' I asked His Highness, for there was only one cup; 'or have you had your tea already?'

This amused them both, and the Maharajah explained that, although it was all very silly and nothing to do with him, Hindoos were not permitted to eat with Europeans. I apologised for my blunder; but he waved it aside with a small jewelled hand, saying that, as a matter of fact, he didn't conform strictly to the rule, and sometimes took a cup of tea with his guests, but that he didn't feel inclined for one just now.

'Now take your tea,' he said, 'and I will keep my questions for when you have finished.'

So, rather self-consciously, I chewed leathery buttered toast, while they sat and watched me and exchanged remarks in Hindi—His Highness smoking a cigarette with a purple tip; Babaji Rao with his legs wide apart, his elbows out, and his hands planted firmly upon his knees. He was not much better to look at than his master, I thought. Smallpox had ravaged his face; a ragged moustache drooped untidily over his big, loose mouth, and behind large spectacles his small brown eyes seemed evasive and sly. His costume was much the same as the Maharajah's, but dingy and of coarse material; he wore neither socks nor collar, and a brass stud shone beneath his unshaven chin. When he took off his round black hat I saw that the top of his head was bald, and that the thick untidy fringe round the sides and back was turning grey.

His Highness did not manage however to keep all his questions for when I had finished.

'How do you say your name?' he asked.

I told him, and he repeated it after me until he got it right, and then glanced at his secretary as much as to say, 'Remember that.'

'Do you like this?' He indicated the walls. 'Is it comfortable? If there is anything you want you must tell Babaji Rao. I thought you would like to stay here instead of in the Guest House with my other guests.'

'Is that the Guest House?' I asked, looking at the square building outside. 'I thought it was your Palace.'

'No, no, no,' he said, subsiding into wheezy laughter, and I was astonished to see that his tongue was bright orange— almost the colour of nasturtium.

I put the last piece of toast into my mouth, and no sooner had I done so than he asked—

'Have you finished your tea?'

—and called the waiter to clear it away before I could manoeuvre the toast into a position that would enable me to reply.

Then began a very bewildering examination of my history. It jumped from one thing to another without pause, and was too long and confusing to reproduce.

How old was I? So old? He had been under the impression

that I was only twenty-two. Did I come from London? Of whom did my family consist? Could I speak Latin and Greek? Did I know Rider Haggard? Had I read his books? Was I religious? Did I believe that the tragedy of Jesus Christ was the greatest tragedy that had ever happened? Was I a pragmatist? Had I read Hall Caine? Had I read Darwin, Huxley, and Marie Corelli? . . .

His Highness seemed very disappointed. I didn't know what 'Pragmatism' meant, and had read practically none of the authors he named. I must read them at once, he said, for they were all very good authors indeed, and he wished me to explain them to him. He had them all in his library in the Palace; I must gett hem out and read them. He was practically toothless, I noticed, and his brown lips sank in and blew out tremulously as he mumbled his questions.

'Have you read Spencer's *First Principles*, and *Problems of Life and Mind* by Lewes?' he asked.

'No, Maharajah Sahib, I'm afraid I haven't.'

His face took on a very grave expression.

'But you must do so. It is very important. You must do so at once. It is the first thing I wish you to do.'

'Very well, Maharajah Sahib.'

'Babaji Rao will give them to you. You must give them to him to-night, Babaji Rao. Lewes refutes Spencer. Spencer says . . . What does he say, Babaji Rao? Explain it.'

The Secretary cleared his throat, and passed a nervous hand over his bald head.

'Spencer says that there is a reality behind appearances, and Lewes . . .'

'Is there a God or is there no God?' rapped out His Highness impatiently. 'That is the question. That is what I want to know. Spencer says there *is* a God, Lewes says no. So you must read them, Mr. Ackerley, and tell me which of them is right.'

He got up to go. I felt I had not made at all a good impression and that he was disappointed in me. Before leaving he asked me about the expenses I had incurred during my journey, and told me to give an account of them to the Secretary, for he wished to refund them at once.

When he reached the doorway he turned:

'At last we are face to face!' he said, and then shuffled out, very stiffly, on splayed feet, to his car.

December 29th

THE 'other guests'—who are living in the large Guest House—are five persons and two dogs. The five persons are Captain Montgomery, I.M.S., and his wife; Major Pomby of the Gunners; a naval Commander on leave from his ship in the Persian Gulf, and Miss Gibbins. All of them, with the exception of the Commander, are from Shikaripur, the chief military station in the Province. The two dogs are Titus and Lulu.

They were all just returning from a jackal-hunt yesterday evening when Babaji Rao took me over; I felt I did not like any of them very much—though the men seemed kinder and were certainly quieter than the women—and I rather resented their presence here.

Perhaps they resented mine; at any rate after giving me the most perfunctory welcome, they paid practically no further attention to me, and by the time we were all dressed and sitting down to dinner I felt quite excluded from their society. I sat stolidly among them and took in my surroundings—the spacious and enormously high rooms of the Guest House, furnished with carpets, rugs, easy-chairs, and pictures of Queen Mary and the Prince of Wales. The conversation, which was chiefly between the two women, who talked very loudly in an easy, smart manner, was frequently amusing; but they employed so many Anglo-Indian words that I found it rather difficult to follow.

'I suppose you think we're all crazy?' Mrs. Montgomery asked.

'A little incomprehensible,' I said.

An incident had occurred while they were out riding, and Mrs. Montgomery related it with indignation.

PART ONE

'Vera (Miss Gibbins) had to dismount to pick up a glove she'd dropped, and had difficulty in mounting again. There was a cultivator standing close by, doing absolutely nothing to help—just looking on—so I called out, "Boy! Come and hold this lady's horse!" And what d'you think he said? "I'm not your slave, miss." Would you believe it? Dirty brute! "Come here at once and do what you're told!" I shouted. "Then I come," he said, as impudent as you please. But Vera was trembling with rage by that time, and wouldn't let him touch her horse. I never heard such damned cheek!'

The two dogs wandered round the table begging, and the Commander said that when he and Miss Gibbins had gone for a walk before breakfast she had hit a pie-dog with a stone.

'Yes, wasn't it awful?' cried Miss Gibbins. 'And I never do hit anything. I picked up a stone, and with unerring precision hit the wretched animal in the stomach. I *was* surprised!'

Mrs. Montgomery laughed.

'And I remember throwing a stone at a septic little boy,' she said, 'and it hit a Tommy instead—a huge rock struck him on the chest! And all he said was "That's all right, miss. Don't you take on!" '

'Titus and Lulu had a fight in my bedroom this morning,' remarked Miss Gibbins. 'It was Lulu's fault. She gave Titus such an ugly look and made a grab at him as I hauled him rapidly on to the bed, and if he hadn't been an expert in giving corkscrew twists to his idiot tail he would never have evaded her clutches! Then I gave Lulu a good swift kick through the door, and she rose about six feet in the air, and disappeared in a cloud of dust and small stones.'

This caused general amusement.

'Do you remember Maggie?' she asked Mrs. Montgomery. 'She was a toy dog about this size—ever so small. We called her "The Dustbin Queen." She used to get into enormously high dustbins—Heaven knows how she did it—and gorge on garbage until her brain was inflamed with meat. Once she stayed in a dustbin for forty-eight hours.'

I found this kind of conversation so remarkable that I began to note it down on the backs of envelopes under cover of the table.

Babaji Rao took me and the two women down to see the Dewan's garden this morning. It is on the outskirts of the town and is called the garden of Dilkhusha or Heart's Ease. The Dewan, or Prime Minister, himself accompanied us. He is an enormously fat man, with small well-shaped hands, with which he frequently gesticulated. He was very voluble and excitable, and his voice, which even normally was surprisingly high for his age and bulk, rose often to a shrill cry. His features, too, were strangely small and refined in the midst of his heavy cheeks and jowls, and his colour was much paler than Babaji Rao's or the Maharajah's. It was a large and pretty garden, and he showed us a fine banyan tree, which, he said, lives for ever, each branch thrusting down a new root into the earth. Before we left, his gardener brought garlands of jasmine and marigold which the Dewan hung round our necks.

We all drove to Mahua this afternoon, a village about ten miles away, where the Maharajah has another palace. It is empty, and is never used by His Highness, I am told, except to entertain his guests to tea; but it is much more beautiful in itself and in its setting than the rather dingy stuccoed palace he inhabits here. The garden was luxuriant, but carefully kept, and monkeys could be seen hopping about on the walls, behind the purple shrubs and the heavy foliage of banana-trees, or peering anxiously round the ornamentation of the roof. Passing through the courtyard where a guard was stationed, and mounting a long flight of stone steps, we reached, through a narrow walled passage, a beautiful arcaded upper court of red gravel; on to it the reception room opened in its whole length front of us, its roof supported on slender columns. It was gaily carpeted, and a long table was already spread with tea, cakes, sweets, and fruit. We passed through this room on to the quayside of a lovely reservoir, a great clear lake stretching away for half a mile or more, and locked by rocky hills with wooded slopes. There were two ancient royal tombs among the trees upon the farther borders of the lake. Just in front of us on the quayside, where the water was rimmed with steps and two dinghies lay moored, a carpet had been spread and set with chairs and a table; and there sat His Highness in the shade of a *peepal* tree.

After we had had tea, the women, the Commander, and Major Pomby went out in one of the dinghies, which had been fitted with an engine; and Captain Montgomery and I were left with His Highness. We discussed books in a desultory fashion—Sir Philip Gibbs, Hall Caine, Meredith, Marie Corelli; and His Highness said he was very anxious that I should read *The Eternal City*, but it was unaccountably missing from the library, and Babaji Rao, who was searching everywhere for it, had not yet found it.

He then took us up on to the roof of the Palace, where we had a view of some very beautiful ruined temples, two hundred years old, which his grandfather had destroyed.

'Why are ruins beautiful?' he asked. 'And what is beauty? Is it the cloak of God?'

Hindoos believe in one impersonal God, Brăhma, the Universal Spirit or Energy, pervading, constituting everything. Like the banyan tree in the Dewan's garden, it is forever evolving itself out of itself. Brăhma is neuter; but it has developed a triple personality, three masculine deities called Brāhma, the Creator; Vishnu, the Preserver; and Siva, the Dissolver and Reproducer. These three principal personalities are sometimes considered as co-equal and their functions interchangeable; they are constantly manifested and finally reabsorbed into the one eternal, impersonal Essence, Brăhma.

December 30th

ANOTHER jackal-hunt was arranged this morning, and Mrs. Montgomery asked me if I would like to join. I said that although I had done a little riding and had always, so far, managed to stay on my horse, I had never hunted in my life and was afraid I might be a nuisance to the party; but she said it was not really a hunt, but only a way of passing the time and exercising themselves and Titus. She is reputed to be a very good horsewoman, the best in Shikaripur.

Hitherto I had not liked her; her rather small eyes behind her pince-nez had seemed severe and hard; but now she was making herself agreeable to me, and looked more kind and attractive. I accepted. The Commander was not riding with us, and Miss Gibbins borrowed his hat to wear. It didn't fit.

'I detest your septic hat,' she remarked. 'It wobbles up and down on my idiot bun.'

But she kept it nevertheless. The words 'idiot' and 'septic' are used very frequently in this sense as terms of disparagement by both the women. Also the word 'lethal.' All Indians, it seems, are either 'lethal' or 'septic.'

While we rode, Mrs. Montgomery drew me back and said:

'You know you gave us all a bit of a shock here at the first kick-off. You didn't introduce yourself. That isn't done in India. You ought to have labelled yourself at once—we all have labels out here, so that we know where we are, so to speak; so you should have told us all about yourself at once —where you come from, your parents, school, 'varsity, profession, business, and so on. But you didn't. You just sat still and left us guessing, and that creates a bad impression. Luckily for you, we're rather different; we're jolly, un-conventional sorts; but if you don't label yourself at once to the people round here, the Rajgarh ladies, for instance— especially the old ones—won't know you after the first five minutes.'

PART ONE

'I'm sorry,' I said, 'I didn't know.'

'I thought you didn't; and *we* don't mind so much, you understand, but I thought I'd better warn you so that you'll know what's expected of you in future.'

'Did you want a kind of recitation?' I asked.

'No, of course not. But at the least opportunity you should have produced information about yourself.'

'I was really quite willing, you know,' I said, 'only there didn't seem to *be* the least opportunity.'

'Of course there was. You see, when we asked you one thing about yourself it meant that we wanted to hear all. It isn't inquisitiveness exactly; you needn't think that; but considering our position in this country it's just necessary that we should know and have confidence in each other. We have to stick together. How do you suppose we'd get on if every one was like you?'

'But I think you all knew all about me before I arrived,' I said slyly.

'That's quite true,' she replied, 'but it doesn't excuse you.' We rode on for a little in silence.

'Now tell me about yourself,' she said.

I walked through the city this morning.

'What on earth do you want to do that for?' asked Mrs. Montgomery, as I set out. 'You're sure to catch something —if it's only a flea.'

But I wanted to see the place. Chhokrapur was once a walled city; it has long since spread outside its walls, but parts of these and some of the old gateways are still standing. I entered through the main gateway, by the caravanserai, which lies on the Rajgarh road at the foot of the Guest House hill, and found myself in a wide, straight street. It was in good repair but very dusty, and bordered by crude dwellings of mud or whitewashed brick, all raised on low brick platforms which formed a kind of wide step in front on which the inhabitants might squat in the shade of the eaves. There were a number of people about, and before I had gone very far I began to feel timid. Curiosity had brought me out; but I now found *myself* an object of curiosity, and this embarrassed me. Every one stared at me; people who were squatting on their heels in front of their houses rose up, salaamed, called others out and stood staring; groups of men interrupted their conversation to watch me pass; children followed me, and women concealed their faces, no matter how old and ugly they might be, in the long red cloths in which they were draped. I felt intrusive and self-conscious in my English clothes, and omitted to return salutes in case the saluters should be encouraged to speak to me and I should not understand what they said.

I turned down another street which crossed at right angles, hoping for less frequented ways, but this led into a kind of bazaar and was more crowded still. Salaams came from all sides; a brass vendor called to me from his stall; goats, fowls, and an occasional cow wandered at large. I hurried along in a panic, trying to appear as though I knew where I was going and had but little time to spare, and soon got lost. The streets became narrower and narrower as I turned and turned, until I felt I was back in the trenches, the houses upon either side being so much of the same colour and substance as the rough ground between.

Eventually I came out by a lake which I remembered having passed on the way to the Garden of Dilkhusha, and so found my way back.

We all drove to Garha after lunch. It is about thirty-five miles distant, and is the home of the Maharani, the Queen.

Once, about a thousand years ago, said Babaji Rao, it was a large city, the capital of the province, and contained about forty great temples, of which a small group of seven still remain and are famous all over India.

We went in two cars: Babaji Rao and the two women in the first, Major Pomby, the Commander, and myself in the second. On the way Major Pomby warned us that one of the temples—and he described its exact position in the

16

group—had some highly indecent sculptures on its walls. We must therefore keep clear of it, he said, in case the ladies followed us. He also told us not to try to enter any of the temples, for this was not permitted.

Garha Palace, the back of which was the first thing we saw, had little of the beauty of the Mahua Palace, but again was pleasanter than the Palace at Chhokrapur. It also stood on the edge of an artificial lake. Beyond it was another imposing white building, whose cupola and *chhatris* appeared over a high surrounding wall. I supposed it to be yet another palace; but Babaji Rao smiled and said it was the tomb of His Highness's grandfather. I peeped in and saw a pretty bush with pink flowers growing at the entrance to the tomb. The temples were facing this, standing against the trees on the far edge of the great clearing which fronted the Palace. They were all close together, and rose from high stone platforms reached by wide flights of steps. Very beautiful they were, like huge grey plants, ribbed and groined, springing up from their wide bases and evolving out of themselves. Built without mortar, they had a loose, self-developed appearance; one felt that if one pressed them down from the top they would collapse and close up into something like an artichoke. Every inch of them, it seemed, was carved and sculptured with countless figures of gods and men. These were of all sizes, and extraordinarily beautiful in their separate form and detail and in their harmony with the general plan. They were Jain temples, Babaji Rao said, dedicated to Siva, the Dissolver and Reproducer, and we might enter them so long as we removed our shoes. I did so; but the two women did not want to spoil their stockings, and remained outside in the charge of Major Pomby and the Commander. Perhaps this was as well, since one of the temples enshrined a gigantic black stone *lingam* which, incidentally, was alleged to contain in its midst a rare and priceless jewel. There was so much sculpture that I should certainly have missed the indecencies if Major Pomby had not been considerate enough to mention them; as it was, it took me a long time to locate them, but I found them at last, a long file of soldiers marching gaily along, and another smaller, more elaborate, design which was frequently repeated. They were both sodomitic.

The village of Garha we did not see; it lies behind His Highness's grandfather's tomb, and consists now, Babaji Rao said, of only about two hundred houses.

I told His Highness that I had mistaken the tomb of his grandfather for a palace.

'He was poisoned,' he remarked.

'Indeed?' I said. 'How did that happen?'

'My great-grandmother. They quarrelled, and she poisoned him.'

He added that a king could never trust his relatives, they were always scheming and giving trouble of some sort; in fact, he said gravely, he had just received a report that some of his own kinsmen were plotting together in a neighbouring State to destroy his son by Black Magic.

Mrs. Montgomery gave me some advice this evening after dinner. Fixing me with her lorgnettes as we sat alone together over the dining-room fire, she said:

'Look here, young man, I'll give you a word of advice. Keep clear of Indian women! Do you understand me? Don't look at them! Don't notice them! They don't exist!'

December 31st

THIS morning His Highness took me out for a drive in one of his cars. He knows no more about cars than I do, and chooses them by the appeal of their names. So he bought a 'Sunbeam.' It would surely be a very pretty car; but it seemed much the same as any other, and he was equally disappointed by a 'Moon.' He asked me to-day what his next car should be, for two of the four he already has are getting very old, and I suggested a 'Buick,' which was the only make I could call to mind; but after pronouncing the word two or three times with evident disfavour, and making it sound like a sneeze, he did not refer to the matter again. He was wearing a purple overcoat, of European cut, lined with pink; the yellow spots down the collapsed bridge of his nose had been renewed; he had not shaved. A travelling-rug was draped about his knees, and over the top of his green and gold bonnet and beneath his chin a bright red woollen muffler was bound.

It is the last day of the old year, and he said he was extremely anxious to see a mongoose, for a mongoose is a very good omen; so we passed slowly along the Deori road about in search of one, while he fired rapid questions at me my circumstances, nodding briefly at my answers but never taking his eyes off the landscape.

How many members were there of my family? Was I the only son? Did I have to support the family? Oh, not while my father lived? And what was my father's business? And his income? And was he old? How old? Was he strong? Did he move, like His Highness himself, stiffly, with diffi-culty? And so on, to the object of them all—Would I stay with him and be tutor to his son (now aged two) when he should be old enough to need one, and be also his private secretary, and even, later on, his Prime Minister? Would I stay with him for—sixteen years? I said I didn't know if I would, postponing a definite refusal by saying I could hardly be expected yet to know my own mind. Meanwhile, no mongoose having been observed, he had ordered the chauffeur to turn the car off the road, and we were now rocking and bumping over the open country among stones and bushes; but the only life I could see were large black-faced monkeys scampering off with their babies clinging to their stomachs.

'Look!' I said, pointing suddenly. ' What's that?'

'Where? Where?' he cried, following my direction anxiously.

Then he leaned back abruptly in the car, and turned his face away.

'A jackal; a very bad omen,' he said gloomily, and then began to shake with laughter.

'Am I very silly?' he asked, with pathetic charm.

'I should like to see a mongoose myself,' I replied.

After this he began to talk of Political Agents in general, and the local one, Major Jenkins, in particular. He was a nice man, he said, no doubt of that, but he had two sides to his nature—he was weak, and overpowered by wanton and wicked men.

'I want to pursue a good policy, but how am I to pursue a good policy when I am overpowered by wanton and wicked men?'

I had no idea to whom he was alluding, but ventured to suggest that Political Agents were not so powerful as he seemed to think.

'Aren't they merely advisers to you?' I asked.

'But, my dear sir,' he retorted, 'what sort of advice is that when I am obliged to take it?'

He spoke then of some previous Agent he had known.

'He was a most . . . cantankerous . . . what is that?'

'Ill-tempered, quarrelsome.'

'Yes, a most cantankerous man.'

But he did not find me very interesting on this subject. All I know about Political Agents is that they are usually unpopular with the rulers of the native States, and that there was trouble between His Highness and Major Jenkins over my engagement. For I am receiving a salary as well as my return fare, and I dare say the P.A. considered me a quite unnecessary extravagance, which—no doubt—I am. Mrs. Montgomery gave me some information about all this. Major Jenkins, she said, had not been at all disposed to receive me favourably.

'But I saw him the other day in Rajgarh,' she said, 'and told him you were quite harmless; so it'll be all right now.' She added that he was 'a horrid man and a fool.'

His Highness turned to the subject of literature. Had I ever read a book called . . . some Latin title . . . '*Quo . . . quo . . .*'

'*Quo Vadis?*' I guessed.

'Yes, you are right, you are right.' He was very pleased. 'How do you say it?'

'*Quo Vadis?*'

'You have read it?'

'Yes,' I said. This was a lie; but I felt he must be thinking me a very ill-educated young man considering the number of well-known books I had already confessed to not having read; and I also thought I knew enough about *Quo Vadis?* to be able to support my lie.

'It is about Nero,' observed His Highness, as though to make sure.

'I know,' I said.

'A very good book! A very good book! What did it mean about Nero marrying Pythagoras in public?'

'I think you've got that wrong,' I said.

'No, no; I have not got it wrong. It says so.'

'Well,' I replied, after some consideration, 'it may mean either that Nero, as a patron, gave Pythagoras in marriage to some young lady; or that he publicly embraced Pythagorean philosophy.'

'But, my good sir,' said His Highness, 'this was not *that* Pythagoras; this was another Pythagoras, a boy.'

'Oh,' I said hastily. 'Well, in that case perhaps it means exactly what it says.'

His Highness simpered into his sleeve.

'Nero was a pupil of Seneca's,' he remarked later. 'Why didn't Seneca overpower him? Was he too strong for him?'

'I expect so,' I said feebly.

'I want to be like the Roman Emperors,' he mumbled; and then asked: 'Do you believe in kings, or are you . . . Bol . . . Bol . . . Bolshevist?'

'I'm Bolshevist,' I replied.

He began to shake with laughter.

'I had a friend,' he spluttered, 'who used to say, "Kings! Tcha! Chop off their heads! Chop off their heads!"'

We had returned to the road again, and the scenery was becoming very beautiful.

'Why aren't you satisfied with this lovely State?' I asked.

'But, my dear sir, this is not *my* State! This is the Maharajah of Deori's State. We have come out of Chhokrapur.'

'What is he like—the Maharajah of Deori?'

His Highness waved a small dark hand.

'I do not know. We are not at . . . speaking terms.'

'Well, he's got a beautiful State,' I said.

'Very beautiful,' agreed His Highness irritably. 'I should like to *grab* it—like the Roman Emperors.'

We didn't see a mongoose.

Talking of snakes, Mrs. Montgomery told me that once she nearly trod upon a krait—one of the most venomous snakes in India. She had been very ill at the time, suffering from acute facial neuralgia, 'so that I didn't care if I trod on fifty kraits. I was quite stupid with pain, and was going back in the evening to my bungalow, preceded by a servant who was carrying a lamp. Suddenly he stopped and said "Krait, Mem-sahib!"—but I was far too ill to notice what he was saying, and went straight on, and the krait was lying right in the middle of the path! Then the servant did a thing absolutely without precedent in India—he touched me!—he put his hand on my shoulder and pulled me back. My shoe came off and I stopped. Of course if he hadn't done that I should undoubtedly have been killed; but I didn't like it all the same, and got rid of him soon after.'

Babaji Rao, the Secretary, took me into Rajgarh this afternoon, so that I might leave cards at the British Cantonment.

The Cantonment presents a neat, orderly, well-disciplined appearance with its trim hedges and gardens, its bungalows and gravelled roads. Every bungalow had a little box inscribed 'Not at home' outside its front gates, for in British India no one is ever at home to a first caller. One drops cards into the little boxes, and awaits the results of investigation. My cards were printed in Italy, and are not therefore, I thought to myself as I popped them in, in very good taste.

On the way back I asked Babaji Rao why Hindoos allow a lock of hair at the top of their heads to grow longer than the rest. He himself has a grey wisp about six inches long; the Dewan has a short stump of hair like a little tail, and a young man who has some work up here connected with the Guest House has a beautiful thick black tress, quite a foot long, which I saw him one day twist skilfully into a 'bun' as he sat under the tree by the cook-house. But the Dewan's tail is particularly striking because the rest of his hair has been cropped close to the skin.

Babaji Rao informed me that, with the Sacred Thread worn round the neck, this tail of hair is the chief distinguishing mark of the Hindoo. It was the custom, he said, to grow it much longer; but European influence and education tended to curtail it.

But he could not tell me what it meant.

An armed guard is now posted on my verandah at night as well as on the Guest House steps. When I return from dinner I find them there—three or four dim shapes huddled together round a brazier on the concrete floor of my front loggia. Their rifles are stacked beside them. I do not know what they are intended to be guarding me from—unless from sleep, for they never stop chattering until midnight, and begin again at six in the morning. And even when they sleep they are not quiet, but moan and cry out in their dreams.

January 1st

THE other guests left this morning, and just before starting Mrs. Montgomery gave me final advice.

'You'll never understand the dark and tortuous minds of

the natives,' she said ; 'and if you do I shan't like you—
you won't be healthy.'

His Highness and I went out again to-day in search of a
mongoose. He asked the support of my arm down the Guest
House steps to the car, stopping for a moment to say:

'Now you shall decide for me, Mr. Ackerley, for I *must*
see a mongoose to-day. I *must* see one. So shall we drive
north, south, east, or west?'

'West,' I said, after pondering the question deeply.

When we were seated I asked him about omens, and he
told me it was a good omen to see black buck, foxes or
chinkara (deer) so long as they were on the right-hand
side; if they were on the left-hand side it was a bad omen.
But it didn't matter on which side one saw one's mongoose.
There was also, he said, a blue bird, but it was very, very
rare; indeed he himself had only seen it once and did not
know its name, and had been unable to discover any other
person who had ever seen it at all.

'Like a robin-redbreast,' said he, 'only blue.'

'Not a blue jay?' I queried.

'No, no, no,' he laughed, moving his hand protestingly;
'I know the blue jay. It is a tiresome bird.'

'And this blue bird of yours is a good omen?'

'A *very* good omen! A *very* good omen!' he answered
gravely. 'But on the left side.'

For some time we drove along in silence, and I watched
the people on the road bowing low as the car passed, and
making the gesture of scattering dust on their heads; then
I studied the two men sitting in front of us, who always
accompanied His Highness on his drives.

One was the chauffeur, a small man of about thirty-five,
with good features and small well-shaped hands, very neat
in his brown round hat and jacket. I had once commented
favourably on his appearance to the King, but had been
met with the subtle argument of lowered eyelids and a faint
smile, followed by the whisper:

PART ONE

'He is a wolf.'

The other was a much older man, who, like the storeroom
keeper, St. Peter, always reminded me of pictures, dimly
remembered from childhood, of the prophets of the Old
Testament. When first I saw him I thought that he should
have been the King, for, with his thick black-and-grey
curling beard and fine, noble features, surmounted by his
big white turban, he was a very majestic figure indeed;
but as a matter of fact he was His Highness's first cousin,
and his only duty in life, so far as my observation went, was
to hold the King's silver cigarette case and box of matches
and produce them when required. They very frequently
were required; His Highness smoked incessantly, large dry
Turkish cigarettes, and coughed a good deal over them,
and wasn't good at lighting matches.

According to him, this cousin was very vain, and once,
when I remarked on the beauty of his beard, His Highness
had said: 'Tell him! Tell him! He will be very pleased. He
thinks of nothing else,' and had then dissolved into wheezy
laughter. Also, like the chauffeur, he was 'no good,' he was
not to be trusted and was only employed so as to keep him
out of mischief. Whether this was true I do not know; his
appearance was that of a very benevolent old gentleman,
but I was never under the necessity of putting my trust in it.

'Is there an·Absolute?' asked His Highness suddenly.
'That is what I want you to tell me. I look upon you as a
kind of *weezard*; you must tell me these things. Is there an
Absolute? Is there a God? Is there a future life?'

'Well,' I said, 'you know the prayer of one of the Cato
Street conspirators before his head was chopped off?'

'No,' said His Highness, looking at me with great expec-
tancy. 'What was the prayer?'

'He said, "O God—if there is a God—save my soul—if I
have a soul." '

I smiled, and he hid his face in his sleeve and his small
body shook with laughter; then looking up at me again, he
said: 'What did he mean?'

25

I explained.

'You are right,' he said, with a gesture of despair, gazing gloomily out of the window; 'it is unknowable. But do you say it is hidden from us on purpose? Do you think we are meant *not* to know it?'

'But that's the same question all over again,' I said, feeling very sorry for the little man. 'Why don't you just believe what seems most agreeable to you, Maharajah Sahib? Why don't you pick the nicest God you know—Krishna, for example, if you don't get on with Christ—and then give up all further philosophic readings?'

It was at this moment that we came across some deer.

The chauffeur saw them first and nudged the old gentleman, who became very excited, waving his arms and calling to the King. Unhappily the deer were on the left-hand side of the road. His Highness plunged forward.

'Turn the car! Turn the car!' he cried, and the car was whisked round with such speed that he was thrown against me and his hat slid over his nose. But the fleeing deer were now safely on the right.

'So!' breathed His Highness, leaning back again with obvious satisfaction. Then he gave me a quizzical, sidelong glance from beneath lowered lids.

'Now if you can do that with your omens,' I said, 'why in the world can't you do the same thing with your faith—take the most comforting belief and keep it always on your right-hand side, even if it means turning round and round to do so?'

He was most pleased with this, and clapped his hands together. 'Oh, that is very good! That is very good!' he cried, and then remained silent for some time during which I thought he was considering it; but apparently this was not so.

'What is the difference between lust, passion, and love?' he suddenly asked.

I tried to think.

'I asked Major Pomby that,' he resumed, 'and he said to me, "Maharajah! you are a very bad man!" Am I a very bad man to ask such a question?'

'What nonsense!' I said. 'Major Pomby is a very bad man to have said so.'

This encouraged him, and he reached the subject of friendship as understood by the classic Greeks, and spoke of a book he had in his library which contained some beautiful photographs of Greek and Roman statuary. But now, he said, young men were never wholly beautiful. Some had beautiful faces, but ugly bodies; some beautiful faces and bodies, but ugly hands or feet; some were physically completely beautiful, but these were stupid—and spiritual beauty alone was not enough.

'There must be beautiful form to excite my cupidity,' he said.

'Your what, Maharajah Sahib?'

'Cupidity. What does it mean?'

'Lust.'

'But you have Cupid, the God of Love?'

This floored me; and while I was considering Latin derivations, he continued:

'Now, take Mr. Lowes Dickinson. I like him very much; very, very much, and honour and respect his wisdom and goodness . . . but he does not excite my cupidity. Goodness, wisdom, and beauty—that is what the Greeks worshipped, and that is what I want . . . a good, wise, and beautiful friend.'

'Well,' I said, 'if I come back here to remain with you we will join in cultivating beauty in Chhokrapur; we'll wed beauty to beauty and beget beauty. In fact, we'll turn your realm between us into a classic Greek state.'

He clapped his hands.

'You are quite right! You are quite right!' he said enthusiastically. 'Now I love you.'

The huge Guest House is now empty and the waiter Hashim has only me to look after. He is a queer, inscrutable man, a Mohammedan, rather handsome in his blue-and-white turban and his long close-fitting blue uniform coat.

But he seems vaguely hostile. At any rate he doesn't respond to friendliness; his broad face reflects nothing, and his steady, expressionless eyes discourage me. He is a little alarming too. Although he produces nothing more than an occasional low mutter when I attempt to convey my wishes to him, I often feel that he really understands English quite well; and since he walks with bare feet I can't hear him move about, and am frequently startled to find him beside me or close behind my chair.

January 2nd

DURING our drive to-day His Highness returned to the subject of the ancient Greeks.

'Would you call me an imaginary man?' he asked.

I said I thought it suited him very well.

'There was an English lady staying with me once,' he continued, 'who said to me, "Maharajah, you soar like a skylark and then fall on the ground." '

He was overcome with merriment, and hid his face in his sleeve. 'What did she mean?' he asked, when he had recovered himself.

'She meant,' I said, 'that although they sometimes came down to earth, your thoughts are usually on higher things.'

'Yes, yes; that I am an imaginary and not a practical man?'

'Quite so, Maharajah Sahib.'

'You know, Mr. Ackerley, I like the old times. I like the Greeks and Romans. I think of them always, always. I would like to have all my people dressed like Greeks and Romans. In my Palace I keep a Greek toga, and when my friends in England used to come to stay with me and talk about those times, I would put on my toga and recline on my couch like this.' He laid the palm of one hand against his cheek, setting the other on his hip, and sank sideways into the corner of the car, which pushed his hat rather tipsily to one side. 'And my friends would clap their hands

and say "The Greeks have been born again in Chhokrapur." '
He sat up. 'Ah, I like those old times. And Charles the First
and all the Stuarts. I like them very much.'

'Why Charles the First?' I asked, very bewildered.

'I find many things in him like myself. And the Tsar.
Don't they say "Like likes like"?'

Some monkeys fled into the bushes before the car's
approach, and their antics were so absurd that I burst out
laughing.

'They are disgraced monkeys,' remarked His Highness
contemptuously; 'for when the God Rama went to fight
against Ravana he was helped by monkeys . . . all the monkeys . . . every kind. But these monkeys fled away from the
battle . . . they were all white then; but they were cursed
because they fled away, and their faces turned black; so we
call them disgraced monkeys.'

We were now about a mile from Chhokrapur, returning
along the Deori road, and I was noticing with interest a
hill in the near distance which, although I had not seen it
before from this angle, I suddenly recognised as being the
southern end and highest point of the stony ridge on the
other end of which, about half a mile away, stood the Guest
House. Covering now the remainder of the ridge, it received,
from its apparent isolation, a prominent and single character,
like the near man in a passing line of soldiers; and I noticed
that it carried on its summit a small, ruined, cairn-like
shrine.

'That's a pleasant little hill,' I said, pointing to it.

'It is a very bad hill,' retorted the King flatly, turning
away his face. 'Every year some man is bitten there by a
snake. It is called Tom-tom Hill.'

'Somebody's lighted a bonfire at the foot of it,' I said; 'is
that to frighten away the snakes?'

'No, no, my dear sir; they are burning a body. All bodies
are burnt there. It is full of ghosts. It is a very bad hill.'

It was clear that he did not like this subject, and he
changed it immediately.

'One day you shall come to my Palace,' he said, 'and I will show the Gods to you.'

I had heard of this entertainment from other sources, and had been anxiously hoping for an invitation, rarely extended to Europeans.

'I should like that very much,' I said.

'And you shall tell me which of the boys you like best.'

I readily agreed and he was very pleased.

'Will you come the day after to-morrow?'

'Yes, whenever you like.'

'Or perhaps to-morrow late I could arrange something. If I can, I will send a carriage for you.'

'That will be very nice,' I said. 'And will there be dancing?'

'Yes, yes. Music and dancing. And the boys will be dressed like the Gods.'

'Will they paint their faces?'

'No, no paint. I have done away with paint. I don't like all this . . . tattooing. But you must tell me which you like best.'

'Of course I will,' I said. 'Are they very beautiful?'

'Very beautiful. But you will see.'

'It will be good to see a beautiful face,' I said; 'for I haven't yet seen one in Chhokrapur, and I've been looking about for a bearer for myself. In fact, only yesterday I was saying to your Tahsildar,[1] "I want a bearer, please, but he must be young and beautiful." '

'I have the son of my barber,' said His Highness. 'He works for me. I will show him to you. He is very beautiful . . . . fair, but unreadable. I call him the White Sphinx. He is sixteen, and has been with me for two years; but he does nothing, nothing, but look at motors and go to sleep.'

For some time after this he was thoughtful; then he asked: 'Haven't you a saying in England, "No man can be a hero to his valet"?'

'Yes. Why?'

---

[1] A subcollector of revenue.

PART ONE

'I will tell you to-morrow,' he said mysteriously, and called for a cigarette.

January 3rd

AT eight o'clock to-night His Highness sent a carriage for me to bring me to the Palace. I was reading in my house when I heard the trampling of horses up the drive, and ran out in time to see the royal coach come thundering up out of the darkness.

A pair of spirited piebald stallions drew it, and two erect postillions were balanced so lightly behind that in their floating white cotton garments they seemed to fly, winged figures, unsupported through the air.

Up towards the Guest House it went, and then, deflecting, swept a grand circle round the plateau to where I stood, and as the charioteer pulled up abruptly in front of me, the postboys vaulted lightly to the ground and ran, one to the horses' heads, the other to open the carriage door for me. All three salaamed. The dust subsided. It was very impressive.

'Salaam,' I said, and climbed up into the shabby open victoria.

Nothing more was said. The door was closed, the coachman cracked his whip, and the postboys swung themselves back on to their perches as we rolled off down the hill. The coachman had a clapper bell beside him, which he rang all the time as though we were a fire-engine. We drew up at the back of the Palace, where a canvas screen is always stretched at night to conceal the King's private entrance and form a small enclosure in which he may walk. A servant was awaiting me here and guided me behind, where another white-clad servant, a good-looking boy with very bright teeth and a single ear-ring, took charge and beckoned me past the sentries and up the steps to an enormous plaster porch. I followed him through the entrance, and found myself in a small dark stone room which contained a cow.

Another doorway opposite brought me into the 'theatre.'
This was an open courtyard with a concrete floor. Ordi-
narily, it seemed, it was quite bare; but now it was prepared
for the 'Gods.' I was entering from the back, I found, for
the scene was set facing away from me towards the wall
on my left. From the audience's point of view, then,
there was a dais in the centre of the court on which two
wooden chairs were set arm to arm. A carpet was spread in
front of it. To the left, along the edge of the carpet, squatted
four musicians, having between them two tom-toms, a pair
of small brass cymbals, and three instruments resembling
fiddles. On the right, rather removed, was a low divan,
covered with a sheet. A charcoal fire in an earthenware basin
glowed beside it. Over all, under the sky, a huge carpet was
spread like an umbrella, a stout pole supporting it in the
middle and supplying the handle. I took these things in
gradually. The four musicians salaamed. Except for them
the place seemed empty. My guide indicated the divan.
I was to sit on it. I did so, leaving room for His Highness
beside me.

'How do you do, Mr. Ackerley?'

I scrambled to my feet again and looked round, but could
not see him anywhere; then his husky laughter drew my
attention to the wall which the scene faced, and I realised
that he was on the other side of it. There was a green reed
blind in the centre which covered a doorway, and on both
sides of this the stone wall had been grilled to form windows
of a latticed design.

'Are you comfortable there? Are you warm? Would you
like to come in here? Then come.'

The servant held the reed blind aside for me, and I
stepped into His Highness's private closet. It was a very
small room, measuring about six feet by twelve, furnished
with a *charpai* (a simple low wooden Indian bedstead, without back or sides, strung with hempen bands), and, a little
removed from it, a *chaise-longue*, both draped in white sheets.
A small three-legged table, provided with an ashtray and

32

some loose brown cigarettes, stood by each, the *charpai* being further equipped with a second small table which carried a tray of betel-leaves, and, on the floor, a basin of charcoal and a spittoon. An oil lamp by the chair shed light and completed the furniture. There was no carpet and no decoration. A second curtained doorway diagonally opposed the one by which I had entered, and one of the walls had been recessed to form what looked like a large sink.

Among the cushions on the bed sat the King, smoking a cigarette. His legs had disappeared; they were folded up and tucked away beneath him, and only a small fragile body could be seen, sitting up erect on its base, like a nine-pin. How small, how thin he is! I thought, for I have never before seen him so lightly clad. He wore a fine white cambric nightshirt, on which a necklace gleamed, and a claret-coloured silk shawl hung over his shoulder. His small head, with its soft untidy greying hair, was bare, and I saw for the first time his Hindoo lock hanging low down on the nape of his neck. Like a little monkey he looked; charming, I thought. I advanced to shake hands with him.

'No! no! You must not touch me,' he said, shrinking away. 'Nor my bed,' he added. Then he laughed at my bewilderment.

'To-night I am holy,' he explained, still laughing as though it were the greatest joke, 'because I have had my bath; and no one may touch me. Did you not know that? You must always say to me when you come here, "Is the Maharajah touchable or untouchable?" '

'I'm sorry,' I said, 'I must begin again. Is the Maharajah Sahib touchable or untouchable?'

'Untouchable,' he nodded, and directed me to sit down in the long chair.

'Is this your theatre box?' I asked, looking round the room. He was amused.

'This is my . . . living-room. I do everything here. I sleep and read here, and do all my business here. My wife used to live above.'

He laughed again at my obvious surprise and then called out some order in Hindi. The musicians tuned up.

'Now the Gods are coming,' he said; 'and you must tell me which you like best.'

Immediately some servants came forward from the back and held outstretched between us and the scene a pretty blue velvet cloth, bordered with silver thread. The music began, a strange thrilling sound, accompanied by chanting; then the cloth was dropped, and Rama, one of the earthly manifestations of the God Vishnu, was revealed seated upon his throne with his wife Sita beside him. A maidservant stood on each side of the dais. All were boys. Rama was splendidly dressed in bright colours, a pink coat and gold silk trousers fastened round the ankles. He wore an enormous headdress and ropes of artificial pearls, and had a line of red and yellow paint down the bridge of his nose. Sita was also gilded, but not so gay, and wore a coronet. She sat in a heap with her chin on her chest, and looked very peevish. Both of them wore a single pearl suspended from the tips of their noses. The maidservants were also dressed in gold; they were very young, about twelve years old, and blinked self-consciously.

'What do you think of him? What do you think of him?' His Highness kept repeating.

'I don't think I'm very impressed by him,' I said.

'No?' said His Highness, astonished.

'Will he dance?'

'No, he cannot dance.'

'May I go out and have a closer look?'—It was difficult to get a comprehensive view through the holes in the wall.

'Of course. But you must not smoke in front of the God, or tread on his carpet.'

The music still continued, repeating a perpetual phrase, but the Gods sat immovable. Then an elderly man dressed in female attire appeared upon the carpet in front of Rama. He wore a long heavy dark-blue silk skirt, a pink veil over his head and bells round his ankles. Addressing himself to

34

the God, he performed a heel-and-toe dance, gyrating slowly with outstretched arms and chanting.

I returned to ask the King who this personage was, but he gave me no opportunity.

'What do you think of him?' he at once asked, still referring to Rama.

I said I thought he had good physique, but that he looked stupid, and I didn't think him very nice.

His Highness seemed very surprised at this, and rather pained.

'And you do not think he is beautiful?' he asked.

'No, I don't. Do you?'

'Of course; I think he is very beautiful.'

'How old is he?' I asked.

'Sixteen.'

'And what else does he do besides being a God?'

'Nothing. The Gods are not allowed to do any other work. And when they are seventeen years old they cannot be Gods any more.'

'What happens to them then?'

'They are all fools,' was all he said.

Meanwhile the dance had ended, the cloth was spread again, and when it was removed Rama had retired to be replaced by Krishna, with his favourite Gopi maiden, Radha, who was impersonated by the same boy who had played Sita. Krishna was a much nicer-looking boy than Rama, and I said so at once to His Highness's prompt and inevitable question—a reply which seemed to intensify his astonishment. Krishna was dressed in bright green and wore bells round his ankles, which indicated that he was not a lily of the field like Rama, but was able, at any rate, to spin; but he began his performance by singing from his throne in a pleasant, rather monotonous voice, gesticulating awkwardly from side to side with stiff brown hands. Then he rose to his feet and performed a fine exhilarating dance (in which the elderly 'lady,' who was now seated in the 'wings,' eventually joined), beginning with heel taps and

35

slow, stiff, dignified gyrations, which got faster and faster until he sank to the carpet and whirled like a top on his knees. This excited me to applaud, until I remembered Rama, and stopped for fear of causing jealousy. This boy was replaced by another, also impersonating Krishna, while Radha still occupied the other chair and took no part, and apparently little interest, in the proceedings.

This third boy was dressed in dark blue silk and was not at all attractive. He was stunted and had a tendency to spinal curvature; but he was said to act well in the play about to be performed. This was opened by the entry of a priest made fat with many pillows, which were supported by a broad green cummerbund. He carried a staff in one hand and some cooking utensils in the other, and was rendered still more farcical by the addition of a false beard, which seemed to sprout from his nostrils, and a string of wooden beads the size of cricket balls round his neck. The elderly 'lady,' who was sitting patiently on the carpet, received him, and I was told that he was a Brahman come, according to custom, to honour her by eating in her presence on the occasion of the birth of her child.

Stones and sticks were brought, and a fire actually lighted to boil the priest's pot; in the preparation of which he pretended that his beard had caught fire, a jest which provoked even Radha to merriment. Then, with the 'lady' (she was a rich woman, a daughter of one of the Shepherd Kings, and inhabited a palace) opposite him, he sat down in front of the fire, and raising his eyes to heaven, called on the God Vishnu to bless the cooked food. But, taking advantage of the Brahman's momentary abstraction, Krishna, who was supposed to represent the lady's newly-born babe, slid from his throne, and crawling over to the priest's food, touched it.

This angered the priest very much.

How dare a child of a woman of that caste touch the food of a Brahman! How dare the woman allow her child to do so! The child must be beaten! So he chased Krishna round the carpet, waving his rod and making irate noises until the woman pacified him and persuaded him to begin the ceremony all over again. This necessitated throwing the food away and washing not only the contaminated utensils but himself also; so he retired to a corner of the carpet and rolled about on his face and back as though he were in water, until one of Krishna's maidservants said she was a tortoise and seized him by the leg, much to his indignation.

His Highness who was chewing betel-leaves and explaining the action of the play to me, was so amused by this incident that he choked and was obliged to eject most of his leaf into the spittoon.

So again the meal was prepared—and again the same thing happened. No sooner did the priest raise his eyes to invoke the blessing of Vishnu upon his food than' the baby crawled over and touched it. Again the priest stormed and chased the child, and again the woman pacified him and persuaded him to begin all over again. But when it occurred the third time, and the priest seemed too discouraged to do more than glare morosely at the provoking baby, the woman said:

'Why do you trouble this poor old man? Can you not leave him in peace?'

And the child answered:

'But he called upon me and I came. I am the God Vishnu.'

And so it was . . . Krishna the Shepherd King, the eighth incarnation of Vishnu; the priest bowed before him and praised him, and the play ended in a general dance.

'Did you like it?' asked His Highness.

'Yes, indeed! I thought it was all——'

'And which of the Gods did you like the best?'

'Krishna.'

'Hookah!' remarked the King.

'I beg your pardon?' I said.

But his remark was not addressed to me. From the shadows behind the *charpai*, where, unnoticed by me, he had been squatting, a white-turbaned servant rose and left the chamber by the other door, returning in a few moments with a hookah pipe, ready lighted, which he set on the ground by the spittoon, laying the stem upon the table.

I looked at him with interest.

He was young and tall, with big bony hands and feet, but his face was strikingly handsome—fairer than usual and lighted by large glowing dark eyes, which every now and then rested curiously upon me.

He returned to the shadows, moving silently; and then I noticed that the King was watching me. He had uncurled, and his little thin legs were dangling over the edge of the *charpai* above the brazier.

'That is the barber's son I spoke of,' he said, removing the stem of the hookah from his mouth. 'He is my personal servant—my valet. Do you like him?'

'Well, I've hardly seen him,' I said, 'but he seemed very handsome indeed.'

He opened wide his eyes, as though surprised.

'I will show him to you,' he said, and with a slight movement of his hand he brought the magnificent boy out of the shadows again into the patch of light that filtered through the reed blind. He moved noiselessly into it and stood there facing me, motionless, expressionless, awaiting my inspection.

But I couldn't manage that—sitting there studying him as though he were a slave; so I hurriedly murmured my satisfaction, and another motion of the royal hand restored him to his shadows.

'Would you call him beautiful?' asked the King at once.

'Very beautiful,' I answered. 'More beautiful than any of your Gods.'

'Oh—h!' The filmy eyes widened again. 'More beautiful than Ram'?'

'Yes, more beautiful than Rama.'

'Oh—h!'

For a few moments he bubbled into his hookah, then he laid the stem on the table beside him, clasped his hands round one updrawn knee, and turning his face towards me, asked:

'Would you call me an ugly man?'

This was a little disconcerting. Among the general descriptive words, 'ugly' was certainly the most appropriate, and I do not think that any one would have contradicted it as misrepresentative; but I couldn't very well say so, and his face was certainly not repellent, nor even disagreeable.

'Certainly not, Maharajah Sahib.'

He received this without the least sign, so that I wondered whether he had been listening; then drawing his legs beneath him again, he called his servant and gave him some order which sent him out of the room.

'I will show you something,' he said, throwing me a veiled glance and popping a betel-leaf into his mouth. In a few moments the boy returned with a small package of papers bound with tape which he handed to the King, or, rather, dropped into the royal hand from a height so that there should be no physical contact between them. His Highness undid the bundle and extracted a letter which he returned, by the same method, to the valet, who brought it to me.

'Read it,' said the King, 'and tell me what you think. Tell me frankly. Don't be beaten in the bush.'

It was a confidential letter from a British official to some friend of his, and the very last person by whom the writer would have wished it to be seen was the King—for he was its subject.

I do not remember very much about it. True, I read it through, and was aware of good criticism while I blushed for it; but I was thinking all the time of the letters that I myself had written home, and for the fate of which I was suddenly deeply concerned. Here, indeed, for all its merciless exposure, was impartial thought and strict, respectful treatment; the writer had not been betrayed, as I had been, into the easy ways of ridicule; there were no caricatures in the margin. I remembered those caricatures, which I had once thought so good, with considerably less appreciation; and I also remembered how I had imprudently dropped them into the State letter-box, or had even entrusted them to a half-witted Mohammedan boy to post for me.

So I do not remember very much about that letter; only one or two sentences recur to me.

' . . . He is a weak man, and a bad ruler, having no real interest in the affairs of the State . . . wasteful . . . generous to a fault . . . a loyal friend . . . he is a very ugly man.'

When I had finished reading it I looked up. He was not attending to me, but was gazing into the air; my movement disturbed him, however, and he turned his head.

'Have you finished?'

'Yes.'

Probably I was a little flustered, for I got up to restore it to him, but he restrained me.

'Put it on the table beside you. Now; what do you think of it?'

'I think it's a very good letter, and the writer seems to be friendly on the whole; but I don't agree with many of the things he says.'

'What don't you agree with?'

I'd been talking at random, but I reverted to the subject of ugliness, and then retired into the question of how he had got hold of it.

'It came to me by chance,' he said, without expression.

'And what do *you* think of it, Maharajah Sahib?'

'It is the truth,' he said, with finality. 'I like it very much.'

I began to say something else to him, but he cut me off.

'And now you should go,' he said. 'Good night, Mr. Ackerley.'

I got up, feeling suddenly rather like a schoolboy.

'Good night, Maharajah Sahib,' I said, bowing to him, and went on, past the cow, to where my chariot was awaiting me in the moonlight to convey me back to the house on the hill.

PART ONE

January 4th

THIS evening as I was returning to the Guest House, I met His Highness's 'valet' coming from it. With him was the young man who has that fine tress of black hair I mentioned elsewhere, and who is connected in some official capacity with the Guest House, probably as a clerk or accountant. I have seen him about here a good deal, and have noticed him for his pleasant, clean and dignified appearance. He speaks a little English, always giving me a 'Good morning,' no matter what time of the day.

Hindoo men wear a peculiar nether garment, called a *dhoti*. This is a very long single piece of cloth which they wind round their waists and between their legs. With the poorer people it shrinks to a coarse loincloth, twisted untidily about their middles; but it can be a very graceful garment indeed, when it is made of fine muslin and properly put on so that it drops in front almost to the ankles in two loops which loosely sheathe the legs.

The Dewan in my sketch (page 208) can be seen wearing one; but he has not put it on very well. To arrange it symmetrically, so that the loops fall equally to the most becoming length, requires a certain amount of care which a man like Babaji Rao, for instance, would not trouble to give; also, since it may have to be taken off, or at any rate disarranged for various reasons, a number of times a day, it must be difficult to have it always quite right. Our trousers are no bother; however often we put them off and on we never find one leg shorter than the other; but the *dhoti* requires attention and skill, and is seldom properly worn.

The young man with the tress of black hair looks particularly graceful in his. It is of the finest, softest muslin, with a narrow border of dark blue, and falls almost to the silver buckles of his black shoes. And as he moves, one catches glimpses behind of his slim brown calves and ankles.

41

January 5th

His Highness has told his 'valet' that I thought him more beautiful than the Gods. This morning, after breakfast, the young clerk whom I saw with the valet yesterday followed me to the house and asked if he might come in. He told me at once that he knew I had seen the Gods dance.

'How do you know?' I asked.

'My friend,' he murmured, 'he tell me . . . my friend you say "like Krishna." '

'Better than Krishna,' I said. 'So the Maharajah Sahib told him?'

'Yes,' he answered; then added, after a moment, 'But do not say to Maharajah Sahib, or he will be angry with me.'

I promised.

'Do you like Europeans?' I asked.

'Yes.'

'Why?'

'Because he is so wisdom.'

January 6th

To the Hindoo all life is sacred. He may not kill, and he may not eat meat. If he does eat meat he is outcaste. Babaji Rao, the Secretary Sahib, is extremely orthodox, and the mere mention of meat discomposes him. No doubt this is one of the reasons why the Guest House accounts are in such confusion, and the monthly bill for supplies, which has to be met from the State funds, causes the Dewan much anxiety. The Secretary's signature is required as a check to the stores list; but he signs with averted eyes. He took me off in his tonga this morning to inspect the jail, but the old St. Peter —Munshi, as they call him—who keeps the keys of the storeroom, waylaid us near the Palace with indents for the Secretary to check. The inevitable crowd of small children and loafers at once collected.

PART ONE

'I do not understand these foods,' said the Secretary, gazing with disgust at the papers before him. . . . 'Lungs? . . . Do you eat lungs?'

He repeated the Hindi word that stumped him to the bystanders; but no one had any idea to offer. I suggested kidneys as a possible alternative, and as such it was hastily set down.

'If,' said the Secretary Sahib uneasily as we continued on our way, 'if my father knew that I had to discuss hens and eggs and kidneys in this way, he would be very cross with me.'

The jail is a long, low, distempered building on the outskirts of the town, with an armed guard over its triple iron gates, only one of which is allowed to be open at a time. There must have been some forty or fifty prisoners, all in leg-irons, squatting on their haunches in the sun in the various yards, spinning hemp and yarn with primitive machines, or plaiting rope. Others were weaving coarse sheets and towels, or sat cross-legged on benches in a shed making carpets. One man was sewing treasure-bags. All of them wore round their necks small discs on which their numbers and terms of imprisonment were engraved, and these the Secretary glanced at from time to time with something of the detachment with which one inspects the price tickets on articles in a shop. Many of them were in for a long term of years, he said; some for life; but the worst characters were grinding grain in a building near by—the hardest and most distasteful work of all.

I walked about among them, giving, as far as possible, equal attention to all, in case my visit was as important to them as are the visits of the Prince of Wales on tours of inspection in England, and lent a particular significance to this day otherwise indistinguishable from hundreds of others; and they all seemed pleased to show their skill in the particular work they were doing. But all were miserable, weedy creatures, and I did not feel any personal interest in any of them. The kitchen or cookhouse we also visited, and I

43

tried to walk into it, but was prevented; one may not set foot in Hindoo kitchens—even in a prison—without first removing one's shoes. It was swarming with flies. Meal-cakes were in process of being made—things like very large crumpets which were turned out of the frying-pan into the hot ashes of the fire itself.

Apparently these and some other corn confection formed the staple diet. Still thinking of the Prince of Wales, I asked Babaji Rao whether I should send the prisoners something —some tobacco, for instance; but he said there was not the slightest need to feel pity, for they were far better off than the other peasants who were not in prison.

Some building is in progress here, a garage for the Guest House, and the workmen carry the water for mortar-mixing up the hill in large, round, earthenware pots, or *lutiya*, balanced on their heads. They also water the shrubbery in the drive, and sometimes the pots are brass. I see them through the open doorway of my bungalow, and am often struck by the gracefulness of their carriage as they pass to and fro with these heavy burdens on their heads. The right arm, bare, slim, brown, is raised so that the hand rests lightly against the lip of the jar to steady it, and their bodies glide with an erect and braced, yet easy flowing motion. Elegant they look, like figures in a frieze; and sometimes, coming up behind them as I mount the hill, and seeing their slow-swift, easy-tense movement, the slim dark arm upstretched, and the *dhoti* tucked up round the loins so that the slender legs are bare in their whole length, I think what grace! what beauty! and, looking round as I pass, see an ugly, coarse-featured, ill-nourished peasant with betel-stained lips.

I give them cigarettes, and one of them in particular, a strange gawky boy, often catches my eye. I am amused by the way in which he manages his clothes. He has four garments, besides a pair of broken-down shoes—a tight collarless cotton jacket with short sleeves, an abbreviated white *dhoti*, little more than a loincloth, a pale brown *sāfā*, or small turban, and a cornflower blue cloak (*pichōra*)—and the last three of these seem interchangeable, for sometimes, when perhaps his *dhoti* is being washed, his *sāfā* is wound round his loins, and his *pichōra* round his head. I noticed him gazing wistfully towards my house the other day, so I beckoned to him. He approached obliquely, like a crab, very sun-blackened and angular, his long thin legs bare to the thigh, his coarse blue cloth tumbled anyhow round his head. His face was floury with dust. I held out some cigarettes. He shuffled off his shoes and, after a momentary hesitation, entered timidly, his coarse hands cupped and stretched before him. I dropped the cigarettes into the cup. He retreated and, from the safety of the doorway, wrinkling up his eyes and disclosing hideous stumps of teeth in a grin, murmured '*Bakshish*.' I held out a rupee. Again the cup, more quickly this time, was advanced, and I dropped the rupee in. He bent very low upon this, and touched first my carpet and then his forehead with his right hand.

During our drive in the afternoon His Highness said to me:

'Mr. Ackerley, I wish to give you advice.'

'Yes, Maharajah Sahib?'

'You should keep a dog.'

'But I don't want a dog.'

'Only a little one. Any little dog. One of these pie-dogs will do.'

'But why, Maharajah Sahib?'

'So that before you eat yourself, you can throw it some of the food.'

I looked at him in astonishment.

'Do you mean in case it's poisoned?'

'Of course.'

'But is it likely to be poisoned?'

'I don't know; but I am a suspicious man.'

'Do *you* take such precautions, then?'

45

'Of course. But I do not like dogs. I keep some cats, and throw the food to them. My cooks are always quarrelling.' He chortled. 'So I eat with cats,' he concluded.

'Well,' I said, after a little consideration, 'I think I'll take the risk. I can't imagine why any one should want to poison me. Besides, if I used a dog to prevent myself from being poisoned in that way, it might develop rabies and bite me, so that I should only be poisoned in another way.'

'You are quite right,' remarked His Highness, without, however, appearing to have heard what I said. But the thought of my comfort remained with him, for, before taking leave of me, he said:

'If you want anything you must at once tell me. You must not lurk anything from me. Lurk? What does that mean?'

January 7th

I SPOKE to His Highness yesterday about a tutor for myself (he is very anxious for me to learn to speak Hindi), and taking advantage of some remark of his on Zeus and Ganymede, asked whether I might not have his valet to teach me.

'I suppose he is indispensable to you?' I asked.

'No, he is not indispensable to me. I will send him to you if you wish. I will send him to you tomorrow morning.'

'Do you think he will be pleased to come?'

'Oh, he will be very pleased—especially if you pay him two or three rupees a month.'

After this neither of us said anything for some time, and then His Highness remarked with finality:

'No, he is not at all indispensable to me.'

But this morning a tonga arrived at the Guest House bearing two men I had never seen before, with a letter from His Highness. It ran as follows:

'DEAR MR. ACKERLEY,—Here are two men who know English and Hindi very well. The bearer of this is called Gupta, he is my assistant librarian of Hindi Books; and the other called Champa

Lal, he is my icemaker. You can choose any one of them, and they will do for preliminary work well. Perhaps they might ask for some wages, and I think two rupees per month will do. Excuse pencil and paper.'

To which I replied:

'DEAR MAHARAJAH SAHIB,—Your messengers have arrived, but I do not know quite what to do. Indeed they have both uttered remarks in English, but neither of them appears to understand my replies. I thought to myself, there is nothing to choose between them in looks, I will take the one who is the sharper in wits. So I returned to them and said:

"I only want one of you. Which of you speaks the better English, for I will engage him?"

The silence was at last broken by the icemaker, who said:

"I do not understand."

—and then by the assistant librarian, who said:

"Your English is very high."

I return them both, and hope I may still be allowed to have the dispensable valet, this morning or at 2.30 P.M., for even if he cannot teach me Hindi, I should like to make a drawing of him.'

The valet came this afternoon. I was lying on my sofa reading, when the light flicked across the page, and looking up I saw him standing in the curtained doorway. He bobbed a nervous salaam; I beckoned him inside and, throwing a rapid glance over his shoulder, he shuffled his laceless European shoes from his bare feet, pulled the curtain right back so that the open doorway was unveiled, and came a few paces further into the room. I indicated a chair, but it was too near me; he took the first at hand, and moved it back so that it stood in the doorway.

I had already learnt a few Hindi phrases by heart: 'Good day,' 'How are you?' 'It is a nice day,' 'Don't talk so fast'; but I found I did not now believe in their pronunciation as much as when I had addressed them to myself; and since he only nodded to the first three, or uttered a throaty monosyllabic sound, I had no opportunity to air my 'Don't talk so fast' composition, which therefore remains in my memory as the only phrase I got right. He was clearly very ill at ease and anxious to please me; but I soon realised that he did not really understand anything I said and was trying to guess from my expression what his response should be, so that most of the time a timid smile trembled on his lips and eyes, ready to vanish at the slightest sign of severity. And whenever I looked down for a moment to consult my dictionary, his head went round at once, I noticed, to the open door, through which he could see across the gravel space the usual crowd of servants drowsing in the shade of the *neem* tree in front of the kitchen. So I gave it up at last and said I was going to draw him, but the moment I rose to get my sketch-book he was out of his chair and watching me in apparent alarm. I tried to convey with smiles and gestures that my intention was quite harmless, but although I got him to sit down again, I could not get him to sit still, and at length, in despair, told him to curtain the doorway, for I could not go on if he kept turning round to look out of it. He began immediately to talk to me very rapidly, and since I did not know what he was saying, I got up to curtain it myself; but again he sprang up and barred my way, still chattering and gazing at me in what seemed to be a pleading manner. I stood still, wondering what was the trouble, and he at once began beckoning, in great agitation, to one of his friends outside, throwing me, at the same time, nervous, placating smiles. Soon the friend arrived, the young clerk who called on me the other day.

'What is the matter with your friend?' I asked.

'He say I must stay with him,' said the clerk.

'Why?'

'He is much frightened.'

This was all I could get. He did not know why his friend was frightened, or if he did know he would not say. But at any rate it was clear enough that I must have both or neither, so I told the clerk he had better stay, though I did not want him—being a shy and, as will perhaps already have been noticed, a rather inexpert artist.

A little later, forgetting the valet's fear, I asked his friend, who had access to the storeroom, if he would get me some more cigarettes, for I had run out of them; but the moment he moved, the valet caught hold of his hand and, even when the mission was explained, would not let him go.

The drawing was indeed not good, and Narayan did not scruple to say so. Narayan is the name of the clerk; his friend, the valet, being called Sharma.

January 8th

TOM-TOM HILL is my favourite walk because of the view. There is a ruined shrine with a fallen idol on its summit, and it is called Tom-tom Hill because a drum used to be beaten there years ago to assemble the people or to notify them of certain times and events. From the backyard of my house the stony slope mounts steadily up to a pretty white temple in its cluster of cypresses. The temple is dedicated to Hanuman, the Monkey-headed God of Physical Power, and the worshippers are often to be seen and heard on its terrace; but I have not yet found courage to enter it, being still ignorant of customs and observances, and afraid of making mistakes. Indeed I have never even ventured close to it, but, at a discreet distance, have always dropped down the western slope of the ridge, and clambered round through the brambles beneath its walls and up again on the other side. As a matter of fact, this also is the only way of getting on, for the temple occupies the whole breadth of the ridge's back and cannot be otherwise passed. It overlooks the town and is reached from that side by means of a long straight staircase of wooden steps which runs steeply up the eastern slope from the Rajgarh-Deori road.

Having skirted the temple in this way, walking becomes more difficult, for the ridge continues in a long narrow *arête*, scattered with huge boulders, many of which have to be clambered over; but beyond this it widens and rises gently to the foot of Tom-tom Hill, and the walk up to the ruined shrine is easy, though the gradient is rather steep. Usually I sit there and rest on one of the stones of the shrine, looking down upon the white town, thickly planted with trees, the Palace, imposing at this distance, in its centre, the Sirdar tank immediately below. But to-day I saw smoke rising again from among the trees and bushes at the base of the hill on the far side, and descended to verify His Highness's information that this was a crematorium. This slope of the hill had an even steeper gradient, and as I zig-zagged down I was able to keep the fires in sight, and took no precautions against observation, believing myself to be the only person about. But soon I perceived two Indians squatting on their heels by the nearer fire, apparently extinguishing the last embers and collecting some of the grey ashes in a metal pot. Realising now that the King had probably been right, and fearing that I might be intruding upon sacred ground, I took cover behind a large boulder and watched them for a little from this shelter. Then I noticed that the other fire, which was a little further down, seemed unattended, so as quietly as I could, I made a detour and approached it.

It was clearly a funeral pyre. The charred skull of the corpse, which was towards me, was split open, for it is customary, I believe, to break the skull of the dead when the body is being consumed, so that the soul may have its exit; and curving out of the centre of the pile, like wings, were the blackened ribs which, released by the heat, had sprung away from the vertebrae. In all directions I noticed the remains of earlier cremations. As I returned home I passed the other fire and saw that the two Indians had just finished and were disappearing among the bushes; but their place had already been taken by two evil-looking vultures with yellow beaks which were picking scraps from among the extinct and smokeless ashes.

His Highness sent the carriage for me again this evening to bring me to the Palace. He was extremely interested in my meeting with his valet, Sharma, the barber's son, and put me through such a cross-examination about him that I began to feel rather uncomfortable. I had been quite expecting such questions as to how I had liked him, and what had occurred, and how long he had stayed, but could not understand why he should require such accuracy as to the time of the boy's arrival and the manner of his dress, or why, when I replied to this last question that Sharma had worn a very becoming long-skirted blue serge coat with velveteen cuffs and collar, he should have said 'Ah!' with an appearance of such immense satisfaction.

I had brought my drawing with me, but he did not look at it. He was untouchable again, and bade me leave it on the table by my chair. Narayan's name was apparently known to him, and evoked another volley of questions the significance of which I was unable to understand; but, remembering Narayan's request a few days previously not to repeat something he had said, I answered with cautious vagueness, in case I should unintentionally get either of the two young men into trouble, and, as soon as I could, diverted his attention a little by remarking on Sharma's timidity.

'Yes, he spoke to me,' said His Highness. 'He told me he was frightened. He saw you closing the doors and thought you were going to confine him.'

'But frightened of what?' I asked.

'That you would beat him.'

'Beat him?' Nothing had been further from my thoughts, and it took me some moments to get hold of this.

'Do you beat him much?' I asked.

'Oh yes! I have to. I beat him very much.'

'But, Maharajah Sahib, didn't you explain to him that, apart from anything else, your guests were hardly in a position to beat your servants?'

'Yes, I did, I did, and he said, of his own accord, that he would come and see you to-morrow.'

He went on to speak of some friend of his, the wife of an English officer, who had told him that she was convinced, after long experience of India, that no servant could be expected to be faithful to his employers until he had cuts on his back two fingers deep; and, from her, passed on to another English friend of his—this time a man. I do not now remember the connection between the two friends, but cannot refrain from expressing a hope that it was matrimonial.

'He was a very strange man,' said he. 'He used to say to me, "Maharajah! do you see those clouds together up there?" "Yes, I see those clouds." "Do you see my dead wife's face looking down from them?" "No, I don't." "Damn!"

'Then again, when we were sitting together here, he said to me, "Maharajah, do you see this wall over here by me?" "Yes, I see that wall." "Well, it is talking to me. All the stones are talking. They are telling me everything that has passed in this room. Put your ear here. Do you hear them?" "No, I don't hear them." "Damn!" '

For a few moments His Highness was shaken with laughter, then—'He suicided himself,' he concluded.

January 9th

'AND how are the Gods this morning, Maharajah Sahib?'
'They are very well.'
'Where did you get them all from?'
'Mostly from Chhokrapur.'
'And where did the others come from?'
'My dear sir, there are only five, and three are from Chhokrapur.'
'Then where did the other two come from?' I persisted. 'Did they fall off Olympus, or were they a Christmas present?'
'No, no, no,' he spluttered, shaking with laughter; 'I bought them. They were not very expensive.'

He then embarked upon a long story about a twelve-year-old boy he had seen dancing in some travelling company of players which had visited Chhokrapur.

'He is very beautiful—like Napoleon the Third.'

'Napoleon the Third?' I asked, mystified. 'Do you mean Napoleon the Second?'

'No, no; Napoleon the Third; I have a picture of him in a history book in my library. I will show you.'

He had been so taken with this boy's appearance that he had wanted to buy him, and had asked how much he was. But the manager of the company, who was the boy's uncle, had named too high a price—fifty rupees a month for the boy's life, for he was irreplaceable.

'I said it was too much,' concluded His Highness; then, after a pause—'But I want him. Should I pay it? Please advise me.'

'What about the boy's parents?' I asked.

'Both dead,' said His Highness promptly.

'Well, if you want him so much and can afford him, you'd better buy him.'

'What would a European do? An Englishman?'

'The same thing, no doubt.'

'And an ancient Greek?'

'I believe they sternly discountenanced such transactions,' I said.

His Highness seemed to ponder this for a moment, then, 'He's black, not fair,' he observed. 'Do you like black?'

'I prefer fair.'

'Ah!' he breathed, nodding his head in agreement.

The sun was setting in front of us in a blaze of pink and golden light. His Highness waved a regretful hand towards it.

'I want a friend like that,' he said.

January 10*th*

PERHAPS His Highness was not pleased with the answer I returned him by his icemaker and assistant librarian; at any rate neither of them came back to me, and he never alluded to the subject again, but placed the matter in the hands of Babaji Rao, who sent me a very alarming young man, the son of a pundit, who seemed to think the letter of introduction he bore was a letter of engagement, for almost before I had finished reading it he had begun to teach me Hindi, shouting pronunciations at me in an abrupt, metallic voice which was actually hurtful, and jumping and gesticulating about the room as though he were composed of steel springs.

He was clearly bent upon making an impression on me (which indeed he did), and tried very hard to conceal the fact that he didn't in the least understand me; for whatever I said struck him at once, in the middle of some gesture, into a state of marionette-like immobility, an injured expression on his face. He would then complete his gesture and make a little rush at me with another staccato sentence, as though no interruption worthy of notice had occurred.

As is always the case when I have a visitor, he had been conducted into my room by curious sightseers—the waiter Hashim and two small boys, all Mohammedans. Hashim is easy to dismiss; one can do it with a nod, for he is accustomed to Europeans, though he would prefer to stay.

But the boys are very difficult and very exasperating. They stand about, quite quiet and expressionless, their wide gaze fixed upon me. A nod or gesture is quite useless. 'Jao!' (Go!) moves them slightly, and may drive the older of the two out on to the verandah, where he will linger, rather bewildered, looking back; but the younger and smaller, whose name is Habib (Lover), might almost be under some hypnotic influence; he moves his thick lips a little . . . and remains. The other day, all else having failed, I made a threatening advance towards him, and then he went, but slowly, reluctantly, rearranging the door-curtains as he left, and staring at me all the time with large astonished eyes as though to say 'This Sahib is certainly peculiar.'

But to return. When the son of the pundit had given me a headache I managed to convey to him that I had had enough instruction in Hindi for one day and would call him if I wanted more, intending to do so if I could not find some one more efficient and less mercurial; but this morning

54

I received another candidate. My new visitor was a grave,
tall, thin-featured Mohammedan, not unhandsome, with a
long aquiline nose and a slight black moustache.

His dress was that odd mixture of European and Indian
garments which all the educated men here affect. A red
tarbush was set squarely on his close-cropped skull, and

from beneath an Army drill tunic, stained green, the tails of
an ordinary European shirt hung down over narrow white
cotton trousers. He wore no collar. Socks, patent leather
slippers, and a long gold watch-chain round his neck, completed his attire. He carried an umbrella.

Holding himself very erect, he said that his name was
Abdul Haq, and that he had heard I was looking for a tutor,
and had come to present himself. I began to explain that I

already had a tutor, but he interrupted me, almost apologetically, to say that he had heard that also, but that—although he did not wish to speak ill of any man—the pundit's son was not nearly as well qualified to be my tutor as he himself was, and would not give such satisfaction.

This I felt might be true, and such self-confidence was disarming.

'I am very interested in you, gentleman, and will teach you well.'

He smiled at me, compressing his lips, his head on one side, his chin drawn in, very persuasive, very smooth, very confident, his umbrella beneath his arm, his toes turned out, and one foot a little in advance of the other as though he were about to begin a prim, decorous dance.

I engaged him, and he said 'Thank you, Mr. Ackerley' three times and thrust out a clawlike hand; but I felt, while I grasped it, that he was really shaking hands with himself. He went, and rather dubiously I watched him down the drive, a thin, stiff figure with toes turned out, twitching back his shoulders, his left arm stiff down his body, his right sweeping the handle of the umbrella in expansive circles. Every now and then he jerked a swift, rather haughty, glance from side to side, so that the tassel on his cap leapt and swung.

It appears that Napoleon the Third is once more in the vicinity of Chhokrapur. The travelling players have returned, His Highness said, but he said it with so little emotion that I cannot help wondering whether they ever really left. At any rate they have not lowered the price of Napoleon, though they now make an alternative offer for a lump sum of two thousand rupees, which is about one hundred and fifty pounds. This is absurd. His Highness has never before paid more than about five shillings for any God. Moreover, for performing in Chhokrapur they now want fifty rupees a night, instead of fifty for the whole visit. They are robbers . . . wolves . . .

PART ONE

'What must I do?' he asked. 'Should I buy him? Thirty years I have dreamed of that face, it is entangled in my heart, and then (he clapped his hands together) suddenly I see it! Why did I see it? How do these things happen? Did God put it before me? Is it God's wish that I should buy? If it is not God's wish, then He is a very wicked man! What must I do?'

'Do you suppose his mind, too, is like Napoleon the Third's?' I asked.

'No, like a donkey's!' he retorted emphatically, and then began to laugh silently, shielding his face with a letter he had just received from the Acting Governor-General of the Province. For some time, it appears, he has been angling for a decoration. All the neighbouring potentates have, at one time or another, been honoured with the K.C.S.I. or K.C.I.E. on the King Emperor's birthday, but so far His Highness of Chhokrapur has been passed over, which is a source of continual irritation to him. He said he could not explain the reason for this neglect, but went on at once to tell me that, at the time of his son's birth, one of his enemies had written an anonymous letter to the Political Agent, stating that the child was illegitimate and not his son at all, and further hinting that an investigation of His Highness's private amusements would prove instructive.

Apparently some sort of investigation had been made, but nothing had been discovered—nothing, that is to say, except the 'Gods,' whose number had been forthwith curtailed. This His Highness called 'political interference with my luxuries.' No doubt it is this suspicion that is operating still against his chances of a decoration; but he does not admit it, nor abate his efforts on his own behalf. The A.G.G. himself has recently been knighted, and His Highness, while congratulating him, had not scrupled to inquire again in the same letter when he himself was to be remembered. The letter that he had brought out to-day to show me was the answer to this, in which the A.G.G. assured His Highness that he would do his best to settle favourably the matter of which His Highness had spoken. The letter seemed sincere and cordial, so he was in a good humour—or would have been if it weren't for Napoleon the Third.

'I cannot afford two thousand rupees,' he repeated. 'It is the boy's uncle who makes the demand. I should like to poison him.'

January 14th

FOR some time past His Highness has been cherishing a desire to erect a 'Greek Villa' where, wrapped in a toga, he may hold symposia with his European friends and his Indian Gods; and to-day a Mr. Bramble, an English architect, friend to the A.G.G., arrived in Chhokrapur to stay for a few days in the Guest House. There are some other guests here as well, two women and their children; and we were all present when His Highness drove up this afternoon. A chair and cigarettes were put ready for him in front of the fire, and as soon as he was seated he addressed himself to Mr. Bramble.

'How old are you, Mr. Bramble?'

'Well, Maharajah Sahib,' said the architect good-humouredly, His Highness's peculiarities having already been explained to him by the women, 'I tell my bearer that I'm a hundred, and he believes me.'

This caused general amusement, in which the King joined; but he obviously did not quite understand the joke, for did not Mr. Bramble, with his silver hair, look very old indeed? So as soon as the laughter had ceased, he asked politely:

'Are you seventy-six?'

'Well—er—no,' said Mr. Bramble, rather taken aback. 'Let me think . . . when was I born? In '66. That makes me sixty-four.'

'And where is your wife?' asked His Highness, without the slightest pause—and also without the slightest knowledge of Mr. Bramble's domestic affairs; but then surely so old and successful a man must have a wife. There was an awkward silence.

58

PART ONE

'I'm very sorry to say that . . . Mrs. Bramble is . . . no more . . . no more.'

He was clearly distressed; but His Highness did not appear to notice it.

'Dead?' he asked briefly.

'Yes,' said Mr. Bramble sadly.

'And have you children?' continued His Highness, without pause.

'One boy.'

There was a silence after this, and I awaited, with considerable apprehension, the King's next association of thought. But it was quite harmless.

'And where is he?'

'Well—at the moment he's in Portsmouth, I believe.'

'Ah, yes—Portsmouth. Where is Portsmouth?'

Mr. Bramble was by now so confused and intimidated that he was quite unable to remember where Portsmouth was; so I came to his rescue.

'It's in the south of England, Maharajah Sahib.'

'Near the Isle of Wight,' said Mr. Bramble, with presence of mind.

'Which,' I added, 'is not the Isle of Man, you know, Maharajah Sahib.'

His Highness at once looked very intelligent, and I knew I had succeeded in diverting his attention from Mr. Bramble's personal history.

'Have you read Hall Caine, Mr. Bramble?' he asked.

'Hall Caine? Yes, I think I have—something or other.'

'*The Eternal City*?' asked His Highness enthusiastically. 'A *very* good book. You *must* read it. He is Manx. Are you Manx, Mr. Bramble?'

'No, no, I'm not Manx,' said the architect, laughing.

His Highness seemed disappointed.

'Ah, I like Manx,' he said, nodding his head. 'They have a separate Parliament, you know. The House of Keys. Do you know Edward Carpenter?'

'Yes, I know Edward Carpenter,' said Mr. Bramble

59

fatiguedly, and began to talk about the weather to one of
the women. But their conversation was at once interrupted.
His Highness had remembered the 'Greek Villa,' and, as
always when he has an idea to impart, was far too impatient
to wait quietly for an opening.

'You mean you want a villa in the Classic style, isn't that
it?' asked Mr. Bramble. 'Yes, I could do it for you certainly;
but we shall have to talk about it first. You will have to
show me the proposed site, and tell me how many rooms
you want and how much you are prepared to spend, and
then I'll make a design for you.'

The King nodded sagely, but he had left off listening; he
was groping in his mind after something else, which in a
moment or two he triumphantly produced.

'Parthenon! Like Parthenon!' he cried; and then, rather
dimly: 'What is Parthenon?'

Hindoos are of four main castes: (1) the Brahman, or
Priestly caste, to which the Dewan and Narayan belong;
(2) the Kshatriya, or Warrior caste, to which His Highness
belongs; (3) the Vaishya, or Tradesman and Agriculturist
caste, to which Babaji Rao belongs; and (4) the Sudra, or
Servant and Labourer caste, to which Sharma, the barber's
son, belongs. The Brahmans are the Lips of God; the
Kshatriyas the Arms; the Vaishyas the Loins; and the
Sudras the Feet. I believe that Rabindranath Tagore in
one of his poems says: 'How can I worship my God better
than by kissing His Feet?'

Babaji Rao was explaining this to me, and also talking a
little on the subject of Hindoo vegetarianism. His own daily
meals are more or less as follows: at 9 A.M. he eats nuts,
pistachios and almonds, and drinks milk from his own cow;
for lunch at about midday he takes rice, *dal* (pulse), vegetables (probably potatoes), and bread; and in the afternoon
he likes fruit, but owing to the difficulty of obtaining it here,
he usually contents himself with cream, and sometimes a
little porridge. Evening dinner at about 6 P.M. is the big

meal and consists of several kinds of vegetables and meal-cakes fried in butter. At 9 P.M. he drinks a glass of milk. He is very fond of sweets, but his doctor has forbidden them.

I have been thinking of buying some little present for Sharma, the barber's son, as a peace-offering, so keeping the question general, I asked Babaji Rao what sort of thing would be acceptable to the poorer classes.

'What about betel-leaves?' I asked.

He smoothed his mouth to hide a smile.

'You cannot give betel-leaves to a Hindoo,' he said. 'He would not accept them from you; though he might be tempted, for they are not easily affordable. But cardamom seeds or cloves would be acceptable, or a few pice (small copper coins).'

'Then why not betel? It is all food.'

'But betel-leaves contain water. The others are dry.'

'I see. What about cloth?'

'Yes, that would be very acceptable. To a person like Narayan, the clerk here, for example, a pair of stockings or socks would be a very good thing.'

Abdul Haq came, this afternoon, to give me an hour's lesson, and I told him that, whilst watching a Mohamme-dan cricket-match on the outskirts of the town, I had met a friend of his named Ali. Abdul was at once very interested.

'When was that?'

'This morning some time.'

'At about what time?'

'At about one, I think.'

'You think? Do you not know?'

I shook my head, amused by his anxiety.

'Did you talk with him?'

'Yes.'

'What did you talk about?'

'Oh, nothing much.'

'Nothing? But you must have talked of something.'

'Never mind, Abdul. I shall not tell you what we talked about.'

'Oh, you will not tell me?'

'No, I won't.'

Keeping his lips compressed, he made a little titter of laughter at the back of his throat, and writhed his hands together in his lap. But how it worried him! He rustled his pages of notes and began to teach me again, asking me questions in Hindi; but soon his questions became purposeful.

'Did you go walking to-day?'

'Yes.'

'No,' he said in English, 'you must always give me the full answer in Hindi—the full and truthful answer. "Yes, I went walking to-day." So. Now say it again.' (I said it again.) 'So. Did you meet anyone?'

'Yes, I met Ali.'

'Did you speak with him?'

'Yes, I spoke with him.'

'What did you speak about?' Then in English: 'And do not forget to make your answer full and truthful.'

But I wouldn't tell him.

January 15th

OVER the main entrance to the Palace, which leads into the marble hall of state or council chamber, there is a board on which the English word 'Welcome' is inscribed. They say that when the board was painted there was a slight mis-understanding as to its intended destination, and it was hung originally over the jail; but after a time the mistake was perceived, and it was transferred to its present position.

There is a very beautiful tank on this side lapping the white walls of the old Palace buildings. It is a large circular pool, bordered on one side by an arc of steps which drop steeply down from the dusty path into the depth of the water. For some two hundred yards they curve round; where they end trees begin, enclosing in a feathery fringe the further circumference of the lake. To this tank, as to the others round the town, the people come to wash themselves and their clothes. There is only one dye, of a claret tint, made in Chhokrapur, and I grow a little tired of the uniformity of colour of the women's *saris*, the single long cloths in which they drape themselves.

But the scene this morning was very beautiful, with these red garments spread out to dry upon the steps, between the blue of the water and the blue of the sky, against a background of white cupolas and minarets and bright evergreen trees. I stood there for some time in the sunlight, idly contemplating, while the men came up out of the water, their thin brown bodies flashing and sparkling, the wet loincloth shaping their thighs. But what poor physique all of them had.

The women were abundantly adorned with cheap jewellery—countless coloured glass bangles and rough silver necklaces and anklets; for the poorer people invest their small savings in this way, by converting them into silver ornaments for their womenfolk. They knelt with their red cloths in their hands, beating them with stones. I saw a woman sitting with her child between her knees, catching the lice in its hair and placing them dead on the child's palm, outstretched to receive them. I saw a boy take a handful of dirt, and descending with it to the water's edge, use it to cleanse his face and neck. I saw an old man standing immersed to his waist, facing the sun, making passes across his chest, and lifting handfuls of the water to spill it out again like glittering beads between his fingers. Babaji Rao, whom I questioned later, told me he was offering oblations to the sun, the scattered water representing rice, and the passes across his body meant that he was painting himself with sandal.

Similar oblations are also poured to one's ancestors by the head of any Hindoo house. Apparently, when a person dies the house is considered unclean, and none but the inhabitants will enter it for a period of fourteen days. For seven days after death the male relations of the deceased will not shave; but on the seventh day they shave head and face, and on the fourteenth day, the house being purified by such ritual, a feast is given.

Oblations of water, sesame, or rice are poured, and afterwards white bands will be worn round the arm in sign of mourning, and during a particular fortnight every year the head of the house will not shave. If the deceased had been aged and spent, Babaji Rao reluctantly admitted, the feast might be rather an enjoyable affair. His own father is living, and is therefore responsible for carrying out these duties; but when he dies Babaji Rao himself will be obliged to undertake them.

His Highness and I went in to Rajgarh this afternoon to have tea with the Political Agent. On the way there he told me that Sharma had been very naughty and had had to be punished. He had been poking fun at one of the sentries outside the Palace. So the King had threatened him with a cane.

'Well,' said Sharma impertinently, 'you have your cane— why do you not strike me with it?'

Perhaps he did not believe that His Highness intended, or was able, to use it; but he was mistaken, and at the first stroke implored mercy.

My hair wants cutting, and I asked whether Sharma, being a barber's son, could do it for me; but the King retorted that the boy was a fool and could do nothing— except look at motors and go to sleep. The clean military cut of the Political Agent's thick greying hair reminded me again later of the state of my own.

'Who cuts your hair, Major?' I asked him.

'A boy named Rahim. He's quite good. He cuts your hair, too, Maharajah, doesn't he?'

'Yes, he cut it the other day,' said His Highness, 'but he cut it all off the top. I should like hair like yours, Major Sahib. If you let your hair grow, Major Sahib, would it reach to your shoulders?'

PART ONE

'Good Lord!' said the Major, spilling his tea on his trousers.

Later on I composed, at the Maharajah's request, an answer to the A.G.G.'s letter which His Highness showed me a few days ago. His Highness had already attempted the answer himself, to convey his gratitude for the A.G.G.'s promise, and to keep him up to the mark; but in his anxiety not to say too little or too much he had got muddled, and had given the unfinished letter to me to revise. It was a pathetic document, very ingratiating and 'diplomatic,' and strongly spiced with fulsome compliments. About halfway through it, when the main object, the question of the decoration, was reached, the A.G.G. began to be referred to as 'Your Honour.' I rewrote the whole thing, cutting out most of the compliments and all the 'Your Honours,' and sent it down to the Palace.

This evening when I went up to the Guest House for dinner, Mrs. Bristow, the young wife of one of the Shikaripur officers, was sitting by the fire reading a book.
'What are you chewing?' she asked, looking up at me.
'A clove.'
'Well, for Heaven's sake don't! I can't bear the sight. I suppose you chew gum at home?'
'No, I don't like chewing-gum,' I said.
'Well, do spit that out.'
'But I like cloves.'
'Well, I don't. It's disgusting and irritating. Go on, spit it out!'
'Certainly not.'
'Go on! I'm accustomed to being obeyed.'
'But obedience is a duty,' I said; 'and I have no duty towards you—except to see that you, too, are fed.'
For a moment she tried on me the power of her eye (which works, I believe, upon the subalterns of her husband's regiment), but this also failed to move my clove.

'Look here,' she said, 'let me give you a word of advice: don't go Indian!'

January 16*th*

MRS. BRISTOW apologised to me this evening.

'I'm sorry for what I said yesterday,' she began; 'please forgive me. You must have thought me awful; but I'm not, really. I'm very nice when you get to know me.'

I said I had taken no offence and hoped I had given none. Then she asked if I had a sister, and whether she was beautiful. I said I had, and she was.

'I supposed she was. You're rather beautiful, you know. You do know, don't you?' she asked. I said I did.

'Not that I like it in a man,' she concluded. 'I hate beauty in a man.'

Anyway, it was a very handsome apology.

In my lesson this morning Abdul asked me, in Hindi:

'What did you think when you saw Ali and me sitting on the steps of that house yesterday?' Then, in English: 'Now give me your answer, and let it be the truthful answer.'

Laboriously I pieced out a sentence which I hoped would be understood to mean, 'I wondered whose house it was'; but I wasn't surprised when Abdul pulled me up.

'No, that is not good.'

'It's the best I can do,' I returned.

'Try again,' he said encouragingly.

I started off once more, but he interrupted me almost immediately with a movement of impatience.

'What are you trying to say?'

'I'm trying to say that I wondered whose house it was, whether it was yours or Ali's.'

'But that is the first answer you made,' said Abdul. 'I want the right answer.'

'The right answer?' I said, mystified. 'You asked me what

I thought when I saw you and Ali sitting together on the steps of a house yesterday?'

'Yes?' Abdul leant a little forward.

'Well, that is what I thought.'

'But I asked for the right and truthful answer,' said he. 'You should have said, "I wondered what you were both saying about me." You see? In this way.'

'Such a thought never entered my head,' I said indignantly.

But he scarcely believed me.

'No?' he said. 'That is what I or any man would have thought.'

I stared at him speechlessly, which caused him to titter self-consciously and twist his hands in his lap. It was only after he had gone that it occurred to me that this was probably another attempt to induce me to answer his question of the other day, for had I been the reasonable-minded person he expected, I would have been consumed with curiosity to know what Ali and he had been saying about me, and he would not have satisfied my curiosity until I had satisfied his as to what Ali and I had been saying—of course about him.

MRS. BRISTOW: 'And did you like Mrs. Montgomery?'
MYSELF: 'Partly, not altogether.'
MRS. BRISTOW: 'O but you *must* like her! She's a great friend of mine.'
MYSELF: 'I like her better already.'
MRS. BRISTOW: 'Tell me all about her and what she did here. Did you go out hunting with her?'
MYSELF: 'Yes, once—if it could be called hunting.'
MRS. BRISTOW: 'And did you ask to go home in the middle of it?'
MYSELF: 'No, not like that. I got a bit sore and tired, and pretended some interest, as a joke against myself, in the direction of home. But I never actually asked to return.'
MRS. BRISTOW: 'What a liar she is!'

In the bazaar to-day I noticed a shop-keeper sitting cross-legged on the platform of his shop making up his ledger. A common sight—and yet there was something wrong, I could not at first see what. Then I understood: what was his heavy ledger resting on? It was lying open before him, on his stomach, but unsupported by his free hand, not resting against his knees. What on earth was propping it up?

The problem teased my mind so much that I had to retrace my steps for another look. There he still was, comfortably scribbling away in the large ledger, which was standing up, apparently unsupported, in his lap. Then, as I stared, he closed it and got to his feet—and the mystery was explained. He had elephantiasis of the scrotum, and had been utilising this huge football of tissue as a book-rest.

I asked His Highness some time ago whether he would allow me to take a short holiday so that I might travel a little and visit such places as Delhi, Agra and Benares. He agreed at once to my request, saying that I must certainly see more of India than just Chhokrapur during my stay, for that would help me to make up my mind to return and live here. Much encouraged by this generous response to a request I felt I had little right to make, I further asked that I might be allowed to go as soon as possible so that I could make my tour in the comfort of the cool weather, which lasts until about the end of February or the beginning of March. This, too, he agreed to, saying that he himself was making a religious pilgrimage of a month's duration at the end of this month, and that we would synchronize our separate tours. He said this in such a business-like and decisive manner, as though the entire pilgrimage were already mapped out and fixed in time as immutably as a season of the year, that I was quite contented, although I had heard that he feared and disliked travelling, and never left Chhokrapur, and had, on one pretext or another, been putting off this very important pilgrimage for some years. And, indeed, yesterday the first complication arose, for when I asked him whether his day of departure had been selected, he told me that the pundits, without whose advice I doubt whether he would even leave his Palace, had informed him that the only two days propitious for starting were January 31st and February 18th.

'I have to decide which day I will go,' he said.

This was ominous; I felt little doubt that he would choose the remoter of the two days merely because it was the remoter, and the weather was getting appreciably warmer all the time. I pulled out my calendar and looked them up.

'January 31st is a Friday,' I said; 'that is a very lucky day.'

'A very *un*lucky day,' he at once replied flatly.

This was discouraging; but I thought the issue worth another attempt.

'In England we consider it a lucky day,' I said, 'except when it falls on the 13th of the month.'

'Oh?' he said, raising his brows and inclining his head; but the sound was more polite than interested.

'It will be nice weather, too, for travelling,' I added.

'Won't it be very cold?' he asked.

'Oh no, not a bit. It's getting warmer every day.'

But to-day is unfortunately colder, and he has now definitely decided to go on February 18th.

Sharma paid me a call in the late afternoon. I had not seen him for four days, and asked in Hindi why I had been neglected; but I did not understand his reply. He did not seem in the least nervous of me now, made no attempt to hang the curtain over the door so as to have his friend Narayan in view, and even came and sat by me on the sofa while I traced for him my intended journey on the map.

I looked at him sitting there, all bunched up, his bony hands on his knee, his toes turned in. He had not removed his shoes on entering, I noticed, which I have been told is a very grave discourtesy. They were ordinary black laced shoes, but the laces had been taken out, and since he was not wearing socks or stockings I asked whether he would like me to give him some; but he said he had plenty at home.

'Who is more beautiful than the Gods?' I asked, looking at his wild eyes and childish mouth, and he was pleased and smiled, exposing small, undeveloped teeth discoloured with betel-juice. I had never seen him without his turban, and asked him to take it off, which he did; but the result was disappointing and a little shocking, for he showed very large ears and a skull as undeveloped as his teeth, with a low narrow brow towards which his short coarse hairs pointed. I told him to put it on again.

'You are not frightened of me now?' I asked, when he was once more beautiful.

'No.'

'Then we are friends?' He nodded, smiling.

'Then give me a kiss.' Still smiling, he shook his head. Then, after idly turning over the pages of a book on Indian architecture, and pointing, without comment, to some of the illustrations, he got up and, taking another cigarette from the table, shambled off.

'Good . . . bye,' he said in childish English as he left.

January 18*th*

A PLAY was performed for me to-day by a party of travelling players (not, however, the company to which Napoleon the Third belongs), assisted by His Highness's Gods. A general invitation to the Guest House had been issued, but I begged the Maharajah to confine it to myself, for I had already attended a play with those two women, and my note-taking had so irritated them both (especially Mrs. Bristow: 'What are you writing down all this rubbish for?') that at last I had been prevented from continuing it, to the deprivation of this journal. He gave in to me, and only Babaji Rao, the Secretary, and his little son Ram Chandra, attended this performance with me. It was not, of course, a private Palace entertainment like the other I had seen, or the women would never have been invited, but took place on a low wooden platform, roughly constructed in the open space near the sundial, just behind the Palace. A canvas screen enclosed it, and a carpet roofed it in. Inside we found everything ready. A white drugget was spread in front of the stage, and down the centre of it, from under the drop-curtain, ran a narrow strip of carpet. Red cloths were stretched on strings from both sides of the proscenium to the canvas enclosure; the one on the left concealed the orchestra and its friends, the other formed the actors' dressing-room.

An incandescent light on a stand glared in front of each of these curtains. I took longer to remove my shoes, which were laced, than Babaji Rao and his son took to remove theirs, which were not; so Babaji Rao said I might retain them if I wished, but if I did so I must not point my feet at the actors. In these circumstances I thought it safer to take them off, and we seated ourselves on the low divan, covered with a sheet, which was prepared for us. The drop-curtain represented Vishnu enthroned and attended; it was set between two flat cardboard pillars—pink on a green ground. The orchestra begins to throb, like a quick, irregular pulse—there seems to be a harmonium as well as tom-toms and fiddles—and the curtain rises, disclosing the Manager (*Sutradhar*), who always introduces 'orthodox drama.'

He is dressed in white vestments, with a puce hat and 'scapulary,' which give him the appearance of a priest, and stands in the left wing in front of another drop-curtain which represents an ornate, pinky street, deserted and un-inhabited except for one almost invisible figure, apparently female—and probably a domestic servant, for she stands at the highest window of one of the houses peeping out. As the music works up, the Manager begins to chant and to beat incessantly two small cymbals. He is invoking the blessing of the Gods on this his play. To him, from the opposite wing, comes the clown (*Bidoushak*). He is dressed in rags, and a bundle of thorny branches is bound across his face with a white napkin.

He dances, and when he has finished the Manager remarks:

71

'I was praying to the Gods for a *blessing*—and look what has come!'

He then addresses himself to the clown.

'What are you wearing over your face?'

'The good deeds of my wife,' answers the clown, removing the bush. 'And what might you be doing?'

'I am making a play of the Gods.'

'What! You are making an auction of the Gods?'

This is a poor pun on the Hindoo word involved, and the conversation continues for a time in this strain.

'Do you know English?' asks the Manager.

'Yes,' answers the clown.

'How much?'

'Only "Yes." '

At length the clown is told to go and get the blessing of Ganesh, the Elephant-headed God, who is supplicated at the outset of all undertakings owing to his particular faculty for warding off evil; so he retires with instructions as to where the God may be found, and after the Manager has done a little more chanting, the raising of the street-drop gives him his cue for departure and discloses Ganesh, seated upon his throne before a curtain representing a marble hall with a vista of stumpy pink pillars. He is hideously ugly. He wears a red elephant's head (the symbol of great wisdom) with large human ears, and a gold hat. His right hand is raised, his left extended, in the attitude of bead-counting.

The remainder of his costume is red, and there are cardboard shields upon his shoulders and upper arms. Why has he been invoked? he inquires of the entering clown. The clown explains; Ganesh gives his blessing, and the former returns to convey the glad tidings to the Manager in the deserted street. But Ganesh's protection is not enough. The negative preventive blessing having been obtained, the positive favour of success and fluency for the actors is now required, and for this Saraswati, wife to the Creator, Brāhma, and Goddess of the Arts, is invoked. She appears, in a forest scene, riding upon her peacock (which is in two pieces, tacked on to her fore and aft) and executes a slow, joyless dance.

I recognised her at once, by her sullen, spiteful expression, as the young man who had espoused the three Gods at His Highness's private view, and since she does not appear now any better pleased with her peacock than she had been with three husbands, maybe there is no pleasing her at all. When she comes to a standstill, the Manager respectfully requests her to bless his actors with fluency, and she consents, rather ungraciously observing that she can make the mute to speak, let alone actors.

She then says she is going back to Heaven (*Nak*); whereupon the clown exclaims:

'What! She is going up my nose (*Nak*)? Indeed she isn't! I shall hold it.' Which he does.

Upon this the abandoned street is again unrolled, and the Manager returns with his chant and cymbals. He is again visited by the clown, who carries a sword upon his shoulder, and describes how he once caught a lion in a parrot's cage. I forget how this was done, and it doesn't matter; as Babaji Rao said, they were just doing a little gagging until the play was ready. So the clown tells another story of how he went to stay with his father-in-law. He was given a room at the top of the house, and desiring to go downstairs at night to make water (*peshab karna*), and being unused to the house and unable to see in the dark, he tied one end of his turban to his bedrail and took the other end with him so that he might find his way back. Unfortunately a buffalo which happened to be in the house chewed the turban through, and the clown, returning, lost himself and got into bed with his mother-in-law by mistake.

At length the Manager and the clown retire, and their place is taken by a boy dressed as a dancing girl. He raises his hands aloft and stamps slowly and awkwardly round the stage, jingling the bells on his ankles, and much impeded by a very heavy pink skirt and several tawdry yellow veils edged with silver. From time to time he glances anxiously into the wings, and is clearly prepared to go stamping on until fatigue overtakes him or some one tells him to stop; which some one eventually does, and he exits with obvious relief, his dance uncompleted.

This concludes the preamble; in orthodox drama it is invariable in form, though not in dialogue.

The play itself now begins. The curtain rises discovering another woodland scene, more elaborate than the last, in which Siva, the Dissolver and Reproducer, is squatting with his wife, Parwati. Siva wears a red cloak and the River Ganges on his head in the form of a rag doll, for he is said to have intercepted this stream as it flowed out of the foot of Vishnu, so that the earth should not be swamped by the rush of water. He looks very silly and gaga in his unconvincing grey beard, and is indeed recognised as being the simplest of the Hindoo Gods; but his consort, Parwati, is a handsome young man and has a ring in his nose. It seems that Siva has called a council of the Gods to discuss some problem, and soon they arrive, heralded by the clown; first Indra, the Rain God and Hindoo 'Zeus'; then Brāhma, the Creator, who has four faces so that he can see all round; and finally Vishnu, the Preserver, carrying his bow. Each is accompanied by his wife; they all kneel to Siva and seat themselves on either side of him in a semicircle, and when the party is complete Siva bids Parwati take the ladies for a walk and show them the beauties of Mount Kylash. Rid of their wives, the Gods now get to business. Apparently the trouble is that Siva has sent one of his demon devotees to bring him some ashes from a funeral pyre, and he has not yet returned. What can have happened? But scarcely has the question been put when flames and smoke spurt from the right wing, and, uttering fierce cries, the demon rushes on with a drawn sword and executes a wild dance.

His aspect is truly terrifying. Black and unkempt are his wig and moustache; across his forehead streaks of red paint have been drawn; dark rings encircle his eyes, and from his upper jaw two small tusks protrude. His costume is less

74

impressive. It begins all right at the top with shoulder-
guards and a monstrous silver helmet decorated with peacocks' feathers; but below this there is a muddle of yellow
chiffon swathed about his torso and spreading forth, beneath a metal belt, like a ballet dancer's skirt, and below
this again are red stockings, so that his general appearance resembles that of the comic pirate in a Christmas
pantomime.

'Why are you so late in bringing me my ashes from the
funeral pyre?' asks Siva testily.

'To-day no one has died,' replies the Demon. 'You cannot
have a funeral pyre without a dead man. Grant me a boon
that I may be able to destroy any one upon whose head I
lay my hand, so that there will be none of this delay in
future.'

Any one else would have given this request a few moments' consideration, but Siva is a simple God and merely
says:

'Very well, have your wish; but see you use it carefully,
and only when you cannot get hold of ashes in any other
way, mind!'

The other Gods, however, are rather dismayed; they think
that Siva has been foolishly rash, and, when the Demon has
retired looking eminently untrustworthy, they do not scruple
to tell him so; but Siva merely remarks that he always finds
it difficult to refuse a request. After this no one seems to have
anything more to say; a sheepish exeunt takes place, and
two men in black enter and dance together on the empty
stage. They look like executioners in a melodrama, and in
fact they are the Demon's attendants; and it is not long
before he himself returns, still uttering ominous cries, and
joins the dance. And now we learn, what we have already
been inclined to suspect, that he is a thorough bad lot. He
got his annihilating power, he tells his satellites, by a trick,
for he never made any attempt whatever to find a corpse,
and intends now to use it upon the Gods themselves and
make himself master of the world. The curtain falls upon

him hurrying off upon his fell work, and rises again upon Indra enthroned.

To Indra comes Bidoushak the clown, with word that the Demon's two attendants have called and are waiting outside. They are admitted, and, without delay, curtly inform Indra that he must immediately abdicate his throne as the Demon wants it. Indra refuses haughtily, and descending on to the drugget in front of the proscenium, dances a battle-dance with each of them in turn; but while the issue is still un-decided the Demon himself irrupts, and Indra, to evade the destructive touch, flees incontinently into the wings. The curtain falls.

The next scene is the same, but now it is Brāhma who is seated on the throne. He is visited by the perturbed Indra, who explains the mischief afoot and what a narrow squeak he himself has just had; but even while they are discussing it and saying they told Siva so, in come the two attendants unannounced. Now it is Brāhma who dances with them; but again, while the result is in the balance, the Demon appears and drives both the Gods before him. Vishnu's turn comes next, and we have a repetition of the preceding action; he also is put to flight. Then the scene changes, and we are back again in the wood. Here is Siva, seated beneath a tree. He welcomes his Demon with cordial speech, which the latter rudely interrupts, and the old man is at last brought to his senses.

He is very upset.

'You are my disciple, my son,' he says; 'it doesn't become you to speak to me like this.'

But alas! even the Gods themselves, it seems, cannot move the heartless; the Demon becomes truculent, and the poor old man is obliged to draw his sword, and is soon driven ignominiously from the stage.

Parwati, his wife, now enters. She has come to seek her lord, but is met instead by the returning Demon (for whom even Siva, it seems, has been too nimble), who makes improper suggestions to her. She escapes, pursued; but returns almost immediately and prays softly to Vishnu to preserve her chastity and save Siva. If she had seen, as we have seen, Vishnu's inglorious defeat, perhaps she would have taken other measures to protect herself; but as it is, she departs apparently well satisfied, and Vishnu appears.

He says that something must certainly be done at once to help Parwati, and goes off to make arrangements for a scheme he has in mind. This does not take long; he returns at once, but in a new form—as a young and beautiful maiden.

(As a matter of fact another actor took the part of Vishnu transformed—the spiteful-looking young man who in the prologue had been Saraswati—so that I found this a little confusing; but Babaji Rao appeared to have no difficulty in following, nor did Ram Chandra, his son.)

Opportunely the Demon returns, and falls in love at first sight. The disguised Vishnu receives his protestations with unconcealed satisfaction, saying that she too feels herself considerably attracted towards him and would like to dance with him. But the suggestion is received with the loftiest scorn; he has never learned to dance, the Demon says, only to fight, and she must either fight with him or marry him. But she pleads so prettily for this first favour that at length he gives way, and, to gratify her, joins her in a dance.

'That shows,' whispered the stout Secretary in my ear, 'to what absurd lengths a man will go when he believes himself to be in love.'

And indeed it was a pitiable sight to see this mighty Demon, who aspired to the seat of the Gods, befooled by a mere girl, divine though she might be, into dancing a minuet. Clearly he is no good at it, but clumsily copies her every movement of hand and foot, and becomes at last so confused that when she raises her hand to her head he does likewise, forgetful of the dangerous power granted him by Siva. He touches himself; there is a flash of pink flame from the left wing to signalize his internal combustion, and screaming in the agony of death he rushes from the scene. Whereupon all the Gods flock in and congratulate Vishnu,

77

now in his proper shape, on his cunning ruse, and the final curtain falls.

'My son is very pleased with you,' said Babaji Rao as we parted. 'He says you are a good man, so you must be all right, for he is very difficult to please.'

Babaji Rao is only about thirty, not much older than myself, in fact. I was astonished to hear this, for with his corpulence, his spectacles, and his scanty greying hair, he looks quite forty, and his serious, rather pedantic manner, too, is that of a much older man. But it is very difficult to guess the age of Indians. I had always thought that Abdul, for instance, must be about thirty; but when I asked him his age to-day he said: 'I am half past twenty-two.'

His Highness's night's rest is of six hours' duration, and is divided into two periods. He sleeps from 11 P.M. to 2 A.M., when he sits up and transacts business or writes letters for six hours. Then he sleeps again from 8 A.M. to 11 A.M.

'Do you mean to say,' I asked him, 'that you call the Dewan and Babaji Rao at two o'clock in the morning?'

He spluttered, and waved a protesting hand.

'No, no, no,' he said, 'I call them at five or six. But I asked them once what they would say if I sent for them at two o'clock, and the Dewan said, "You will be responsible for the murder of a Brahman," and Babaji Rao said, "You will be teaching me my first lesson in disobedience." '

His Highness had told Mrs. Bristow also that he did his writing in the middle of the night.

'What, poems?' she asked, and when he shook his head, 'Oh, what a pity! I was hoping you'd write one to me.'

He did so (she is his idea, he says, of perfect feminine beauty), and sent it to her—a nice little poem, which said among other things that her eyebrows were like drawn bows and her teeth like pomegranate seeds.

'Do you like India?' Mrs. Bristow asked me.

'Oh, yes. I think it's marvellous.'

'And what do you think of the people?'

'I like them very much, and think them most interesting.'

'Oo, aren't you a fibber! What was it you said the other day about "awful Anglo-Indian chatter"?'

'But I thought you were speaking of the Indians just now, not the Anglo-Indians.'

'The Indians! I never think of them.'

'Well, you said "the people," you know.'

'I meant *us* people, stupid!'

'I see. Well now, let's start again.'

January 19*th*

ABDUL HAQ showed me some obscene postcards to-day.

'I have brought with me some pictures, Mr. Ackerley,' he said. 'Do you wish to see them?'

'What are they, Abdul?'

'Postcards,' he said, simpering 'Very *bad* postcards, so I do not wish to show them to you . . . unless you wish to see them. You understand?'

I did not quite understand, perhaps chiefly because, having always, from a vague mistrust, kept my relationship with Abdul strictly scholastic, I was scarcely prepared for a sudden exchange of the schoolroom for the lavatories of sex. There had, indeed, been indications that such an exchange might, at my least encouragement, be easily effected, for among the first things he had taught me were such phrases as 'To have sexual intercourse,' 'To lie down with one's wife,' 'To make water,' and so forth, accompanied by bashful sniggerings and puffings in the nose; and although I had been grateful for such practical information and must count these phrases as among the first learned as well as the first taught, I had never taken advantage of them as short-cuts to intimacy.

'Where are they?' I asked.

'I have them here, in my pocket; but I do not *wish* you

to see them. If you *tell* me to show them to you, then I *must* show them to you. You understand? In *this* way.'

Having made himself clear, he frowned slightly, drew in his chin (a peculiar trick of his), and scrabbled nervously among his notes.

I watched him with great amusement. It was the second time he had played for my curiosity, and this time he certainly won. Bad postcards were irresistible.

'Come on, Abdul,' I said, 'let's have a look at them.'

He looked up brightly, smiling with tight lips.

'You wish to see them?' I nodded. 'You are sure, Mr. Ackerley?' I nodded. 'You will not be angry with me?' I shook my head. 'They are *very* bad.' I held out my hand. 'But I do not *show* them to you, you understand?' he continued, drawing a packet from his pocket. 'You have commanded me—against my wish. Look, I place them here, on the table. It is for you to decide.'

I took them, and he at once craned forward, straining his hands in his lap, watching the expression of my face as I turned the cards, and tittering when one was particularly pornographic. They were mostly photographs, all of extremely unattractive naked Europeans, conventionally or unconventionally amusing themselves and taken from the most spectacular angles. I had seen them before—or pictures very similar—at school, where I was disgusted and returned them quickly to their owner, and later in Paris, or Naples, where I was disgusted and bought them.

Perhaps they differed little in subject from the sodomitic sculptures on the Garha temples—the representation of an act; but their greater reality prevented one from looking at them with such detachment, rendered them more sensational, so that the figures, selected by the photographer with as little concern for physical beauty as, it seemed, the Garha figures had been cut, were here repulsive, whilst the latter, owing to their unreality, had been merely quaint.

'You like them?' asked Abdul slyly when I had turned the last.

'Very interesting,' I said in a cold voice, handing them back.

I had gone with him as far along that road as I intended to go; I had indulged in front of him a coarse appetite; it was quite another matter to share with him my satisfaction.

I was, indeed, as much in need of friendship as he had shown himself ready to supply it; but I did not want Abdul for my friend.

There is a small market fair on the outskirts of the town, and strolling through it this afternoon I thought I would like to taste the queer silvery saffron sweets that were displayed on some of the stalls. Mrs. Bristow appeared at that moment, and asked me what I thought I was doing. I enlightened her. 'You're mad!' she exclaimed. 'Do you want cholera? Because if you do, eat some of those sweets and you'll be dead in a few hours!'

'But quite a lot of people are eating them,' I said. 'Will they all be dead in a few hours?'

'Indians!' Mrs. Bristow snorted. 'Never mind what filth they put into *their* stomachs. That's a very different matter. They're pretty well inoculated by now, I should imagine. But what *they* can eat will kill *you*. All right' (as she saw the doubt in my face), 'you needn't believe me, but I *know*. Nobody, *nobody*, unless he's out of his senses, would *dream* of touching Indian sweets!'

She spoke with such vehemence that I was quite alarmed, and allowed myself to be led sweet-less away.

It appears that Sharma has been very naughty. The Maharajah gave him a small gift of ten rupees last night, and since this was received in silence, asked:

'Are you not pleased?'

'No,' said Sharma sullenly. 'It spoils me.'

'Then why do you not give it back?'

'I do. Here—take it!'

'Very well. Then, since presents spoil you, why do you

not give me back all the other things I have given you—
the money, clothes, and ornaments?'

'I do. I give them all back. I will bring them now.'

'Bring them to-morrow morning,' said His Highness,
exerting what little dignity and authority remained to him;
'and meanwhile go, and do not return until I send for you.'

'He is a very bad boy,' concluded the King morosely
when he had recounted this deplorable incident.

'Oh, no,' I smiled; 'he's a good boy really; he's only a
child!'

'He is a very bad boy,' repeated His Highness, gazing
straight before him. 'He says that when he came up to see
you the other day, you tried to—to—to cling him, that you
threw him down and tried to cling him.'

'What!' I exclaimed, considerably startled.

'That is what he told me,' said His Highness.

'It's an absolute lie,' I said.

'That is what I told him,' he replied, turning upon me
wide eyes that politely reflected my indignation; 'and I
said that if he repeated the lie to anyone else I would send
him to hell. He is a very bad boy!'

'A *very* bad boy!' I warmly agreed.

He did not appear to have anything more to say, and for
some moments we rolled slowly along the empty road in
silence. Then it seemed to me that in justice to Sharma I
should explain what had actually taken place.

'I asked for a kiss,' I said, 'and he refused. That's all that
happened. I didn't lay a finger on him.'

'But you must not do such things, Mr. Ackerley,' remarked His Highness, without the smallest change of tone.

'But good Lord!' I exclaimed. 'I must kiss *somebody*.'

His small body began to shake, and he hid his face in his
sleeve.

'I suppose this explains why he didn't come for a ride
with me this morning?' I asked, after a pause.

'Did he say he *would* come?' He enquired huskily, looking
very grave.

'Yes, he did. However, if he comes to-morrow I will forget that he didn't come to-day.'

'I will tell him he *must* come.'

'Tell him he *may* come,' I said.

January 20*th*

EARLY this afternoon I received a visit from His Highness and Babaji Rao. The latter, who has never in my short experience achieved tidiness, looked particularly dishevelled and careworn. He was carrying a sheaf of papers in his hand.

'We have come to you for help, Mr. Ackerley,' said His Highness; and then to Babaji Rao, abruptly, 'Tell him what it is.'

Babaji Rao was obviously very nervous; he kept clearing his throat and smoothing the top of his head; but he explained, in his halting manner, that 'His Highness the Maharajah Sahib' was not yet satisfied with any of the attempts made to compose that difficult letter to the A.G.G., and my services were again required——

'Give them to him! Give them to him!' interrupted the King, so curtly that Babaji Rao spilt most of the papers on the floor. They were collected and handed to me, and I found about half a dozen letters to the A.G.G., all unfinished, in His Highness's and the Secretary's hand. My own letter was included, and separate from these was the King's latest attempt to combine them all and, at the same time, to express gratitude for the recent introduction to Mr. Bramble, the architect. This also, it appeared, he had been unable to finish, and Babaji Rao's suggestions had been worse than useless.

'You are to read them all,' His Highness said to me, 'and put everything I want to say into one letter, in the best English. Can you do this? Can you do this—miracle?'

I said I could.

'*He* cannot do it,' he remarked bitterly, pointing to Babaji Rao, who cleared his throat again; 'he cannot do anything. How long do you require? Ten minutes?'

83

'Would an hour be too long?' I asked.

'No, that will do. When you have finished, give it to Babaji Rao, and he will bring it to me in the Guest House. Take my letter as your model.'

I had already glanced through it, and noticed that he had retained much of my own letter, but that all the 'Your Honours' which I had cut out had been restored, while the compliments heaped on Mr. Bramble were excessive; he was even alluded to as 'a gem among men.'

'You seem to have changed your opinion of Mr. Bramble, Maharajah Sahib,' I said gravely. 'You told me once you thought he was an awful bore.'

'But the A.G.G. will like it,' explained His Highness with irritation. 'They are very great friends.'

Then he hobbled out, followed by the Secretary, who drew aside the curtain to let him pass. As they retired towards the Guest House I heard the King's voice uttering brief remarks in Hindi which did not sound at all amiable.

Babaji Rao's voice I did not hear at all; but he soon returned, and keeping his face averted, but casting at me every now and then timid, furtive glances, he shuffled off his shoes.

'Shall I disturb you?' he asked.

'No, my dear man, of course not.'

'I do not think I can be of any help, but ask me if you get into difficulties. May I rest on your sofa for a moment?'

'Yes, do.'

He spread himself out, and began to polish his glasses; his feet, encased in mustard-coloured socks, pointing at the ceiling. He is a very loyal subject and servant, and would not have wished me, even implicitly, to show a sympathy for him which would seem to reflect unfavourably upon the King.

I forget the exact letter I wrote for His Highness, but it was based on his own style and ran more or less as follows:

'DEAR SIR,—I feeel that I cannot thank you sufficiently for having introduced Mr. Bramble to me; I have seldom met so

84

charming and courteous a man, and it was a great pleasure to have his company and see his very interesting designs. He has promised to send me a statement of the details, together with the estimated cost, of the Greek Villa which I contemplate having built. We shall then have to consider to what extent the State will be able to support the scheme. The site which he has selected at Garha is ideal, and if the building is raised I am sure, from what I have seen of Mr. Bramble's designs, that it will be a beautiful addition to the State. I was very disappointed that he could not prolong his stay, but hope that our connection may continue. * I shall be very happy to have the photograph you promise me, and so that I may also possess one of your family, may I send a photographer myself to take it? For the message contained in your letter I am very grateful indeed, and am confident in your assurances for the future, remembering your unfailing generosity and kindness to me in the past. If there is anything in the papers which my Dewan has submitted to you which you could wish to have explained, I shall be pleased to send him personally to you at any time that suits your convenience. With kindest regards to yourself, Lady S.—and the children, etc.'

When I had finished this I gave it to Babaji Rao and accompanied him to the Guest House. We found His Highness talking to Mrs. Murphy, a stout, good-natured Irishwoman, wife to one of the medical officers of Shikaripur. She was telling him that one of her children was sick, and I heard him say with deep concern:

'Why did you not tell me? I will send up a magician to him.'

'Whatever for?' asked Mrs. Murphy.

'He will cut——'

'Oh no, please; there's nothing like that!'

'No, no; he will cut something out of paper, and all the badness will fly away.'

His Highness read my letter and professed himself satisfied with it. In the evening one of his messengers arrived bringing his version of it, addressed and stamped but unsealed, with a short note asking if it would do. Up to the asterisk in my own letter he seemed to have followed me closely, but thence onward it proceeded as follows:

' . . . For the kind message contained in your letter of the 6th inst. I am very grateful indeed, and feel confident in Your Honour's assurances for the future, remembering Your Honour's unfailing generosity and kindness to me in the past. . . . Indeed it will be a great pleasure to have the photograph of yourself which you promise to send. . . . For that, if you do not mind, I would like to send the photographer whose address you so kindly sent me the other day. I have written to him about that, and if he agrees to go there you will kindly have a photograph of yourself (in standing posture) and a family group from him.

He will then prepare the copies and send one set to me and the other to you. . . . I hope this will meet with Your Honour's assent. As my long-cherished desire of addressing Mrs. S.—as Lady S.—has been fulfilled by the Almighty, I would now like to open correspondence with her direct. Hope you will allow me to do so. . . .'

I wrote a note to him saying that I did not think it could be improved upon.

January 21*st*

MRS. BRISTOW and Mrs. Murphy are to go to-morrow, so this afternoon His Highness gave them a farewell tea-party at Mahua Palace. The Political Agent was also to be invited; His Highness was going into Rajgarh to bring him back, and Mahua being on the way, he took Mrs. Murphy with him in his car and left me to escort Mrs. Bristow in another. Shall I record the conversation of Mrs. Bristow as we drove through the cool scented air? It hasn't anything to do with India—but then it seldom had; perhaps that is a good reason for recording it. It doesn't much matter which of her remarks we start off with. Let us take this one:

'What nice hands you've got; too nice for a man. I hate effeminacy in a man.'

'Yes, they are nice hands,' I said, looking at them. They

were quite clean and I had given up biting their nails. I was genuinely pleased with them.

'Of course you're frightfully conceited,' she observed. 'That's such a pity. I hate conceit in a man.'

'Do you mean about my hands?'

'Oh no, lots of things. I've been watching you. I rather hate you.'

I did not say anything; there seemed nothing to say, and it was perhaps lucky that I didn't, for shortly afterwards she said:

'I love you now. You don't mind me saying so, do you? I always make a point of telling people if I change my opinion of them. I think it's only fair.'

'But why have you changed your opinion?' I asked.

'I've been observing you. Yes, I love you now. You're a dear. So you must like me too—do you?'

'Yes, rather!' I said enthusiastically. But perhaps I over-did it.

'Well, anyway, you've done me good—not making love to me. Every other man I've ever met has. But I'm not conceited. I'm not, am I? I'm nice really, as you'd find out if you knew me better. You don't know me very well, do you?'

'Very well enough,' I couldn't help saying.

'You're the rudest man I ever met!' she exclaimed. 'Bar none!'

Conversation languished after this; then she began again. 'Of course, you're beyond me. I don't understand you. I'm rather frightened of you. You're always silent and sort of deep. I love superficial people. I hate silent people. I'm one of those awful people who are always frightfully cheerful when others are gloomy. . . . Tell me—you needn't be afraid of telling me things—have you ever been bowled over by a woman?'

'No, never,' I answered, watching a flock of green parrots dart overhead.

'You will! Just you wait!

When we arrived at Mahua I was called by His Highness, and we had a short walk on the terrace before he continued his drive to Rajgarh.

'Did the barber's son ride with you yesterday morning?' he asked.

'Sharma? No, I haven't seen him for days. Did you tell him to?'

'Yes, I told him to. I said, "You must go and ride with the Sahib when he calls you." He did not come?'

'No, he did not come.'

'He is very disobedient. I told him also to come in the morning to massage my legs. They get very stiff. But he did not come.'

'He's a naughty boy!' I said, smiling.

'He is a rogue!' said His Highness emphatically. 'What is a rogue?'

I explained.

'He is a great nuisance,' he murmured dimly.

Mrs. Bristow came up to us shortly after this, and His Highness greeted her with enthusiasm, and asked her where she had bought her hat. It was black and rather of the *chapeau bras* type, but higher in the crown.

'Do you like it, Maharajah Sahib?' she asked.

'Oo, I like, I like!' he said, staring at it childishly. 'Where did you get it? I want one like it for myself.'

She laughed, and said it was a Paris model but that she could not remember where she had got it; but he was not amused, and turned a very serious face to me.

'You must get me such a hat, Mr. Ackerley,' he said. 'You must write to Paris for it. Do not forget. I *must* have it.'

I said I would discuss the matter with Mrs. Bristow, and satisfied with that, he got back into his car and drove off to Rajgarh to fetch the Political Agent. But he returned late, alone and melancholy.

I was sent for, and found him huddled up in a corner of the car looking rather wretched. He didn't speak, but with his hand indicated the seat beside him. I got in, and we drove back to Chhokrapur.

For some time he was silent; then he cried out:

'What is criticism? What should we say to it? Should we allow it?'

Then it all came out. He had spoken about his darling project, the Greek Villa, to the Political Agent; but his enthusiasm had been met with coldness and even with cruelty. What childish scheme was this? the Political Agent had demanded. It was sheer waste of money. His Highness was an old man, and if he lived to see the building finished he could not be expected long to survive its completion. And what earthly use would such an edifice be to his son, or to any one else, for that matter? Instead of wasting money over Greek Villas he would do well to apply it to something useful and necessary—such as road-mending, for example. That was, more or less, the Political Agent's criticism, and no doubt it was sound enough, but its harshness seemed inexcusable. I said something of the kind—rather inconsiderately, for the least approval of Political Agents, never very wise, was at that moment obviously ill-timed, and His Highness relapsed into moody silence. In front of us, going in the same direction, was a slow procession of bullock-waggons. These and buffalo-carts are, except for pedestrians, about the only traffic one meets with; but they are frequent, and usually occupy the crown of the road. The chauffeur sounds his horn on sight, and the wagons stagger, unsystematically, to right and left and come to a halt, while the drivers clamber hastily down, and taking hold of their agitated beasts by the horns, hang on to their heads, and try at the same time to perform a salaam. For, owing no doubt to the infrequency of motor-cars in these parts, the bullocks are terrified of them; they stand rigidly tense until the car is actually passing, and then make a convulsive movement towards the jungle, which their owners, clinging to their heads, can hardly restrain.

Honk! said our car, as we sighted them.

'Are you still troubled?' I asked the King gently.

'To-day I am very pessimist.'

Indeed I had failed him, and he did not any longer want my company.

'Jao! Jao!' (Get on! Get on!) he muttered, and the car, suddenly accelerated, bounced, and then flew over the dusty road. Honk-Honk! Honk-Honk! it said, and the panic-stricken bullocks, as we burst into their midst, stampeded to right and left before their owners could control them, and overturned their loaded wagons in the ditches on either side of the road. I clung to the strap beside me; but His Highness lay back in his corner and beheld with a bilious eye these minor disasters, which were soon left behind us in a thick cloud of dust.

'What do you do next Sunday, Mr. Ackerley?' asked Abdul during our lesson this evening.

'I don't know,' I answered cautiously.

'Have you seen the big tank at Rajgarh?'

'No, I don't think I have.'

'But you should. It is very beautiful. I will take you and explain everything in Hindi. You will learn to speak very well in this way. Sunday is a Holy Day for me, so I shall be able to accompany you.'

I wondered what he was after now. Perhaps he had some business in Rajgarh, or was it just his vanity, for I knew he liked being seen with me in public, and became, on such occasions, very self-important and haughty, walking stiffly beside me, his umbrella beneath his arm, and greeting his friends with dignity. But I did not say anything, and soon he continued:

'You could get His Highness to lend you one of the cars for the day. It is easy for you; he will give it at once because you are the Sahib. There are one, two, three, four cars— and you must ask for the Daimler because it is the best. He cannot refuse you.'

'I usually ask Babaji Rao when I want a car,' I said.

'Then you will ask *him*. That is perhaps better. But do not say *I* asked, or he will be angry with me. You understand?'

'Perfectly,' I said.

'Then what will you say?'

'I shall say,' I answered, knitting my brows—'I shall say, "Abdul wants to know if you will lend me a car on Sunday to take him to Rajgarh where he has some private business to transact." '

Abdul was quivering with anxiety by the time I had finished. 'No, no!' he cried, holding his hands before him as though warding off some unseen danger; 'you must not! You must not really! He will be very angry with me. Listen; I will tell you what to say. Hear me. "How many tanks are there about here, Mr. Babaji Rao?" He will then number them. Then you will say, "Which is the largest? I should like to see it." He will then name the Rajgarh tank, and you will say, "I will go and see it on Sunday. Please let me have a car. The Daimler. And I think I will take my tutor Abdul with me." In this way. You understand? Am I clear?'

'Perfectly,' I said gravely.

'Then how will you say?'

'Let me see,' I said, 'how did it go? "My tutor Abdul wants to know . . ." '

'No, no! no, no! that is *not* the way I told you!' cried Abdul in great agitation; then he perceived that he was being mocked, and drawing in his chin, he twisted his hands together in his lap, and smiled self-consciously down his nose.

January 23rd

SHARMA appears to have recovered from his ill humour. He walked into the Palace this morning, His Highness tells me, in the sunniest of moods.

'How are you to-day?' asked the King, looking at him suspiciously.

'I am very well.'

'Are you going to be obedient to me?'

'Of course. Am I not always obedient?'

His Highness passed this over with the silence it deserved.

'And will you take my gifts?'

'Of course. Are we not your beggars?'

'And will you go and ride with the Sahib when he asks you?'

'Yes, I will gladly go.'

His Highness clapped his hands together, as much as to say to me 'What do you think of that?'

'Yesterday,' he said, 'he was like one in a dream; but to-day—I do not know.'

Chhokrapur is lovely in the evening twilight. Standing by the Dilkhusha tank to-day, I watched for a little the imperceptible transition of day into night. Over the water the spur of hill on which my house stands was black and featureless, but behind it, edging with light the cypresses and the speared dome of the Hanuman temple upon the crest, the sky was pale green and of curious depth, like the eyes of a lover into which we hungrily gaze, believing that here at last, where the light seems so clear, we shall find truth. Above, lifted by the cypress plumes, Venus brightly shone, and lay also at my feet a pale, quivering starfish below the silver surface of the water. The air was full of the sweet scent of the dust. In the far distance a pipe thrilled, and along the stone margin of the lake a turbaned boy walked towards me, salaamed, and gathering earth from the pathway, descended the steps to wash his hands. I continued on my way, and as I walked on I heard him, out of sight, singing to himself, his voice mingling with the reedy music of the pipe.

The night is always full of strange sounds. There is the throb of the tom-tom, at one house or another, keeping up marriage celebrations or other festivities till the dawn, accompanied by the rapid chanting of the musicians; and there is the screaming of the jackals. Encouraged by the darkness, these beasts come foraging into the town itself at night, and the noise they make is human and terrible, like a scream of pain.

Indeed, until this evening, I believed these appalling wails were really uttered by human beings, though I had forgotten to ask why; but when they began to-night, quite close to my house, Babaji Rao was sitting with me, and he told me they were only the voices of the jackals.

'There was once a very simple king,' he began immediately, in his pedantic way, passing a hand over his bald head, and told me this story. 'There was once a very simple king who, hearing the jackals howl constantly outside his palace, said to his minister, "What are they crying for—those poor animals?" "They are cold," said the resourceful minister, "and are crying for warm clothing. Poor brutes! They have nothing to put on at all, not even a loincloth, no matter how cold the weather is." "How much will it cost to clothe all the jackals in my kingdom?" asked his sovereign. "At least ten thousand rupees," said the resourceful minister. "See that it is done," said the simple king. But a few days later he heard them wailing again. "Are those jackals not yet clothed?" he asked. "Yes, sire." "Then why do they still cry?" "They are thanking you for your charity towards them," said the astute minister.'

January 25th

WHEN I walked this morning to the post-office, I met an elephant with a load of rushes and grass entering the town from the Eastern Gate. The Maharajah does not any longer keep elephants, and this is the first I have seen in Chhokrapur. Later on I learnt the reason: this is the birthday of the Elephant-headed God, Ganesh, and a day of fasting. A fair was to be held in commemoration, and in the early part of the afternoon His Highness came to take me to it.

'Maharajah Sahib! Maharajah Sahib!' chattered the

grey-bearded Munshi, appearing in my doorway and pointing down the drive. With the exception of Hashim, whose
wooden impassivity is only relaxed when he is playing with
his baby and a sweet, tender smile lights his face, all the
Guest House servants get excited at His Highness's arrival,
and tidy themselves, and stand up ready to bow their foreheads to the ground. But Munshi is always the most moved,
and indeed seems endowed with a special faculty for sensing
the approach of his royal master, for even before the car is in
sight upon the plain below, he pops out of the storeroom
or the cookhouse and stands gazing towards the Palace.
Narayan says that he is not to be trusted; that if I kept the
keys of the storeroom myself that transfer alone would help
considerably to decrease Guest House expenses; and if this
is true the old man's alertness is explained on other grounds
than those of zeal or devotion. I heard the car arrive, and
putting on my topee went out to meet the Maharajah.

'It is all finished! All finished!' he cried out to me in a
tragic voice as I approached.

'What is all finished?' I inquired, getting in.

'Napoleon the Third. His uncle is very sick. They say he
must die.'

Having announced this, he dropped his hands despairingly
in his lap, and turned his face away.

'Dear, dear! But isn't that exactly what you wanted?' I
asked.

'But, my dear sir, if he dies *now* I shall lose the boy for
ever! *Such* bad news! I have not liked singing or dancing
since I heard it.'

I did not quite follow this, so it was explained to me that
some two hundred miles separated the boy, in Cawnpore,
from his dying uncle, while another two hundred miles
separated the uncle from His Highness, and that if a
definite arrangement was not made and the nephew handed
over to His Highness before the uncle expired, other and
unprincipled persons, like wolves always on the watch for
such morsels, would grab the boy.

PART ONE

'Never a very strong man,' remarked His Highness irritably, referring to the uncle.

'Well,' I said, 'perhaps if Napoleon is a good nephew and has any proper feelings he will go and visit the poor old chap on his death-bed, and so if you send a man along at the same time you will be able to complete the transaction.'

'*Just* what I'm hoping!' exclaimed the King.

The fair was a local one, held round the temple of Ganesh. His Highness stopped the car on the road near by and told me to go and look round and then return to him.

The temple stood on a little knoll, and was hardly more than a shrine containing an image of the God about two hundred and fifty years old, which I was not permitted to see.

The knoll was enclosed by a wall with a gate from which white stone steps mounted to the shrine, and these steps and the slopes of the hill were thronged with Hindoos dressed in bright colours, while outside the wall and round the gateway were merchants and pedlars, selling cloth, sweetmeats, and shoes. There was not a very large number of people there, but then it was getting late in the day; the shrine had been open to supplicants since the early morning and would be closed at eight o'clock. It is an important religious occasion, and by the end of the day every Hindoo in Chhokrapur will have visited the shrine and sacrificed to the God. The sacrifice is a cocoanut, which each worshipper brings with him and breaks before the image; after which a garland of marigolds is hung round his neck by the priest.

His Highness explained all this and about cocoanuts when I returned to him. There was once a monk or sage who, as far as I remember, fought against Indra, the King of the Gods, and was defeated by him. At any rate he was very cross, and told Indra that he would go away and create a world of his own which would be a great improvement on Indra's, and when he had made sufficient men he would fight him again. His idea (which he kept secret) was to grow adult men on trees, instead of having all this protracted business of love, gestation, and upbringing.

95

Indra laughed at him; but when he looked down from Mount Kylash a little later on and saw what was going on he became rather alarmed; for the sage had been as good as his word, and was growing men in plantations. Then all the Gods came down and implored him to desist, which he was eventually persuaded to do, so that of the new men nothing more was grown than their heads, which are still to be seen hanging from the cocoanut palm, and which were smashed to-day, as representing the human head, before the image of the Elephant-headed God.

January 28th

WHEN His Highness came to call for me this afternoon, I was greeted in the same way as on the last occasion.
'It is all finished! All finished!'
So this time I did not require to be told what was all finished. 'Napoleon the Third,' I said.
'He isn't coming! Phutt!' He clapped his hands once to express conclusion.
It appeared that a messenger had been sent with five hundred rupees to the uncle, who, it was thought, now that he was dying, would probably take far less than he had demanded when he was not. But the messenger, in an attempt to win favour with his master, had exceeded his authority and lost all. Hoping to get Napoleon for less money still, he had passed over the uncle in favour of a neighbouring aunt, who had asserted that she was the only person who had the legal right to dispose of the boy, and that His Highness should have him for four hundred rupees. Bundling the messenger forthwith to the railway station, she had taken him to Cawnpore; but on arrival there they had been informed by another uncle, temporarily in charge of the company, that, oddly enough, the boy had just gone to visit this very aunt in her village. They must have passed him on the way. So they returned in haste. But the boy was not there, and had not been there, and was not with his

sick uncle either. So back again they journeyed to Cawnpore, only to learn that the boy had been sold for five
hundred rupees to another company, and was on his way to
Calcutta.

'What must I do? What must I do?' asked His Highness.

I had listened to this story with increasing bewilderment,
and felt, at the end of it, confused and feeble. Somewhere
in the middle, somewhere between Cawnpore and the
abode of the crafty aunt, I too had got lost; but even while
I was preparing to question His Highness he diverted my
attention to a tree growing by the roadside.

'Do you see that tree?' he said. 'It is very rare and is called
"*Kalap*—The Tree of Illusion," because it once grew on
Olympus, in the garden of Zeus, and whatever his supplicants wished for—food, money, friendship, happiness—he
would pluck it from that tree and give it to them.'

'Then why don't you transplant one to your Palace courtyard, King,' I asked, 'and pray beneath it for your heart's
desire? With a little faith you might get Napoleon the Third
to grow on it, like a cocoanut. Why don't you?'

'I have!' he cried. 'I do! In secret. But nothing comes . . .
nothing. All that is—gone!'

But in spite of the melancholy of his words, he seemed, I
thought, less upset than might have been expected by the
reverse he had suffered in this latest Napoleonic campaign,
and became, indeed, as time went on, quite sprightly, remarking, as we passed a pretty grassy slope scattered with trees:

'If there were Greeks and Romans on that I would play
hide and go seek with them.'

We were on our way to the village of Chetla, where a fair
was being held, and where also, His Highness told me, there
was a very beautiful boy, son of a betel-leaf planter, on
whose appearance the King wanted my opinion.

We saw the boy first. The car was stopped soon after
entering the village; there were men standing about outside
their mud-houses, and word was passed along for the boy,
who soon appeared from a neighbouring doorway and came

running up. He was lean and hideous. After they had conversed a little and salutations had again passed, we drove on, His Highness avoiding my eye; but when we were out of sight, he looked at me mischievously and dissolved into hoarse laughter.

'I would not have known him,' he said. 'He is all shrunk away. What did you think?'

'Very disappointing,' I answered.

'*Very* disappointing,' he echoed.

The chief industry of Chetla is the cultivation of the betel-leaf, for which the soil of Chhokrapur is not suited; it is a thriving trade, and Chetla is the most prosperous village in the State, its people being so rich and independent that when His Highness has tried to hire servants from among them he has always met with the same reply: 'Why should we come and serve you? We keep servants of our own.'

'They are very quarrelsome and cantankerous,' he remarked bitterly.

We were passing between betel-leaf plantations while he spoke; large areas enclosed in rush and bamboo fencing to a height of about ten feet, and lightly roofed with the same materials. I asked to be allowed to enter one, and His Highness stopped the car and told his cousin to take me. From the door of the plantation into the interior a long straight pathway ran, two or three feet wide, and at right angles to this, on either side, regular lines of bamboos, up which the plants crawled, had been set very close together, so that there was left only sufficient room for one man to pass between them. The atmosphere was cold, odorous, and subaqueous, the large bright green leaves colouring the light. Very thick and luxuriant they grew, constantly in need of water; and for my benefit a farmer, naked except for a loincloth, brought a large earthenware *lutiya* of water and showed me how the watering was done. It was simple and graceful. Retreating backwards down one of the narrow ways between the bamboo stems, he thrust his left hand, palm upwards, into the mouth of the vessel, which was on his left shoulder, and pulling it forward allowed the water to flow out in front of him. Then extending his right hand into the stream, he distributed it, by a slight manual movement, to the betel roots on either side.

When we came out again into the sunlight a little boy presented me with a pile of stemless marigolds which he had been told to pick for me from the small garden that brightened the entrance to the plantation. Thanking him, I took them in the palms of my hands, and nursed them while we visited the fair. It was concentrated in what I suppose was the high street; stalls of sweetmeats and merchandise lined the gutters, and a large crowd of people pressed round them, filling up the road. We did no more than push slowly up and down again in the car, pressing the people back to either side like bushes which swung together again behind us. There was a good deal of noise, laughter, and commentary, and not nearly as much obeisance as the King received when driving through the streets of Chhokrapur; but it all looked to me good-natured enough, though I did not understand the comments. His Highness sat well back, raising his hand perfunctorily every now and then whether he was saluted or not, and shaking gently with laughter when anything particularly amusing happened—as when, for instance, an old man was rolled into the gutter by the mudguard, or a boy pressed a rude grimace against the window. Soon, however, we were clear of the crowd— except for two or three small boys who were adhering to the sides of the car like burrs to clothes, and had to be flicked off by the King's cousin with a long whip always carried for dispersing goats or cows or other nuisances.

'King,' I said, as we left Chetla behind; 'can I throw these lovely flowers away?'

'Yes,' he said; 'but throw them into a bush, so that they will not be trodden under foot.'

I did so; and after a moment he said gently:

'Please do not call me "King"; that is what my dear tutor used to call me; I do not want any one else to use it.'

'Very well,' I said, 'but "Maharajah Sahib" is such a mouthful.'

'Then call me "Prince".'

'All right. Now what about "Mr. Ackerley"? Isn't that rather a mouthful for you?'

'Oh, no,' he said, 'I like it very much. I will tell you something, but you will think me very silly. When I first heard your name, it made me think of a stream of water running over little stones.'

I remember Miss Gibbins, when she was staying in the Guest House a month ago, saying how frequently her night's rest was disturbed by the noises the guard used to make on the verandah outside—coughing and spitting over their brazier, or talking, awake and asleep. Once, when she was disturbed by some sound, she looked through the doorway and saw 'a singular figure in the moonlight—a lean figure upon an emaciated white horse, looking like the White Knight in *Alice through the Looking-Glass*.' In the vigorous language of those accustomed to command and be obeyed, she would order them to be silent or to go away; but I am not very good at this. Always at night, and sometimes, when the weather is bad, in the daytime, my front verandah is thronged with odd, derelict, tattered figures. A small bundle of dirty straw in the corner (eaten during the day by cows, which sometimes blunder into my sitting-room in search of further provender) is used by the guard at night to protect their bodies from the harshness of the concrete floor; and there they lie, wrapped up like mummies in their blankets; or squat smoking over a brazier, passing the pipe from hand to hand, their thin rumps just clear of the ground, their backs curved, their arms dangling over their knees, looking like a cluster of bedraggled birds.

I peer out at them. Besides the guard there are two men, poor, emaciated, huddled face to face under one blanket, and in the far corner is an old woman, shrouded in her rusty red shawl, with rings on her toes and an ornament in her nostril. She too is on her haunches, smoking a fragment of a pipe in solitude, a brazier between her thin brown wrinkled legs.

I peer out at her. She perceives the glint of my eye in the window and draws her shawl across her face. I retreat to my book. Through the cracks of the door the charcoal fumes enter and the muffled conversation of the guard or of the two men lying together under one blanket.

Some one chokes and chokes as though he would die. The pipe is passing. Soon it will return to him, and he will choke again, and there will be muffled laughter. I retreat to my bed, and lie alone under my blanket, while the pipe passes. . . .

February 3rd

NAPOLEON THE THIRD is in Chhokrapur. He arrived last night, under escort and unpaid for. His Highness professes complete innocence. How was he to know that the messenger would go and kidnap the boy? It is a 'great nuisance,' especially since the sick uncle, whose death now would be of considerable assistance, is reported to be rallying. There may be a scandal . . . legal proceedings.

What is he to do? He is 'very upset.' Napoleon also is 'very upset.' Indeed the escort had great trouble with him. He protested shrilly all the way from Cawnpore. He does not want to live in Chhokrapur. He is used to constant change and constant excitement and big cities. He will not live in Chhokrapur. He will make trouble. He will get his aunt to make trouble. She is on her way here now. She, too, is 'very upset.'

Abdul took me for a walk to-day, 'to converse upon natural objects in Hindi—in this way you will learn to speak *very* well.' He was wearing an enormous, rather dirty brown topee, of which he was evidently very proud but which considerably subtracted from his appearance by swallowing up almost all of his head and neck. The indispensable gamp was beneath his arm.

'I have to ask you something, Mr. Ackerley,' he said. 'Three things. Will you promise to grant my wish?'

'State it, Abdul.'

'But you must keep it in your heart, and not tell it to any one.'

'You must leave that to my superior intelligence,' I said.

He smirked at this, and then, after a brief consideration, began volubly to explain. Would I get for him, from the Political Agent, a letter of recommendation so that he could obtain better employment, in one of the neighbouring States, than that which he now has in Chhokrapur—a clerkship at twelve rupees a month in the Forestry and Mining Department.

'How can I support myself and my family members?' he demanded. 'It is not possible.'

'But I don't see any reason why the Political Agent should consider such a request,' I answered. 'He doesn't know you, and he doesn't know me very well either . . .'

But Abdul was already proceeding. Failing that, there were two posts in Chhokrapur he would very much like to obtain: typist in the 'War Office,' or lecturer in Persian and Urdu in the school.

'But are these posts vacant?' I asked.

'Oh no; but the present men can be sent somewhere else. You have only to ask His Highness and he will at once do it for you. And the lecturer is not at all a good man; he should not have been appointed, but my application was passed over because I am a Mohammedan. But I am much better suited for the post than any other man—though I do not say it, of course, because I *want* the post, but because it is *true*. You understand? Am I clear? In *this* way.'

'I see,' I said; 'and you haven't any feelings about getting a man turned out of his job in order that it may be given to you instead?'

'But he can be given another post somewhere else. A

much better post . . . in some other State. In *this* way. So it
would be greatly to his benefit . . .'

'You hypocrite!' I said. 'You don't care à rap if he starves.
No, my dear Abdul, we'll put your alternatives aside, and
consider the question of the Political Agent.'

He sniggered self-consciously, drawing in his chin.

'Ah, Mr. Ackerley,' he said; 'but you always go to
the base of things! But if you will promise to stay in
Chhokrapur, to get some good permanent post here, I
will not want to leave it at all. Why don't you? Do so, for
my sake.'

When I went into my bedroom this morning I disturbed
a rat on my dressing-table. It vanished with alacrity behind
it. Silence ensued. I wondered vaguely what it could have
done with itself, for the piece of furniture was isolated and
the rat had not emerged. I peered underneath, but there
was nothing to be seen, so I concluded that the rat must be
halfway down, between the back of the table and the wall;
and wondering how it could be supporting itself in such a
sheer and difficult place, I peeped cautiously behind.

There it was, a globular, dusky shape, its little beady eyes,
bright in the gloom, looking up at me. It had fixed itself
much in the attitude a mountaineer adopts in negotiating
what I believe is called a 'chimney,' its little legs spread out
and clutching on the one side some roughness in the wall,
on the other the wood of the table. Quite absurd it looked,
its small fat body propped between the two precipices by its
short, spread, match-like legs. We stared at each other for
some time. I would have liked to see it complete the descent,
but it seemed disinclined to move, and not wishing to
trouble it further I went away.

In the evening Babaji Rao drove up in his tonga to chat
with me. He is a good man. I realise now that his shifty,
taciturn manner (by which, together with his general
appearance, I was at first unfavourably impressed) is only

due to timidity, whilst he, having interpreted perhaps my reserve as colour prejudice or the conscious racial superiority which Anglo-Indians exhale, is also delighted to confess himself wrong and has readily responded to my friendly overtures; in fact, we are both now very well pleased with each other. I like his tonga-driver too, though our intercourse consists solely in a frequent exchange of grins. He is a thin, pock-marked Mohammedan boy, and extremely dirty (his neck, indeed, is so disgraceful that I drew Babaji Rao's attention to it), but his smile is so infectious that it always makes me gay. His dress, too—what there is of it—is soiled and unkempt; but of one garment he is obviously very proud, and I never see him without it. It is the last he puts on, a waistcoat, and must, once upon a time, have been a very fine waistcoat indeed; but nothing now remains of it but the back, very greasy and stained, and a few wisps of pink silk which still adhere to the front of the armholes, so that it is only when one sees him from the rear that one realises that he is wearing one more garment than one had reckoned in studying him from the front.

Babaji Rao shook hands with me, and placing his round black hat on the centre table by the lamp, sat down opposite me in a characteristic attitude—his legs wide apart and his hands, fingers inwards, resting on his thighs. I always feel, from the careful way in which he does it, that he dislikes shaking hands with me and is glad when it is over; and apart from the fact that it is not a natural Hindoo salute and therefore awkward, it cannot be pleasant for him to have to touch the hand of a meat-eater. But he is courageous in discussion, and is always ready, in the interests of learning, to converse with me on any topic, however distasteful it may be; so I broached this very subject of meat-eating, and he told me a curious reminiscence.

Two years ago his only son, Ram Chandra, now aged eight, was playing with some fireworks, when one exploded prematurely and his *dhoti* caught fire. With great difficulty, burning his own hands in the process, Babaji Rao tore off the blazing garment, but not before the little boy had received very severe injuries to his thighs and stomach.

Immediate medical aid was of course necessary, and though Babaji Rao knew that his parents, who do not live in Chhokrapur, would prefer him to obtain Indian treatment, he called in the local Indian doctor who follows the European system of medicine. The child was very weak from shock and pain, and could take nothing but a little rice or porridge, which, the doctor said, was not sufficient to nourish him, and the resisting power engendered by nourishment was very necessary, for every day the wounds had to be anointed and dressed, and this was such a painful business that it took about two hours, the least touch causing the little boy to cry out. So the doctor advised Babaji Rao that, since the patient could not digest milk, he must be given something that he *could* digest—he must be given Brand's Essence of Chicken. Babaji Rao's face puckered with disgust as he uttered these dreadful words to me. Was ever man placed in such a terrible dilemma? He had not known what to do. He could not even think. And he was left to settle it alone with his conscience, for he could not go and seek advice from his friends on so repugnant a matter—except, of course, from the Prime Minister, who had said bluntly exactly what one had expected him to say: 'Don't be a fool, my good fellow! Do what the doctor tells you, and don't make such a fuss about it!'

For the Prime Minister was already guilty of the offence of having eaten with his nephews, who, since they had been educated in England, must be presumed to have eaten meat there—or, at any rate, to have eaten with people who had eaten meat. By this act he had become tainted with the same defilement which already disqualified them from being contracted into the best marriages, to which their very high birth entitled them; but a loss of prestige which would undoubtedly have damaged Babaji Rao's self-respect, had upon the Prime Minister the opposite effect; having already suffered, by eating with those who had eaten meat, the same loss of caste in which they were involved, he had then done openly what, it was suspected, he had been doing for some time in private—eaten meat himself. Eggs. He liked them. But Babaji Rao, though he secretly admired the Prime Minister's courage, whilst deploring his taste for eggs, and though he was, perhaps, a little comforted by the unhesitating decision of his advice, could not bring himself to take it. What would his parents say to him if, contrary to their counsel—for they would never permit it—he administered to Ram Chandra Brand's Essence of Chicken—whatever Brand's Essence might be? What would his son say to him afterwards when he learnt that he had been made the victim of such an enormity? And yet, on the other hand . . . He could not decide.

For five or six days he had procrastinated, hoping that the boy's condition would improve naturally, without such desperate remedies; but at length the doctor had told him that unless his instructions were carried out he could not answer for the child's life. And then Babaji Rao had yielded. But still he could not find the courage to take the first step himself; it was the Prime Minister who had bought the horrid stuff, opened the tin, and introduced into Ram Chandra's mouth the first spoonfuls. After that Babaji Rao and his wife had carried on the treatment, until about nine or ten tins were consumed. Indeed Brand's Essence seemed more remotely related to the chicken than was the Prime Minister's egg; but this was small comfort, and the moment the little boy was pronounced to be out of danger, though still terribly weak and tormented, Babaji Rao stopped the treatment, in spite of the doctor's advice to continue it.

However, the child had picked up gradually; but it was nearly three months from the day of the disaster before he was sufficiently restored to enable Babaji Rao, who had been sharing the watch with his wife, to obtain a complete night's rest.

He told me this story with great shame and discomfort and then added:

'I did not tell my father till afterwards, and he was very angry with me and said I had done wrong.'

'And what about the little boy?' I asked. 'Does he know?'

'Yes, he knows,' said Babaji Rao, fixing his gaze on the wall, 'and when he thinks of it, he thinks of it with shame. He wishes that I had not made him eat it, and I often think now that, on his account, perhaps I was not justified. But we did not tell him at the time, so that he did not know what he was doing; and I wish I had not been told myself, but that it had been done without my knowledge.'

'But supposing you *had* told him at the time—told him that unless he ate it he would surely die?'

'He would not have taken it,' said Babaji Rao.

February 5th

I THINK my denial of intimacy with the Political Agent has disheartened Abdul, for he seems to have lost interest in that quarter and is now worrying me to try to get him advancement through the Maharajah instead. I promised nothing; but Abdul does not need positive encouragement; his requests supply their own promises, extracting them, it seems, from any reaction which cannot be called definitely opposed; so that, before long, he was reproaching me with my unreliability. However, an opportunity occurred to-day for speaking a word on his behalf, and I took it.

'How are you getting on with your tutor?' asked His Highness.

'Quite well,' I said. 'If I did as much work for him as he does for me I should be getting on *very* well. He has aptitude for teaching, I think, and it seems a pity that his talent should be wasted on a poorly paid clerkship. Only the other day he was saying how disappointed he had been not to get the position of Lecturer in Persian and Urdu in your school when it fell vacant. Is there, perhaps, room for another lecturer? Can anything be done for him, Prince?'

'What is he getting? Fifteen rupees?'

'No, twelve; and he says he finds it difficult to support himself and his family on that.'

'But he must send in a petition,' said His Highness gravely. 'Why has he not done so? Tell him to write one and give it to you, and you can give it to me, and I will give it to the Dewan.'

In the afternoon, when Abdul appeared to teach me, I was feeling a little tired, so I did not wait as usual to watch him work carefully round in his own way to the subject foremost in his mind, but told him at once that I had spoken to the Maharajah about him. Immediately he was in a twitter.

'And I am to be moved to that post in the school? When? To-morrow? Tell me it is so. If it is not so, do not tell me anything. Is it so?'

I shook my head.

'Then it is bad news!' he moaned. 'I do not want to hear. Do not tell me anything! O my Lord! You have failed. You have not done your best for me. You have not said what I told you. You have not *pestered* him. O my Lord! It is bad news! Then do not tell me anything! I do not want to hear!' He began rapidly to turn the pages of his dictionary; then, without raising his eyes, he started to moan again. 'O my Lord! What is to be done now? In a short time you will go, and I will stay—and you have not done your best for me. O my Lord! But come, tell me, what passed between you?'

I gave him the conversation.

'But it is good!' he cried, his face brightening. 'A petition? Then it is done! I will get the post! He will give it me! That is *good* news! Why did you say it was *bad* news?'

He was greatly excited, pressing his face towards me into the air; but something—the amusement in my eyes, perhaps—made him suddenly self-conscious, and abruptly he withdrew, became decorous and tutorial, and began to teach. But as soon as the hour had elapsed, during which he had displayed unusual absentmindedness and impatience with

my slowness, he asked me if I would do him the favour of
drafting his petition for him 'in the best English and manner
possible,' and with some reluctance I produced this:

> 'May it please His Highness the Maharajah Sahib Bahadur of
> Chhokrapur, I, Abdul Haq, petition that I may be granted
> employment in the High School, as a teacher of Persian and
> Urdu, of both of which languages I have a thorough knowledge;
> or in such other capacity (as a Master in the Preparatory School,
> or as Manager of the Guest House) as may seem suitable to His
> Highness, so long as it be permanent and may bring me a monthly
> salary of twenty-five rupees and as much more as may seem to
> His Highness just and appropriate. I have the honour to be His
> Highness's most obedient servant. . . .'

I read it through to him, and he nodded slowly, his gaze
fixed on the paper. I was surprised at his silence, which he
maintained while I copied the letter out—until I came to
the word 'appropriate': then he held out a lean, detaining
hand.

'Please add there—"For this gracious act of great kindness, I will pray every day for Your Highness, and for
Your Highness's son, the Rajah Bahadur, and for . . ." '

'No, Abdul,' I said firmly. 'If you want anything added
you must add it yourself.'

'What harm there is?'

'It isn't necessary.'

'But he is Hindoo. He will like.'

'Nobody cares tuppence,' I said, 'whether you pray for
him or not.'

But of course he was right. I realised that afterwards,
when my irritation had subsided. He was only treating His
Highness in the same manner as His Highness had treated
the A.G.G. It was customary; it was acceptable; and the
irritation that it started in me was stupid and bad.

When Babaji Rao drove up to see me in the evening, his
tonga-wallah grinned at me even more radiantly than usual;
but I was too astonished to respond. The boy was quite clean.

'What has happened to your tonga-wallah?' I asked.
'Has he fallen into one of the tanks?'

Babaji Rao smiled.

'I noticed his neck myself yesterday,' he answered, 'and
I said to him "Do you ever wash yourself?" Then I gave
him two pice; but I also was a little surprised to find him as
clean as this to-day.'

Two pice is equal to a halfpenny.

'It's a miracle,' I said. 'How do you suppose he did it?'

'He bought a piece of soap.'

'And what did that cost him?'

'Two pice.'

I thought it good of the boy to have spent the two pice
on a piece of soap, for his wages, which the State supplies,
are only one rupee (about 1s. 4d.) a week, and Babaji
Rao, who is himself badly paid, adds little to this—as will
already have been remarked.

To-night I started him off on Hindoo marriage customs,
and he spoke at great length on this subject.

A Hindoo marriage, he said, is divided into three ceremonies—Betrothal, Marriage, and Consummation; and
the first of these takes place when the boy is about five years
old. At about that time his father begins to look about for a
wife for him, and this is sometimes done by means of a
messenger—a professional matchmaker—who visits the
district in search of a baby girl of suitable rank—that is to
say, of at least equal caste.

This is the most important consideration. Usually, I
suppose, the two families are neighbours, well known to each
other, and already perhaps in agreement on this question, so
that the employment of a messenger is either unnecessary or
a mere formality; but when there is no such familiarity,
some inquiry is necessary.

Either this inquiry is considered sufficiently answered by
information brought by the messenger, or sometimes an
actual inspection of the would-be bride is thought desirable;

at any rate Romance can obviously have no part in the
transaction, and when the boy's family have ascertained
that, besides being of the right caste, the girl is a strong and
serviceable article, sound in wind and limb, and in possession of her faculties, then they have learned about her all that
they have any wish to know. But, as Babaji Rao observed,
it is now different in his more advanced society; a photograph is usually required, and, if this is not forthcoming,
some *serious* member of the family—the father, or the elder
brother (the younger brother is not considered serious)—
will visit the young lady and report upon her appearance.
After this, if the reports from both sides are satisfactory, her
father will wish to examine the horoscope of the prospective
bridegroom to see whether it is favourable and agrees with
that of his daughter; and if there is anything wrong, if the
boy's horoscope predicts for him an early grave, or if,
however unexceptionable it may be in itself, in conjunction
with the girl's equally good horoscope it prognosticates a
barren or unhappy union, the marriage is off. All Hindoo
children have a horoscope taken at birth, except the lowest
castes, sweepers and cobblers, who usually cannot afford the
services of a pundit, and are therefore obliged to go through
life without knowing, from day to day, what is about to
happen to them.

But if the two horoscopes are harmonious the marriage is
arranged, the actual proposal always coming from the girl's
side, and the betrothal ceremony takes place. Later on they
are married. The marriageable age varies all over India,
but in Chhokrapur the boy should be ten or more, the girl
seven or more.

'But,' said Babaji Rao, 'in my society, where we consider
ourselves more advanced, the bride should be not less than
fourteen.'

On the day fixed for this second ceremony the bridegroom
goes with his parents and a great company to the house of
the bride's father. But he does not enter it in company. At
some distance from it the party halts, and he goes on alone

and empty-handed, for it is the custom that he should seem to arrive a beggar and that the girl should be given to him for charity's sake. And it is scarcely to be wondered at that many of these children when they reach the age of puberty and are better able to appreciate these charitable gifts, the uses of which at the time of giving they did not understand, should begin to doubt the infallibility of horoscopes, and hold, for the remainder of their lives, on the subject of charity, views unlikely to be found in any of the Vedas. Narayan, for instance, does not love his wife; 'she is much ugly,' he complains; but the Prime Minister, speaking the other day about human physical beauty, said that he set no store by it; it was a thing of no account; there was, in fact, a common saying in India—'A beautiful wife is a man's worst enemy.' Nevertheless he admitted that when he had been married by his parents he had resented, for a year or two, the plainness of his wife: 'But I made the best of a bad job, and now I find that it was not a bad job at all, but a good job, for she is an excellent housewife to me, and we are very happy together.'

'Also she does not honeycomb me,' he added; but after a moment's consideration he corrected this to 'henpeck.'

But to return. In the bride's house a great company meet the bridegroom, and another house is allotted to him and his friends, since he will have to stay and feast for some days. This is usually in the spring, the most propitious time for marriages.

The actual ceremony is rather complicated, but as far as I remember, the couple sit on the floor and a sacred fire is lighted between them by the officiating pundit. They then rise and unite—that is to say, their vestments are tied together by a piece of consecrated cloth beneath which their hands are joined—and walk three times round the sacred fire, each time in seven steps, repeating prayers and Vedic hymns. This concludes the ceremony; they are now man and wife, and he takes her with him back to his home, where she stays for a couple of days in order to meet his relations. The marriage is not, of course, consummated; this is another business altogether, and happens one year, three years, or five years later, at the discretion of the parents. If it is a lower-class marriage the wife has complete freedom and may go where she likes (though she will probably veil her face before any strange and undue interest in the streets); but if she is of the upper classes she disappears, after the consummation ceremony, into *purdah*, and save by her husband, her near relations, and female friends, is never seen again.

'And, provided there is no fundamental incompatibility, nor any physical repulsion on either side, love,' said Babaji Rao complacently, 'comes of its own accord.'

There is no divorce in India for the rearrangement of lives to which love does not come; though Hindoos may, if they wish, have more than one wife. But, owing to the great costliness of marriages, on which frequently the savings of a lifetime are spent, polygamy is usually impracticable, and, as in the Prime Minister's case, bad jobs are made the best of. Whether courage and diligent usage generally bring, as in his case again, their own reward, and familiarity breeds content, I do not know, for, says Babaji Rao, Hindoos are averse to discussing their domestic affairs, especially when they are disharmonious; so it is difficult to say whether, on the whole, the Hindoo marriage system produces as much unhappiness as our own, by which a man usually selects his own wife himself and seldom attempts to make the best of a bad job if the divorce laws can be bent to his deliverance.

February 8th

YESTERDAY evening, at the Palace at Garha, Her Highness, the Maharani Sahib, gave birth to a daughter. I learnt this from Abdul, whom I found leaning up against the wall of the doctor's house on my way to the post-office this morning. I was delighted at the thought of what this would mean; there would surely be all kinds of festivities and celebrations, and every one would be gay and excited. His Highness had not been near me for two days—a touch of fever was alleged —but a letter received during breakfast warned me to expect him at three o'clock. At about two the Prime Minister, accompanied by Babaji Rao, arrived at the Guest House, in a pink silk skull-cap. After talking about his own health for a quarter of an hour, he put on a pair of horn-rimmed spectacles and, spreading his enormous bulk on a sofa, began to read an Indian newspaper. He looked like a captive balloon.

He read, as is his habit, in undertones to himself, gesticulating every now and then with a small, well-shaped hand; while Babaji Rao and I sat in deferential silence on opposite sides of the table.

At length, however, when he was turning a page, I ventured to ask:

'Is it true that there's been an addition to the Royal House?'

'Quite true,' he answered, without looking up. 'A daughter was born to His Highness yesterday evening. Why do you ask?'

'I wanted to be sure before congratulating him.'

'A *daughter*, I said,' he remarked, fixing me over the top of his spectacles.

'Yes, but . . .' I began.

'There is nothing for congratulation in that,' he concluded, rather severely, and returned to his reading.

'Is His Highness disappointed, then?' I asked, diffidently, after a pause.

'Of course he is disappointed! Wouldn't you or any man be disappointed? It is an occasion for condolence, not for congratulation.'

'But there is a certain demand for daughters,' I began, seeing disappear the interesting festivities I had hoped for; but as though he were only too accustomed to this childish argument, his high-pitched, excitable voice emphatically cut me short.

'My good sir, that is no consolation to the father. Let a man's neighbours be afflicted with daughters, but let him himself be spared such useless and expensive encumbrances. That is the Indian's attitude. How can any man *want* daughters? What good are they—fed, taught, and clothed to become another man's property? Parents can never feel that a female child really belongs to them. There is always the knowledge that a time must come when a man will have to be paid to marry her and take her away. But with our sons it is different. They are a part of us. We rely upon them for our happiness in this world and the next, and when they marry they bring their wives under our roof, as we and our fathers did before them.'

'But His Highness has one son already,' I said.

'Yes, one. But how can a man feel secure with only one son? Consider how much depends on him, to comfort and support us here, and, by his prayers, to get us peace and happiness hereafter. One son is not enough.'

'Then won't there be any festivities?' I inquired despondently.

'Certainly not!' replied the Prime Minister, and after reading his paper again for a few minutes and breaking wind audibly once or twice, he said, in a drowsy voice, 'I did not have my accustomed rest to-day; excuse me if I sleep.'

Babaji Rao had contributed nothing to the conversation; he had just sat and sniggered and rubbed his chin deprecatingly. His mild, sedate, deliberate thought is always overborne by the Prime Minister's assertiveness and sweeping volubility, and he is obviously amused and, at the same time, slightly shocked by the latter's bold arguments—clearly too extreme for his own advanced society. Soon His Highness hobbled upon the scene, and there took place a short discussion, which I did not understand, about some mysterious proposal which Babaji Rao was to submit for the Prime Minister's consideration. It was, it appeared, very important to His Highness that the Prime Minister should accept it—so important, in fact, that Babaji Rao was forbidden to submit it to-day, since to-day is a Friday. When this had been settled, His Highness beckoned me to lend him the support of my arm and returned to the car. He complained of great stiffness and acute pains all over his body, and seemed very gloomy.

'How does one make a decision?' he cried in a fretful voice, after we had been driving for some time. 'How does one make up one's mind? *That* is what I want to know.'

'Is there anything in particular?' I said.

'This tour of mine. If I do not go, I fail in my duty; but if I do go I may fall ill upon the way, for I am broken in health, and this might cause a fatal delay. I might even have to return in the middle of it, which would make a very bad impression. What must I do?'

'You must go, of course,' I said hastily, feeling that my own tour was in jeopardy. 'You know yourself how important it is that you should make this pilgrimage, so you must make up your mind to do it now, and get it over. And really, Prince, I don't think your health is as bad as all that; you'll be better to-morrow, I expect.'

'I get so stiff in my legs,' he said dismally; and then, after a pause: 'I do not understand. We are born, and we enjoy life—and then we must die. Why must we die? Nobody *wants* to die.'

'Perhaps not; but doesn't it make a lot of difference not knowing *when* we must die?' I asked; 'for in the ordinary course of events we have no previous information about our death; we only know that it will happen some time, somehow—perhaps without our knowing anything about it—so it's silly to try to prepare for it.'

'Why did they shoot the Czar?' asked His Highness mournfully. 'Such a kind, weak man.'

'That's why,' I retorted grumpily. 'He was weak and irresolute. He couldn't make up his mind.'

For some time after this we travelled along in silence; then suddenly His Highness remarked:

PART ONE

'A daughter was born to me yesterday.'

'I know,' I said. 'I was going to congratulate you, but the Prime Minister says it is rather a subject for condolence.'

'No, no,' he said; 'you *may* congratulate me. I am pleased. I wanted a daughter.'

'But aren't they rather a nuisance on the whole?'

'You are *quite* right; a *very* great nuisance.'

I took out my handkerchief and dried my neck inside the collar. It was very hot; too hot to go into the question of why His Highness wanted a nuisance; but I supposed that really he did not care very much about it one way or another, and had not given the matter much thought. Later on this supposition seemed to receive confirmation. The Prime Minister was still at the Guest House when we returned; he was standing on the steps talking to Babaji Rao. His Highness beckoned to him from inside the car.

'You know,' he said dimly, 'a daughter was born to me at Garha last night?'

'Yes, yes, I have heard.'

'I am very pleased,' mumbled His Highness sombrely. 'I wanted a daughter.' Then, after a moment's pause: 'Are you *sure* it was a daughter?'

The Sacred Thread, Babaji Rao says, is of three interwoven strands, each strand being again of three interwoven strands, and they are all tied together at one place in a small sacred knot. It is a symbol of the great Hindoo trinity, Brāhma, Vishnu, and Siva, the main personalities of the one eternal spirit Brăhma; and when it has been consecrated and blessed by Brahmans it acquires spiritually regenerating, purifying properties.

Only the three highest castes may wear it; they are solemnly invested with it when they are about ten years old at their initiation ceremony, up to which time they are not permitted to pray or participate in any religious service;

but immediately upon investiture they become entitled to
the name of 'Twice-born,' and their religious and spiritual
life begins.

This life was divided up into four periods or states—
'unmarried religious student,' 'married householder,'
'anchorite,' and 'renouncer of all worldly concerns,' when
even the Sacred Thread itself was given up. Originally,
then, after the investiture, the child, whoever he might be,
would at once leave home and go and live for several years
as an unmarried student in the house of a religious preceptor, and do, in return for education, such services as were
required of him—begging alms in the city, tilling the soil,
or grazing the cattle, for education was thought too high
a thing to be acquired for money; and when his religious education was complete he would return home to
marry, and enter the second state. But now that early
marriages are the rule, the investiture is often solemnised at
the same time as the marriage, and the child no longer
leaves home.

But he pretends to do so. He takes a stick and a small
bundle of food and prepares to leave.

'Where are you going?' ask his parents.

'To Benares to my preceptor,' answers the child.

'Please do not go as far as Benares,' they say; 'stay with us,
and we will find you a preceptor here,' and he is given over
to the priest who performed the ceremony.

The Sacred Thread is worn round the neck ; but its position is altered for religious ceremonies, according to whether
the wearer is going to worship his Gods, or his departed
ancestors, or the saints. When he relieves nature he twines it
round his ear; for a Hindoo squats even to urinate, and if the
dangling thread were to come into contact with his genitals
it would be defiled, and another Thread would have to be
procured and consecrated, which, if he were not a Brahman
and able, therefore, to consecrate it himself, would be rather
expensive.

So when one sees a Hindoo coming out of the jungle,

usually in the company of a friend, with his little brass *lota* of water in his hand and his Sacred Thread twined round his ear, one knows what he's been up to.

February 9th

'You know—I am unholy to-day,' remarked His Highness as we started off this afternoon.

'Unholy? Why?'

'Because of the birth of my daughter.'

He went on to explain that for a certain length of time after a birth or a death a family is considered to be unholy, unclean. The period varies according to caste; so the stigma clings to a Brahman for ten days, to a warrior for twelve, to a tradesman for fourteen, and to a labourer for a month, during which periods the afflicted houses are shunned, since contact, even indirect, with their inmates is considered to spread defilement.

'So,' said His Highness gravely, 'if the birth had taken place a day later I could not have gone on my pilgrimage, for then the twelve days would have included the eighteenth, the only auspicious day. As it is, it is a great misfortune; no one will come near to me or attend to me: "You are unholy!" they say.'

He gazed mournfully at the passing scenery, and then added with a touch of bitterness:

'Of course my servants are very pleased. They are always praying for a birth or a death so that they may be idle. It is all they think about.'

I laughed aloud, thinking of Sharma, whom I do not now see. He was undoubtedly making the most of it, I thought, and having a fine old time.

'And I dare say they go so far as to create fictitious births and deaths?' I said.

'You are *quite* right. That is what they all do.'

'What occurs if a child is still-born?' I inquired. 'Is that counted as a birth *and* a death, or as neither?'

But he seemed unable to answer this difficult, and perhaps frivolous, question.

In the *Pioneer* the other day I was reading of a murder in which a Brahman and a Chamar were involved.

'What is the Chamar caste?' I asked Babaji Rao who was beside me. 'Is it a division of your caste?'

There was a shrill cry of delight from the Dewan who was stretched on the sofa. 'If *I* had said that to him he would have taken it as the greatest insult,' he called over; 'but because it is you he smiles.'

It was true that the Secretary's face wore a sickly smile.

'O dear!' I said. 'Is it the lowest caste?'

'Not quite,' said Babaji Rao bravely; 'but it is *one* of the lowest, the shoemakers.'

Abdul is rather a nuisance. He grows increasingly fidgety at our schoolroom relationship, and is always trying to turn it into something more intimate and more public.

At first it seemed enough that I should walk with him. It was very satisfactory to lead me in front of the houses of his Mohammedan friends, or through the bazaar, the most populous part of the town.

Walking a little in front of me, when the crowd was very thick, he would call out haughtily to the people to make way for me, or prod them with the ferrule of his umbrella; and once he actually took hold of an inattentive peasant by the shoulder and dragged him roughly out of my path—a thing I feel sure he would never have dared to do if my presence had not appeared to sanction it. Naturally such practices made me extremely uncomfortable and angry, and I had constantly to correct him for them. But even apart from this, I do not much enjoy these excursions 'to converse upon natural objects in Hindi,' for his mind is always busy with his own affairs and countless plans by which he can make use of me. I do not blame him for this, of course; being English and a friend to His Highness I am an influential person, and I suppose he would be thought a fool if he did not make the most, while he could, of the opportunities afforded him as my tutor. But it becomes boring nevertheless.

I should add, in his favour, however, that he does not worry me for money, which he might very easily do, but accepts with at any rate a moderate grace the salary I give him.

I went to Babaji Rao for advice as to how much this should be, for he is always reproving me for my extravagance. I asked him to advise me on the generous side, and he said that eight rupees a month would be quite enough; so I give Abdul ten. And this, as I say, he receives without comment; if his manner suggests that it could hardly be less, he does not actually ask for more.

Now his latest request, produced alternately with questions relating to his petition, is that I should consent to be entertained by him to dinner at his house.

'I am giving a feast to my friends,' he said; 'and I have promised them your company, Mr. Ackerley. Will you grant my feast?'

I resist Abdul's invitations. I cannot help it. I distrust his motives too much. This is not to say that I believe he has no genuine affection for me; I think he has; but I cannot welcome it; it is too closely bound up with self-interest. So I made excuses, quite at random, and not very good ones, as he promptly showed. Indian food was not good for European stomachs, I said; it might upset me. But, he hastened to say, he would provide English food for me, whatever I liked; he would give me just the same food as I eat in the Guest House. I then said that in any case I was not free to accept, since I never knew when His Highness might want my company in the evening. Though there was far less truth in this, it seemed to me more impressive than my first line of argument; but, with merciless persistence, he at once exposed its worthlessness. If I could go to dinner with the Sahibs in Rajgarh, I could go to dinner with him. It was

121

easily arranged with His Highness. I was the Sahib and could do as I wished. But perhaps I did not wish? I didn't, but was too polite to say so. Besides, he said, the feast need not be in the evening at all, but in the morning or the afternoon if I preferred; and I need not stay long, only long enough to eat and drink a little, and to see his house, and his little son, and his cat. He wished to show me these things; how could I refuse him?

'You are my friend and I wish to honour you,' he said. 'So you must grant my feast because we are friends. You see? In *this* way. So I have your permission? It is granted? Yes, I think so.'

'I'll think about it,' I said feebly.

'But what reason there is? Ah, Mr. Ackerley, if you will not grant my feast, what shall I say to my friends? For I told them all that you would surely grant my feast because of your love for me. They will say you do not love me.'

'And they'll be quite right,' I said with a smile, feeling that if I did not immediately arrest this rapid growth of intimacy there was no knowing where it might not end.

'How is that?' he asked, as though perplexed. 'You do not love me?'

'No, Abdul, I don't love you.'

He seemed very concerned.

'Ah, gentleman, but that is not good! If I love you, then you must love me.'

'Why?'

'Indian rule!'

'Nonsense!' I said.

He smirked at this, and then continued, shaking his head:

'Ah, then I was mistaken. I am much ashamed. I said to myself, "The Sahib loves me in his heart and will grant my feast." I said so to my wife, and to my mother, and to my little son. What shall I say to them now?'

'I've no idea what you will say,' I replied, rather crossly.

'I shall be much ashamed before them. What can I do to make you love me?'

He looked at me appealingly, and I did not know how much of all this was honest and how much bunkum.

'Look here, Abdul,' I said, 'I'm not much given to feasting and parties, but one day I'll come and have a quiet cup of tea with you alone in your house.'

'And I may not ask my friends?'

'I'd rather come alone.'

'But why may I not ask my friends, Mr. Ackerley?' he inquired, with an impudent smile.

'Oh, English rule!' I said.

He seemed to consider this for a moment or two; then made the best of it.

'Thank you, Mr. Ackerley; thank you. And when shall it be?'

'One day,' I said.

But one cannot evade Abdul. He is quite merciless. My promise is now about a week old, and he has plagued me with it ever since, varying his method of approach according to my temper. If I show irritation at a direct attack he gets at me slyly under the cloak of tuition. Thus I have been made to add to my written vocabulary the Hindi for 'to grant,' 'feast,' 'promise,' 'faithless,' and 'liar,' and to learn by heart the translation of such phrases as 'Can you come to-day?' or 'I am disappointed in you,' and it is remarkable how such a process, working upon a sensitive mind, is able to trouble the nerves. In the employment of some such organisation as the Inquisition, Abdul would have rendered invaluable service. I have promised to have tea with him on the 11th.

Babaji Rao came up in the evening, and, after clearing his throat, began to talk about the status of Indian women. That their importance in the general scheme of things is entirely subservient is theoretically true, he said; they are the instruments by which a man may get the son whose prayers are so necessary to the peace of his soul after death; but as a matter of fact, in an Indian household, the wife is often a person of influence and even authority, sometimes actually ruling the house and her husband and children too. In any case, chiefly, no doubt, because her instrumental importance is so considerable, there is supposed to be a communion between husband and wife almost as sacred and personal as that between mortals and God. Until quite recently a husband never addressed his wife in the presence of a third person, nor alluded to her directly in conversation; but owing to the inconvenience of such a rule it is now a little relaxed, and a man will converse with his wife in the presence of a near relative, such as a mother or brother, or of such personal servants as a nurse or companion.

I listened attentively to this lecture, and it suddenly occurred to me that he had come expressly with the intention of trying to correct any bad impression which might have been left upon my mind by the Prime Minister the day before yesterday. It was, at any rate, the kind of conscientious thing he would do, and I was glad to have been shown a private domestic interior in the light of his mild and dutiful orthodoxy, after the somewhat depressing pictures suggested by His Highness's indifference, the Prime Minister's cynicism, and Narayan's discontent.

But he had not said very much; only that marriage was the aim, the beginning and end of a woman's life, and could mean for her love, respect, and spiritual development. Of her first years of monotony and neglect, already too plainly hinted at in the case of the Maharajah's daughter by the manner of her reception into this world, he did not speak; nor did he even theorise any happiness for her in widowhood. For an Indian widow may not marry again, and if, as not uncommonly happens, her boy husband succumbs, before the consummation ceremony, to one of the many epidemics prevalent in India, she is condemned to perpetual mourning for him, whom perhaps she cannot even remember, and to a life of domestic drudgery, the loneliness and thanklessness of which it is easy to imagine. As at her birth, no one wants her, but now the opportunity of disposing of her has gone; a child, if she had been able to have one, would have preserved for her, from the wreckage of her single plan, some reason and contact; but now her only importance lies in the performance of those rites for the peace of her husband's soul which would have been the duty of their unborn son.

I wanted to ask Babaji Rao about his own marriage, but felt a little scared by all the etiquette; however, I thought he would not object if I inquired at what age it had taken place, and was pleased to see him receive the question without apparent discomfort. His early life with regard to marriage had been rather tragic, he said, for his first two wives had died before the consummation ceremonies, and he had not accomplished his present successful union (which was his third) until the late age of twenty-one. Two periods of four years had divided these three marriages, so he must have been about twelve or thirteen at the time of his first. I asked him to what extent he had been distressed by these early losses, and he said that by the first he had been no more affected than he would be by the death of some distant acquaintance; but it had been different when his second wife died. He said no more than this, and I respected what appeared to be a still painful thought, remembering His Highness's treatment of the tender memory of the late Mrs. Bramble. But I did very delicately suggest that, considering the superstitious nature of his people, he might have found it rather difficult to make a third *good* match after such a record, and this he endorsed, but added that, as a matter of fact, he had had no difficulty whatever. True, he had not seen his present wife before the marriage; but his aunt had, and from her report and what he himself had gathered from the girl's brother, whom he already knew, he had believed her to be intelligent and even cultured.

This was of primary importance to him, coming before beauty; and not only were his expectations fully realised, but she was beautiful into the bargain—a pleasing asset which his aunt had not considered important enough, it seemed, to include in her report.

February 10*th*

To-day Abdul gave me the copy he had made of the petition I wrote out for him some days ago, and asked me to present it to His Highness 'in the best manner possible.' He then proceeded to explain precisely what he meant by the best manner possible and to compose the kind of speech he wished me to make on his behalf, until I lost patience with him and told him he had better present the petition himself. At about four o'clock we heard the car drive up, and, going out, I told the Maharajah that Abdul wanted to present his petition.

'Tell him I will see him when we come back,' said His Highness, but immediately changed his mind and called after me, 'I will see him now.'

I sent for Abdul, and then seated myself in the car. He approached with great humility, beginning his salutations while still some distance away, and then, holding the petition in front of his face between the palms of his hands, he produced a flow of speech, pitched on a low, desolate note, in which the word 'Huzoor' (exalted) frequently occurred. He did not once raise his eyes to the royal visage. After his speech had been going on without pause for about two minutes, His Highness suddenly interjected a question, and obtained some information which seemed to give him immense satisfaction, for, ejaculating 'Achchha! Achchha!' (good), he leant back in the car and flicked the ash from his cigarette with a triumphant gesture. Meanwhile Abdul's speech was continuing; his hands, relieved of the petition, which he had been told to drop in the car, were now outspread before him, and his eyes turned upwards, so that I guessed he must be saying that for this gracious act of kindness he would pray for His Highness's soul, and for the soul of the Raja Bahadur, and . . . but His Highness had heard enough. At a word from him the car began to turn and the door was slammed in Abdul's face; but he still continued his prayers and supplications through the open window, moving nimbly round with the car, and even following, till he could not keep up any longer and, still moaning, was left behind. His Highness turned a half-veiled eye upon me.

'No man is hero to his valet,' he observed.

'Meaning, Prince?' I asked.

'I did not know who he was until I spoke with him. But now he has told me. I knew his father very well when I was a boy . . .' He began to giggle.

'Yes?' I encouraged.

'Oh, do not ask me! Do not ask me!' he said, tittering, and hid his face in his sleeve.

'Are you going to help him?' I inquired later.

'Yes, yes. I will do for him,' he answered—a remark which, after a moment of mistrust, I accepted in Abdul's favour.

To-day, he shortly afterwards informed me, is Basant day, the day of Spring. In this province the event is now scarcely marked, but in other parts of India it is the gayest of festivals: every one is happy and puts on a yellow garment and worships Mahadeo, the God of Love. Yellow is the Basant colour, he said, and at the feast of a Rajputana chief every-thing would be yellow: not only the carpets, clothes and flowers, but even the food. As we drove along I noticed a certain amount of this colour about in the streets of Chhok-rapur. I asked if we were to have no celebrations at all, and he said that he had arranged for Napoleon the Third to dance at the Palace in the evening and that I was to come and watch and say exactly what I thought about him. He would be dressed in yellow; but on the following evening I was to come again and see him dance naked and say exactly what I thought about him.

I said that all that would suit me nicely, and asked how the young man was settling down. Apparently he wasn't. Not only were his relatives behaving badly (the second uncle-guardian had now arrived in Chhokrapur to make trouble, while the first still clung disappointingly to life), but Napoleon himself was very restless. In fact he was leaving the State on Monday, probably for ever; that was why His Highness was anxious that I should see him at once. At least, he was *threatening* never to return unless His Highness gave him a present of five hundred rupees as well as the monthly salary of fifty rupees which had been promised him. But if that were granted he would return to His Highness when the latter's pilgrimage was completed. Of course the uncles and aunts were behind all this; they were getting at the boy in private and corrupting him. His Highness had said that it was too much; he would either give Napoleon a lump sum of five hundred rupees, or fifty rupees a month subject to decreasement at the end of a year—and this offer had been refused. So what was His Highness to do? He could not make up his mind.

'What must I do?' he cried mournfully.

'You must be firm,' I said.

But he did not want to lose the boy—for whose future he had already made plans. He had decided that Napoleon should become a lawyer, and I was to take him back to England with me when I returned and have him instructed in this profession. And for a few months every year I was to bring him back to Chhokrapur so that His Highness might see for himself how he was progressing.

'Of course, he is quite illiterate, you know,' he said.

I nodded gravely.

'Is he intelligent?'

'*Very* intelligent. *Very*. He has great . . . *decision*. Indeed he makes me feel quite ashamed.'

But Napoleon the Third was only one of many such troubles. There was His Highness's spiritual leader, for instance, who had been with him for thirty years and was quite indispensable. He also was demanding money. Unless His Highness gave him eight hundred rupees he must leave the State, for he was dying of starvation. . . .

PART ONE

'Like wolves!' said His Highness, with a gesture. 'They are all like wolves . . . wolves!'

'Dreadful!' I said. 'But since you are undergoing this persecution, I think I must add my voice to the general howl and ask whether you don't think it's about time—since I've been here over seven weeks—that I received a month's salary, or even two?'

This remark seemed to amuse him, and quite restored him to his earlier good-humour.

It struck me the other day, while walking with Abdul, that the streets of Chhokrapur have no names and the houses no numbers. I asked him how letters were addressed, and he said either by indicating the quarter (i.e. Talaiya Quarter: the vicinity of the Small Tank), or by describing the position of the house in relation to other houses or public buildings. His own address, for example, was: Near the Kotwali, near the house of Baldeo Deni.

He then showed me the mosque in which, draped in long white robes, he worshipped five times a day. Abdul's God dwells in the shape of a burning light in the seventh heaven, and Abdul has great faith in Him because He frequently grants his requests. Has He not, on various occasions, bestowed upon Abdul a wife, a son, and even a sum of rupees, for all of which blessings Abdul had prayed? Of course, He has not granted *all* Abdul's requests—but then He has not got Abdul for a tutor.

At about nine o'clock this evening the carriage arrived and took me down to the Palace, where the pleasant-looking boy with single ear-ring came forward to receive me. I have learnt from Narayan that his name is Bundi.

'Bund'gi Bundi,' I said.

'Bund'gi' means 'I bow to you,' and is not, therefore, the way to speak to a servant. He seemed very pleased.

The music was in full swing when I entered the theatre, and His Highness, who was sitting just inside the doorway of his sanctum, from which the reed blind had been drawn aside, indicated that I was to sit on a solitary chair placed in front of the carpet with its back to him. There was only one throne on the stage, and the occupant of this, His Highness informed me (by chortling bashfully when I looked to him for confirmation of my supposition), was Napoleon the Third.

He was diminutive and dark, with very large eyes and an air of self-possession. A streak of white paint decorated his forehead, a single pearl his nose, and his cheeks were vividly coloured with vermilion. Whether this description bears any resemblance to the real Napoleon the Third I do not know. If I ever saw a picture of that monarch in his youth, I have forgotten it, and so, I imagine, has His Highness.

He was dressed in the Basant colour; a high-waisted yellow silk dress, heavily ornamented and flecked with gold tissue, and a headdress like the rising sun.

After a time he danced, and danced very prettily, with tremulous, almost imperceptible movements of the head and hands, like a bird fluttering its wings, and the gold tissue, shaken from his whirling skirt, filled the air around him with a glittering dust.

But his singing voice, with which he accompanied his dance, was discordant and rather fretful. My attention wandered after a moment and found more pleasure in the figure of a very old man who sat cross-legged beside the carpet. He was wrapped in a fine soft cream-coloured cloth which fell in beautiful lines from his head, and a bright-red Kashmir shawl hung loosely on his thin shoulders. Round his neck, against his bare brown chest, a garland of jasmine hung. The worn, grey-bearded face in the frame of his garment was very impressive, and his eyes, raised to the dancing god, were full of a gentle benignity. The dance was still in progress when His Highness, unable to contain himself any longer, cried out:

'What do you think of him? What do you think of him?' referring of course, to Napoleon the Third.

'Oh, Prince!' I said; 'he is a bronze Ganymede!'

Gust upon gust of wheezy laughter greeted this sally.

'Then where is the eagle? Where is the eagle?' he cried, clapping his hands together.

'Who should know better than you, O Zeus!' I returned; 'since you sent it to Cawnpore to snatch the little boy!'

Then I had to go. I thought he was going to choke; his betel-stained tongue, like a piece of red flannel, rushed in and out of his mouth; the music stopped, and even Napoleon the Third came to a standstill and was infected by the sovereign mirth.

February 11th

I VISITED Abdul's house with him to-day. It was a low, irregular, whitewashed wall, with a portal and a window above it. The portal was not more than five feet high, and was closed with two solid unvarnished wooden doors, studded with nails, and badly slung on their hinges. The window, behind which, he said, his wife and mother lived, was curtained with sacking. The effect of the whole was that of a blind beggar. Abdul rapped on the door; whereupon a man poked his head out, peered at us and retired. This person, Abdul explained, was his brother-in-law, who lived with him and who had kindly lent his services for the occasion; he had gone in to warn the women of my arrival so that they might conceal themselves. This did not take long; a cry from within signalized that the coast was clear, and we entered. The low portal gave upon three small dark rooms which were quite bare and empty and looked as though they were made of mud. The doorways that gave them intercommunication were even smaller than the street-entrance, so that I had to double up to get through to the little open yard that lay beyond. This was weedy and so neglected that the walls and buildings on the further side had crumbled into ruins. It contained nothing but a puppy, which immediately rolled over on its back. Abdul ignored it. He picked his way past it, and guided me up a short flight of stone steps which were built against the wall on our left and led back on to the roof of the three rooms through which we had passed. This was our destination.

The major part of Abdul's house, a low, one storeyed building with two doors, faced me. One of the doors was curtained and must have been the room into which the women had just been herded—the room whose window was veiled with sacking. The other door was open and probably led to the kitchen.

The minor part of the house was a tiny compartment about five feet square sprouting all by itself from a corner of the roof. It looked like a box, without its cover, standing on end. It was Abdul's private bed-stitting-room. The doorway was open, and a tongue of stained and faded purple cloth protruded across the threshold.

Behind this box, balancing a similar structure on the other corner, rose a low open turret approached by very narrow ladder-like steps. These turrets, said Abdul, were used either as storerooms or as sleeping-out places in summer—each being just large enough to take a *charpai*.

It was very hot standing on the roof in the full glare of the sun, and I was glad when he invited me to enter his room. I shuffled off my shoes and crawled like a fly over the purple tongue. There was no furniture in the room. It was so small that one could neither stand up nor lie down in it at full length. There was a white sheet spread upon the floor, and on this, copying as nearly as I could Abdul's attitude, I squatted beside him. We filled the room.

And yet, in spite of its smallness, it contained all Abdul's worldly goods. These either hung from innumerable nails in the walls, or were neatly piled along the sides; and I never saw such a remarkable collection. One would have thought that never in his life had he thrown anything away, however worthless or useless. Empty tins and boxes; worn-out shoes; remnants of socks and other articles of clothing; books and bits of books—these were neatly stacked and surmounted by a small cotton-tree in a pot; while on the wall were hanging almanacs and photos, a hat, a bladeless knife, a glove, some broken pieces of glass and metal, and all manner of quite useless and unornamental things. It was, somehow, very like Abdul himself, this room of his: very like his mind, small, mean, tidy, uncomfortable, and full of rubbishy things. There was a smell of mould.

'Your tree looks dead,' I said.

'Yes,' said Abdul, 'it is dead.'

I was then introduced to his son, who was brought by the brother-in-law and placed on the purple cloth in front of us. He was a sturdy and rather pretty little chap of about five, with a very large head and *tarbush* and a distended stomach.

Abdul offered me cigarettes, spices, and scent upon a tray. There were three scent-bottles, one containing a brown, gummy Indian scent and another a cheap French perfume bought in Calcutta. The third bottle was shaped like a slender sausage and contained a little transparent fluid. I took it up curiously.

'Is this good?' I asked.

'No very,' said Abdul.

'How does it open?'

'No one can open,' he replied. 'Only my father, who is dead.'

His father had been dead for two years, but I was not discouraged until I perceived that in the small brass neck at either end the glass stopper had been broken off short. I handed it back to him, wondering why, since it could only be opened by his father who was dead, he continued to offer the scent in it to his guests. No doubt it looked mysterious and important on the tray with the others. After I had rubbed a little of the Indian scent upon my hands, he showed me some of his treasures—cheap, highly coloured plates of Mecca, Medina, and Jerusalem, and some 'holy books' which were tied up with string and suspended from nails in the roof. He also showed me an early family group, so faded as to be scarcely discernible, in which he figured as a little boy.

'That is me in my lovelyhood,' he said.

Then, when the attractions of the room were exhausted, he sent his brother-in-law, who, with Abdul's son and two other idle spectators, was hanging about outside, to bring the sweetmeats. In a few moments these arrived, in saucers, on a tray, preceded and accompanied by a cloud of flies and followed by a cat of the most mangy and sinister appearance. It was covered with half-concealed sores, and its almost hairless tail was rigid and twisted like a stiff piece of rope.

Abdul greeted it affectionately.

'I told you I had a cat,' he said.

I gazed with disgust at this wretched object, which, I am thankful to say, did not come into the room. It sat just outside on the purple cloth and peered short-sightedly, from beneath drooping pink lids, at the sweetmeats which were set before us. These were chiefly mustard-coloured or pale grey, and looked rather like bread pellets moulded by grubby schoolboy fingers into various sizes for flipping at other schoolboys across the table. A little sugar clung to them, and a thin, adhesive silver tissue (also edible, said Abdul) which fluttered in the slight breeze. He handed me a spoon, and with his own attempted to beat off the flies which swarmed so obstinately upon the food that they appeared to prefer death to separation from it. Personally I could not pretend to their enthusiasm. but gingerly digging with my spoon to the centre of one of the piles, I selected, with a care which may have seemed rather rude, three of the smallest pellets I could find.

These, which were no larger than peas, I swallowed, and, recollecting Mrs. Bristow's dire prophecy of a month ago, had little doubt but that in a very short space of time I should be dead of cholera.

But Abdul was watching me, and, protesting loudly against my modesty and politeness, pressed other and larger sweetmeats upon me, which I firmly refused.

He seemed very upset. If I did not care for Indian sweet-meats, he said, he had some English cakes he had bought in Calcutta; but I pleaded a recent lunch, remembering that he had not been in Calcutta for over six months. He gazed unhappily at the loaded tray. He had hoped, he said, that we would share it between us. It was a great disappointment. Indeed, so depressed did he look that I suggested that, since I did not feel inclined for food at present, I might be allowed to carry some back with me to my house to eat another time.

This seemed to him an excellent plan; his spirits revived at once, and he sent his son with the sweetmeats to make up a bundle for me to take away. But in a few moments the little boy returned to say that unfortunately nothing could be found in which to tie up the food; whereupon Abdul, never at a loss, drew from his pocket a soiled handkerchief which he tossed over to his son. Then, in spite of my refusal, he ordered tea, which was brought, already mixed with milk and sugar, in a kettle; but owing no doubt to its not having been made with boiling water it was found to be so thick with tea-leaves that it could scarcely trickle through the spout, and was sent back to be strained. I accepted a glass when at last it returned to make up for my refusal of the food; but it was sickly sweet and tepid, and I did not drink much. Shortly afterwards I left, carrying with me the sweetmeats tied up in Abdul's handkerchief.

For a day or two I shall keep them exposed to view on a plate in my sitting-room, throwing away a few from time to time, so that he may think they are being steadily consumed. He said he couldn't express his pride and satisfaction that I had visited his house, which, he added, cost him two rupees a month in rent.

Since his show of irresolution a few days ago His Highness has not spoken to me again about his pilgrimage. Such incidental allusions as he has made to it have implied that he has accepted the inevitable with resignation; and though he does not cease to complain of ill-health, it seems settled that he will depart in four days' time. It is my own fault, I expect, that I don't know much about it. Since the original plan was that we should synchronize our holidays, I naturally tried to keep him up to the mark, feeling that my own tour depended upon his; and, since my urgings have increased with his reluctance, he no doubt feels me to be out of sympathy with him and leaves the subject alone. But now that, what with introductory letters and invitations and one thing and another, it seems assured that, independently of his plans, I am to leave for Benares on the 19th, it makes no difference to me whether he goes on his pilgrimage or not. So while we were driving to-day I carefully approached the subject to find out if he was feeling any more cheerful about it. He wasn't. He was very gloomy, and said there was no improvement in his health, and that the medicine the doctors gave him made his eyes water. I asked what the exact object of his pilgrimage was, and he explained that he was under obligation to perform certain religious rites at certain holy places to obtain absolution for the souls of his ancestors. There was no definite punishment for failing to do this, but the souls would continue in everlasting need of it, and this neglect would count as a bad act against him and, along with such other bad acts as he may have committed, operate to send him to hell and delay his passage through the cycle of transmigrations to reabsorption into the one Universal Spirit.

'What is hell?' I asked.

'Hell is fire and blood, flesh, bones, dung, urine, and serpents and dragons that prey upon you,' he announced, discharging each item in this unsavoury concoction almost with relish, and beating his knee with his hand. I giggled at this.

'Dear me,' I said.

'And pus!' he added with gusto, his sunken lips blowing out as he spat the word at me. Then he giggled himself, but not very good-humouredly.

'Never mind,' I said. 'One doesn't stay there permanently. One is born again, isn't one?'

'Yes,' he said, 'as a pig or a donkey; then back into hell; then as a serpent; then as an insect . . .'

It was clear that he was not feeling very well.

'But there is always hope?' I asked encouragingly.

'Yes, after millions and millions of reincarnations one gets back to the shape of a man and has another chance.'

'Does one ever run across one's injured ancestors on the way?'

'Perhaps by chance. But it is not likely. It is only great love that brings people together again. So that two friends may go on together, or a father and son, a brother and sister, if there was great love between them.'

February 13*th*

ALMOST every morning now, and sometimes in the late afternoon, Narayan, the young Guest House clerk, comes in to see me.

'I may come in?' his soft voice inquires from the threshold, and I smile a welcome and indicate the chair opposite. He is a handsome boy, with very gentle eyes, beneath a broad, intelligent forehead. The lower part of his face is less good; his lips are too thick, his black silky moustache rather untidy, and his teeth badly discoloured by betel. But he is spotlessly clean and wears his *dhoti*, which is always of the finest muslin, more gracefully than any other Hindoo I have seen, so that it falls almost to the level of his insteps. On his bare feet he wears old-fashioned buckle shoes, which are both becoming and sensible, since they have so frequently to be shuffled off; and on his head a round black hat, like Babaji Rao's, into which he crams his long oily tress of blue-black hair. His carriage is calm and dignified, conscious of the superiority of his caste; his demeanour reserved, thoughtful, and attentive.

I have found him very useful as an interpreter in getting

my small wants attended to, or in suppressing the zeal of Habib, the smaller of the two Mohammedan boys, who seems to have elected himself my personal servant; but although Narayan must be aware of my need of him, he does not, like Abdul, take advantage of it, but remains always courteous and deferential.

I do not know why he comes in to me so often; if it is to benefit his English or his mind—Europeans being 'so wisdom'—then his courage must fail him, for he seldom speaks a word, but just sits here, very shy and quiet, with his hands idle in his lap and his gaze bent upon the floor.

I have tried to draw him into conversation, but I dare say he is self-conscious about his English and feels it to be inadequate; for although he has no difficulty in understanding and answering my questions, he seems unable to frame one of his own. Yet his knowledge of the language, though not extensive, is serviceable enough; and he speaks it rather prettily, in a light, musical, rather caressing manner. Now I scarcely interrupt my studies for him; he salaams, and we touch hands; I offer him a chair and a cigarette, which he would not take without my permission, and then go on with my work. Every now and then our glances meet and he responds to my smile shyly and then drops his gaze. And here he sits, smoking, or chewing betel, or doing nothing, until some one calls him or he thinks he ought to go.

'Now I will go,' he says gently, making it half a question and half a statement; I nod smiling, and with a salaam he departs.

I have seen many forms of salutation here, the commonest being to move the tips of the fingers of one or both hands to and from the forehead. This is an abbreviation of the full gesture of scattering dust on the head, which some of the servile peasants still perform, laying their foreheads on the earth. There are various modifications of it, and the Prime Minister does no more than place the palm of his right hand flat on his forehead when he meets the Maharajah. But Narayan's salaam is the sweetest; he puts his hands together, in our attitude of prayer, just below his chin, and moves them a little to and fro, and smiles shyly, and the gesture grows full of love.

When he came to see me to-day he offered me his little silver box of betel-leaves before helping himself. I had never tasted one before, and was curious to try, though I did not like the smell of them in other people's mouths; but after chewing it for a few moments I felt obliged to spit it out, it had such a sickly flavour, heavy and acrid. Narayan was very amused, and pointed at me and then at his mouth, laughing on a high light note—a freer, franker sound than Babaji Rao's snigger, Abdul's titter, or His Highness's wheezy chortlings.

I went to the looking-glass to examine my mouth, and was delighted to see that my tongue and teeth were bright red.

What a pity, I thought, that Mrs. Bristow is no longer here! How smilingly would I have greeted her! But I was expecting Babaji Rao at any moment, he had arranged to walk with me, so I could try my bright-red smile on him.

I told Narayan of my appointment, and he asked whether he might accompany us. I shook my head, being quite unable to imagine what kind of relation existed between them, for whereas Narayan is of a much higher caste, he is, at the same time, Babaji Rao's subordinate. But Narayan did not appear to foresee any difficulty. He put his hands together before his face, and said in a pleading voice:

'Ah yes. Please.'

'Why do you want to come?' I asked, teasing him.

'I like.'

'But why do you like?'

'I like.'

'Yes, but *why*?'

'Sim-ply.'

'But there must be a reason.'

'No reason. I like.'

'Well,' I said, 'I don't think that's good enough. If you'll

give me a reason—just one little reason—I'll take you;
otherwise not.'

But, although he looked hard at the floor, he seemed
unable to find a reason; so, when Babaji Rao arrived, I said
to him:

'Narayan wants to come with us, but he won't say why.
Shall we take him?'

'Certainly. With pleasure,' said Babaji Rao.

But perhaps I had carried my teasing too far and Narayan believed that he was not wanted, for now that permission
had at last been obtained he held back, and I had to take
him by the hand and draw him along with us. Just as we
were leaving I noticed the remainder of Abdul's sweetmeats
on the table and asked Babaji Rao whether they might not
be acceptable to his Mohammedan tonga-wallah. He said
he thought the boy would be very pleased indeed; so I
wrapped them up in a piece of paper and carried them with
me.

'Look,' I said to Babaji Rao, since he had not noticed it;
'I am becoming an Indian indeed.' And I showed him my
red teeth.

'Do not make yourself ill,' was all he said, with a smile.

I questioned him, as we strolled along the Deori road,
about the small shrines that were scattered over the countryside, and he said that they commemorated *Suttees*—faithful
wives who had burned themselves alive upon their husbands'
funeral pyres. This, not so long ago, was quite a common
practice among the highest castes; the faithful wife (unless
she had young children, for the community naturally did
not wish to be burdened with orphans) went voluntarily
with her husband even into the fire, and was afterwards
deified; and indeed so desirable did such loyalty and devotion seem, that if a widow tried to get out of it, the only possible explanation was that she had *not* been a faithful wife,
and she was accordingly ostracised and outcaste. When a
king died, not only his wives but his servants and household
goods also sometimes went with him into the fire, so that he

should not lack in the next world anything to which he had been accustomed in this; and about this gigantic funeral pyre guards armed with spears were set to drive back upon the flames any one who tried to escape. The custom of *Suttee* has been prohibited by the Indian penal code, and now, save in very rare, isolated cases of fanaticism, never takes place; but the beliefs from which it sprang remain unaltered, so that there seems no reason why, when British rule passes, it should not gradually revive. And considering how unenviable the lot of a Hindoo widow is at the present day, especially if she is a child and childless, it could hardly be more unkind to allow her to end her life in this way than to oblige her to preserve it in perpetual asceticism and mourning. Narayan did not contribute to the conversation; he walked quietly beside me, and when we turned into the town and reached Babaji Rao's house he took his leave of us. I asked Babaji Rao what he thought of him, and he said he was a good boy; but he seemed reluctant to go into the question of their relationship. He agreed, however, that Narayan would feel himself superior to lower castes, and therefore, in this respect, superior to his master Babaji Rao, and that whereas he could not, if invited, come and take food in Babaji Rao's house, the latter could and would (though he would not feel very comfortable about it owing to his superiority in *rank*) go and take food in Narayan's house.

We had entered Babaji Rao's house by now, and were sitting in his study on the ground floor—a room sparsely furnished with a desk, a few rickety chairs, some books, and a number of almanacs and photos on the walls—and it suddenly occurred to me that perhaps I had done wrong to bring Abdul's sweetmeats with me into the house.

'Do you mind?' I asked.

'No. Why should I mind?'

'I've touched them.'

'That does not matter; but if it had been cooked meat I would not have taken it.'

When his little son Ram Chandra came into the room, Babaji Rao asked him playfully whether he would eat the sweets, and the child said he wouldn't for they came from the hands of a European. But I blundered later on. While we were talking, a mosquito bit me on the hand and I slapped at it and killed it. Then, looking up, I saw that Babaji Rao's brows were contracted.

'I say! I am sorry!' I exclaimed. 'I wasn't thinking.'

'It doesn't matter,' he said, not meeting my eye.

But clearly it did. There may be lives which for one reason or another it might not seem wanton to take—the life of a snake, for instance, of a rat, or of an offensive insect —and Babaji Rao would, I think, agree to this; but he would have to be hard put to it, nevertheless, before he would take even such a life himself, and by this much sensitiveness shrinks from seeing it done by others.

February 14*th*

AND Habib. He cannot be ignored, excluded from this picture. Looking back, I see that he has already introduced himself at the beginning of a process of obstinate attachment which has ended in his becoming my personal servant. I didn't engage him. I didn't want him. And I don't know whether he just took me over of his own accord, or was detailed to do so, or, being denser than the other dozen or so servants, was left behind by them as a piece of wood is left by an ebbing tide upon the shore, in their languid withdrawal, after the first fuss and excitement of my arrival had subsided, from an unaccustomed life of action to their interrupted slumbers under the *neem* tree. At any rate it is very clear that he now belongs to me. The first occasion on which I remember noticing him as something more than an obstruction of the line of vision was one morning about a month ago. I had just got out of bed and was brushing my hair at the dressing-table when I heard the sound of heavy breathing behind me, and saw in the looking-glass a small, dusky boy of about twelve, with thick brown lips, eyes like wet toffee, and very dirty feet.

He was making the bed. That is to say, that after patting the pillow with a hand which, I was surprised to see, left no stain upon it, he drew up and tucked in the clothes I had just thrown back; then, picking up a clean pair of shoes, he made off with them. But I called him back by the only name which, as far as I then knew, he possessed—Boy!—and taking hold of the mattress by one corner I turned the whole caboodle on to the floor.

It wasn't a very good thing to have done. I knew that, as soon as I perceived, from the blankness of his face, that I should now have to explain, if I could, why I had done it.

And why had I, anyway? What did it matter whether the bed was aired or not, or the mattress turned? No doubt my bed had been made after that fashion ever since I had been here, and I had slept in it without the least discomfort. But so accustomed was I at home to having my bedding turned and aired every morning, that I had come to think that such procedure was an indispensable part of bed-making, whereas in fact it made no difference to me at all. However, some explanation of my mysterious conduct was now clearly necessary, and the best way seemed to be to pick up the clothes and remake the bed myself. When I had finished, it did not look anything like as tidy as before; but I gazed hopefully at Habib. He presented an appearance wholly devoid of intelligence.

'Do you understand?' I asked in Hindi.

His thick lips unstuck a little and then cohered again.

'Oh, never mind!' I said irritably, feeling rather ridiculous; 'Go away! Jao!' and I turned back to the dressing-table. But he stood there as though rooted to the spot, looking inquiringly from me to the bed, and I had at last to open the curtains and point his exit before he want, still gazing at me over his shoulder.

After this I began to observe that, among all the servants,

he was the one upon whom chiefly I was depending; that what little was done for me was done by him.

Whenever I ran out of cigarettes and drew attention to this, which would otherwise not have been noticed, by placing the Gold Flake tin in the centre of the verandah, it was always Habib who, apparently suspecting some connection between the emptiness and the exposure of the object, brought it back to me to elicit, by gesture, the reason for its having been placed where he found it. At the end of a month I gave him two rupees.

And now he haunts me. In a long, dingy, plum-coloured coat buttoned up to the throat, and a dusty black skull-cap tied under the chin, he tidies the room from morning till night. I was never so much looked after in my life.

If I put a match in my ash-tray he patters in at once, picks it out, and bears it off to the rubbish-heap. But not, of course, without my permission. He never does anything without first getting my nod of assent. He holds the match towards me, almost under my nose. I am trying very hard to learn my lesson for Abdul, so I pretend not to notice. But it is no good.

'Sahib!' he urges confidingly, or sometimes 'Huzoor!'—a very respectful form of address, usually reserved, I believe, for royalty.

I glance crossly at him. He waves the match towards the door. The gesture is expressive:

'Are you willing that this match shall be thrown away and for ever lost?'

'Yes, yes—for Heaven's sake!'

He departs happily, and I go on with my lesson, writing down the new words on a sheet of paper and learning them off by heart. Perhaps if that match had been Abdul's, I think to myself, he would not have permitted it to be thrown away. Or, at any rate, he would have given the question more careful consideration. Might not the match be put to other uses, as a toothpick, a nail in the wall for light articles such as pretty empty match-boxes, or to dangle before the

cat at the end of a piece of string? No doubt, I think to myself, Abdul has a tin box in which he collects his match-
sticks. Having learned my words, I tear up the sheet of
paper, and since there is no wastepaper-basket, drop the
pieces absent-mindedly on the floor beside my chair. In
patters Habib, and carefully collecting them, holds them
under my nose.

'Huzoor!'

'Oh, *do* go away!' I groan.

But it is all of no use. I have begged and commanded him,
both through Narayan and Babaji Rao, to leave my ash-
tray alone, but it is all of no use. It is still emptied about
thirty times a day, and wiped on the door-curtains afterwards, so that I myself now hastily take out again anything
which I inadvertently put into it. The bed is still made
according to his original plan, and for a whole month the
house has not been swept or dusted, so that when I walk
about my rooms little puffs of dust rise up from under my
feet. Lampblack and cigarette-ash lie thick on my books and
papers, and rat-droppings all over the dressing-table; and
while I dismally survey this dreary scene of dust and deso-
lation, in patters the devoted Habib to pick the latest match
out of the ash-tray. I gaze mournfully at him. Then I smile;
he looks so absurd; and the thick brown lips part to disclose
dazzling teeth in response, while he holds out the offensive,
untidy match:

'Huzoor!'

February 15*th*

HIS HIGHNESS's pilgrimage has been postponed for a month.
He is not well enough, and also the weather is too cold, he
says, though personally I find it uncomfortably warm. It is a
great disappointment to him; and perhaps it is; but the real
cause of his disappointment, I suspect, dates back to the
days when, believing his own departure unavoidable, he
gave Napoleon III. and me permission to take a holiday

running concurrently with his. Napoleon III. has already gone, and I'm off on Wednesday; but he himself now stays. Perhaps he is really unwell; but probably it is only an attack of the nervous disorders to which he is especially prone whenever this pilgrimage to Gaya is attempted. He is really very nervous about his health, and consults every doctor he meets, and seldom takes their medicine because it is not the same as the medicine the last doctor prescribed, or because it *is* the same, or because his pundits advise him against it, or because the moon is in its eighth zodiac, or for some other reason. Most of the friends he invites here are army medical men, and we have an I.M.S. man, Captain Drood, and his wife staying in the Guest House at present. They are unusually pleasant Anglo-Indians, and are kind and patient with the little man. One needs patience. Captain Drood examined him the other day, and told me that the Maharajah's complaint was locomotor ataxia and that he had made out a prescription for him to have dispensed at the local hospital. But the Maharajah brought it back next day. He had had it explained to him at the hospital and had recognised it. It was the same prescription that an Allahabad doctor had sent him recently. It contained potassium iodide, which was very disagreeable; it made his eyes water. Could not the Doctor Sahib put something else into the medicine instead of potassium iodide? Could he not put in, for example, nux vomica? Captain Drood told him that nux vomica was of no use for his particular trouble. His Highness quoted other drugs at random. Could he not have one of these—anything but that horrid potassium iodide? But Captain Drood, who was attending the Maharajah for the first time, continued to be reasonable. The most that he could do, he said, was to diminish the amount of potassium iodide he had prescribed, and if it still made His Highness's eyes water this could be obviated by lengthening the intervals between the doses.

With this concession the Maharajah hobbled off, apparently reassured; but the next day Captain Drood learnt

that the local doctor, a Hindoo following the European
system, had cut out the potassium iodide altogether and
substituted something else—no one seemed to know what.
This vexed Drood considerably, no doubt in his professional
dignity, though he pretended alarm for the Maharajah's
welfare in the hands of 'these damned unscrupulous pundits,' and expressed a determination to give the little King
a 'good talking to.' But the 'good talking to' did not long
survive an interruptive question suddenly put by His Highness, who for some time had appeared inattentive, as to
whether the Doctor Sahib (who happened to be slightly
bald) shaved the top of his head.

After all, His Highness had already got from Captain
Drood all that he really wanted—his medical opinion that
the Maharajah was not in a fit state of health to undertake
the pilgrimage to Gaya. Mrs. Drood also used her talents to
bring about the happy result of another postponement.
His Highness loves her. As is common among large, blowsy,
highly coloured women, she is amiable and kind-hearted;
but this is not the point: she tells his fortune with cards. He
never tires of this; it is one of his invariable claims upon all
his new female visitors, and he seems quite surprised when
he is told by any one of them that she does not know how to
do it, as though he has always considered this talent an
accomplishment possessed by all women of the West. As a
matter of fact, Mrs. Drood herself pleaded ignorance at his
first request; but His Highness begged her so earnestly at
any rate to try, that she gave way and, on what little she
remembered of the subject, contrived a system by which not
only His Highness but she herself, it seems, is now quite taken
in. She allows him to have two or three wishes a day—the
wish-card being the nine of hearts, and, while she spreads
out the cards into a pattern, he sits beside her with his eyes
closed and a very solemn expression indeed on his face,
concentratedly wishing.

What is he wishing for? For health, perhaps, for friendship, or for everlasting life; for a vision of heaven, or revision

147

of earth; for the art of the classic Greeks, or the power of the Roman Emperors—or for the return of Napoleon the Third.

Sometimes he gets his nine of hearts and is contented and grateful; when it does not occur he grows ill at ease. But Mrs. Drood usually manages to offer him some compensation. If the nine itself is not turned up, something near to it may be—the seven, eight, or ten; and she tells him that though it does not seem that he is yet to be granted his *full* wish, it will be realised at any rate in part.

'How many annas?' he cries, never slow to accept the opportunity of twisting omens to his advantage, as once he turned his car to keep the blackbuck on the right. If the nine of hearts is fullness—sixteen annas to the rupee—what is the eight of hearts? How many annas?

She helps him; his chances are never less than ten annas, and even when, as invariably happens, he drops the cards in shuffling (for this is an accomplishment which no amount of practice can teach him), she is never impatient, but finds good omens in those that fall to the ground.

When the moon was in its seventh zodiac he was always coming to Mrs. Drood for wishes, for this was a very propitious time for him; but only for three days. Then the moon would be in its eighth zodiac, which, he told her, was predicted to be such an unlucky period for him that he would be ill advised then to have his fortune told. He could not, however, refrain, but came to her during this unfavourable period too, and anxiously begged that he might be allowed to have one wish, just *one*.

'Of course, Maharajah Sahib,' she said at once; 'and if the nine of hearts does not turn up we shall blame the moon for muddling the cards.'

'You are *quite* right! That is *very* true!' he agreed, immediately restored to confidence, and glanced at me as much as to say 'Did you hear? *Such* intelligence!'

The occurrence or non-occurrence of the wish-card, though of primary importance, is not of course the end of the matter; there is all sorts of interesting information to be gleaned from the combinations of the cards when they are spread, and one of His Highness's most frequent inquiries is for news of his future health. This news, Mrs. Drood sees to it, is always good; though once she told me, with a solemnity quite equal to his, that the cards had clearly indicated that he was soon to be very seriously ill. However, since I now find myself, when driving out with him, quite infected by his anxiety over the mongoose, and experience relief or depression according to whether we see one or not, I can hardly say anything more about that. Anyway, his pilgrimage has been postponed until March; the stethoscope and the cards have gone into the scale of his disinclination against the advice of the pundits and of Babaji Rao, who has already made all the elaborate arrangements for his transport; and His Highness is 'very disappointed.'

If Habib is a pest, Abdul is a positive incubus.

During the last week I have become so involved in his affairs that now I do not know how to extricate myself; he is an old man of the sea round my neck, and the knowledge that I gave him permission, so to speak, to sit there does not help me to bear his weight philosophically now that I cannot shake him off. After he had presented his petition to the Maharajah I wrote to the latter, at Abdul's request, to confirm it, saying that I hoped he would not forget his promise and that Abdul might be given the managership of the Guest House at twenty-five rupees a month as soon as possible.

I selected that particular employment from among Abdul's other suggestions because it seemed least liable to interfere with any one else's interests, and because the Guest House, according to the bills which upset the Dewan every quarter, is badly in need of management. Narayan says that much of the extravagance is due to the pilferings of the venerable Munshi, who has the keys of the storeroom and is therefore in a splendid position to supply himself, his relations, and his friends, the Doctor and the Collector, with whatever they want. That, says Narayan, is how the port goes, and the whisky goes, and the cigarettes, and Fortnum & Mason's preserved fruits. The Collector is nominally the manager, but he is too busy a man according to Babaji Rao, and too artful a one according to Narayan, to give undivided attention. Advice is always being sought for reducing the terrific expenditure, and it was once suggested that I should take the whole thing over myself as one of my duties; but when I began my campaign against extravagance by cutting out Fortnum & Mason's preserved fruit (which I don't happen to like), I was said to be too extreme an economist and politely released from my new duty. So the appointment of Abdul as a resident manager seemed to me a good idea. Later in the day I was told by His Highness that this was arranged, and that Abdul had been appointed manager on probation from that day at twenty rupees a month. Abdul didn't seem as pleased with this news as I expected.

'Ah, on *probation!*' he said. 'That is their *craftiness*. I shall not be allowed to please them, and when you go they will turn me out! I know!'

However, he thanked me before he left, and offered his hand.

But the order to remove was not given, so I spoke to Babaji Rao about it and was told that Abdul must present his petition to the Dewan in the usual way, and the Dewan, under the Maharajah's instructions, would pass it. But Abdul seemed nervous of the Dewan. Could not the business be done through Babaji Rao? he asked; and, in any case, would I draw up his petition for him? But I was rather fed up with the whole affair, which was eating up more and more of the lesson hours, and told him he'd have to manage the rest by himself. But I was not to get out of it so easily. On the 13th I learnt, to my distress, that the very thing I had been trying to avoid was happening; Narayan was to be moved from the Guest House to make way for Abdul.

This might not have been unfortunate, for Narayan, I knew, wanted a change; but the post to which he was to be moved was not as good as the one he held. And it seemed to me that, at about this time, his manner towards me began to alter. I had had his confidence and respect; but now, I felt, he was avoiding me. On the evening before Abdul was to present his petition, while Babaji Rao and I were discussing this muddle on my front verandah, Narayan, who had been sitting with Sharma under the *neem* tree by the kitchen, came over to us to get a paper signed by Babaji Rao. He salaamed and smiled at me in answer to my smile, and I asked him if he would care to walk with us. He said he would; but when we started off a few minutes later he had returned to his seat under the *neem* tree. He had his face turned away, and was pretending, I thought, not to notice us; but his friend Sharma was watching me. This made me very unhappy, and I wrote to Babaji Rao that night to say that I would be much easier in my mind if he would try to rearrange matters with the Dewan so that Abdul remained in his office with an eight-rupee increase of salary until Narayan was properly suited. He replied very agreeably that he would do his best though he feared the Dewan's reply, and asked me to send Narayan to him at seven o'clock in the morning, before the Dewan's court sat, so that he could find out what the boy wanted. But Narayan had an attack of vomiting in the morning and could not keep his appointment; however, Babaji Rao told me yesterday afternoon, greatly to my relief, that he had fixed it all up satisfactorily in the way I had suggested. The Dewan had been very cross, but had nevertheless agreed, and now a little scene would have to be enacted in which Abdul's officer would feign anger with Abdul and tell him he could not yet be spared. The petition would still have to go through the Dewan, and he would write on it 'Eight rupees advance'— and that would be the end.

February 16th

'WHEN are you going on your tour?' asked His Highness this afternoon as we started on our drive. 'Are you going on Thursday?'

'No, Prince,' I answered firmly; 'you gave me permission to go on Wednesday.'

He inclined his head slightly, widening his eyes, as much as to say that he experienced surprise but was too polite to express it.

'And you will be away for . . . two weeks?' he inquired, glancing at me.

'Two weeks!' I exclaimed, a little crossly. 'Now you know quite well, Prince, that we agreed that . . .'

'Then how long will it be?' he interrupted me.

'You said I might be away for a month, the period of your pilgrimage,' I said, feeling unkind and guilty, but nevertheless obstinate. Once again, without looking at me, he indicated his surprise by a movement of the head and eyes; then in a gentle voice, touching me on the sleeve, he said:

'Do not be away for more than three weeks. I cannot spare you.'

We drove into Chetla. There the Maharajah received presents of betel and fruit, and gave audience to that same young betel-leaf planter whose physical deterioration had disappointed us so much on a previous visit. He was in trouble.

Some wicked man, a relative, was disputing his claim to a certain plantation and had threatened to kill the boy unless he yielded. His Highness gave a merely perfunctory attention to this story, and after instructing the boy to bring the case before the civil court in Chhokrapur, ordered the chauffeur to drive on. Indeed the young man was very disappointing, we once more agreed; and His Highness remarked, with a chuckle, that he could *not* understand what he could be *doing* to have got so thin. For a short time after this we drove in silence, and then he asked:

'Do people in England drink the urine of the cow or any animal?'

I said I'd never heard of any one doing so there.

'Why, do you?' I asked.

PART ONE

'Oh, yes,' he said; 'I must drink it. All Hindoos must take the five products of the cow. It is our religion.'

'What are the five products?' I inquired.

'Urine, dung, milk, curd, butter.'

'What about sweat?' I asked. 'Isn't that a product?'

'Unholy!' he said, tapping his knee with his hand.

'And saliva? How about saliva?'

'Unholy!' he repeated, tapping his knee again. 'The mouth of the cow is unholy and is never worshipped.'

'Will any cow do?' I asked. 'Or must it be a special cow, like the Frenchman's frog?'

'*Any* cow,' he replied.

'Those cows, for instance?' I indicated some scraggy specimens in a passing field.

'They are peasants' cows,' he said, with a deprecating smile.

'And how often do you take the five products, Prince?' I inquired.

'Every day; in small quantities. I *must* do so.' Then he began to giggle. 'Dung and urine are *very* holy,' he added.

'Cow's urine is said to have medicinal properties too, isn't it?' I asked. 'I've heard that most Indian medicines contain it.'

'It is quite true,' he replied; then, after a pause; 'I like it *very* much. I drink it like water.'

I asked him why the cow was reverenced above all other animals, and he said that it was looked upon as the universal Mother, and with the Lion, the Peacock, the Black Bee, the Secretary Bird, the Black Humming-bird, and the perfect male and female human bodies, was thought to be the Seat of the Unknown. He could not account for this selection, he said, any more than he could say why maize, onions, celery, and spinach were unholy, or why the cat was sacred and the dog not; but so it was. As we drove through the outskirts of Chetla I pointed out to His Highness one of the rude tree-shrines one sees frequently hereabouts and asked him what they meant. They are small circular platforms of clay-covered brick, roughly built round the trunks of trees, and the actual shrine is a small knob of clay or mud on top of this, hollowed out to receive some relic. He said that they are built to propitiate ghosts, spirits of the dead—*genii loci*, perhaps—which were often ferocious and harmful. Sacrifices of eggs and coco-nut milk were made. But they were the work and beliefs of the ignorant, superstitious peasants, he said contemptuously, many of whom worshipped demons.

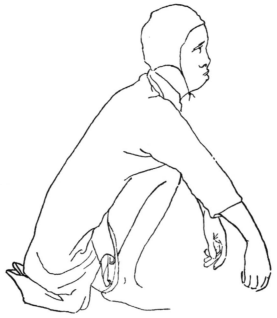

When I was changing for dinner this evening, and had nothing on but my socks, Habib entered the room.

I shouted at him and he vanished. I have tried to teach him that whenever my curtains are closed he must tap for permission to enter; but he always enters without tapping, is always shouted at, and always vanishes. As I went on leisurely dressing I wondered what he had wanted and what had become of him, whether he had left the house or was waiting in the next room. I listened for sounds and heard nothing; but I felt sure, nevertheless, that he would not have left the house before accomplishing his mission—whatever that might be. The idea of going away and coming back later on would not occur to him. When I had my trousers on I peered into the next room. It was empty. Then I looked on the back verandah. There he was, in the gloom, polishing something with a cloth. I gazed at him severely. His thick lips moved nervously, sticking together, then unsticking, as though indicating their readiness to answer to a smile.

'What do you want?' I asked in Hindi.

He presented to view the object he was polishing. It was a soda-water bottle.

With a sigh of resignation I returned to my dressing. A bottle of soda-water is put on the table in my bedroom every evening, and I knew that Habib would patiently await the opportunity to put it in its accustomed place. I might remain in the bedroom for hours and hours; he would stay on the verandah, quietly polishing the bottle with his cloth, awaiting his opportunity. To put it anywhere else would not be right. On the table in the bedroom it was always put; on the table in the bedroom it must therefore go. Eventually, when I had almost finished dressing, I had occasion to go into the bathroom for a moment, and when I returned there was the soda-water bottle on my bedroom table, and Habib had disappeared.

Narayan's vomiting yesterday morning didn't put things straight internally. I met him in the evening and asked him how he felt.

'I have a pain in my belly,' he said.

So I got Captain Drood to examine him. Drood asked him what he ate, and he said rice, milk, and bread; so the doctor warned him off bread for a day or two and gave him some castor-oil, after which he felt better. He came in to see me this evening after dinner.

'Is Sharma angry with me?' I asked him. 'Or am I angry with Sharma?'

'I do not know.'

'Yes, you do. Tell me.'

'He is not angry with you.'

'Well, I am not angry with him.'

'He think so,' said Narayan. 'He say me yesterday, "The Sahib is angry with me." '

'I like him very much,' I said. 'Will you tell him?'

'Yes, I will tell him.'

'*You* were angry with me the other day.'

'No, I was not angry.'

'A little, yes, a little.'

'No. You are my big brother, and I am your little brother.'

February 18*th*

POOR ABDUL! In the afternoon of the day on which he had been told to present his petition to the Dewan, when the Dewan 'would write on it "eight rupees advance," and that would be the end,' he came at his usual time to my house.

But he was clearly not in his usual spirits; he was subdued, jerky, and mysterious; something had clearly gone wrong. He greeted me with a perfunctory movement, and seating himself at the table, began arranging his books and papers without a word.

'Mr. Ackerley,' he said at length, in an uncontrolled voice, 'I want you to know that *nothing* has been done. Your recommendation—your *strong* recommendation—has come to nothing. But do not ask me any more! Do not speak of it any more! We will never talk of it again.'

Nor did we—that afternoon; he drew in his chin, frowned, and concentrated painfully on his books; for the first time for some weeks I had a full hour's lesson. At the end of it he set my next lesson, collected his things beneath his arm, and bowing stiffly, departed.

But yesterday afternoon, when he returned, he was unshaven and did not look as if he had slept very well.

'If I tell you something, Mr. Ackerley,' he began at once, 'will you give me your solemn promise not to speak of it to any man?'

PART ONE

'What is it, Abdul?' I asked, and at once his eyes filled with tears and his voice became husky. His officer had been angry at not having been consulted. There had been a scene in which the officer had said that Abdul had behaved in a deceitful, underhand manner, that he could not be spared from his post, and that an apology was due from him to the Dewan, who had been put, on his account, to considerable annoyance. Abdul's voice shook. The interview had been terrible.

'You are a bad man, a wicked man!' the Dewan had screamed. 'Not one extra pice will I give you, but I will have you dismissed from the office you already hold if I ever hear of you again!' There had been a lot more like this, and then the Dewan had ejected him, saying that if he breathed a word of this to me or any one else he would have him killed.

I couldn't help smiling at this; the 'little scene' that Babaji Rao had spoken of seemed to have been acted with some enthusiasm; but Abdul observed me.

'Ah, you are pleased, Mr. Ackerley?' he said, smirking.

I hastened to correct this impression, without, however, giving the plot away. I said that I simply was not worried by his story; the Maharajah had promised him twenty rupees a month, and this sooner or later he would get, but he must not expect the managership of the Guest House until Narayan was suited. But he had been too badly scared. The Dewan hated him, he said, and would seek to injure him; he was Mohammedan and they Hindoo, and so they hated him. I had done nothing for him, nothing; it was all over, and now the least that I could do was to get him, through the Political Agent, a good job in some other State.

He looked at me appealingly. He was abject with fear and self-pity; the whites and browns of his eyes seemed to have run together. I did not like him at all; but I soothed him as best I could, and said that if nothing had been done by the time I returned from my holiday I would write to His Highness to ask why his promise had not been given effect. He seemed a little comforted, and left repeating his first request:

'And I have your promise not to speak of all this to any man? It will be very bad for me, gentleman; very dangerous for me!'

We had done no work at all.

But to-day he was quite his old self. This was our last lesson but one before my departure, he said, and so he had some requests to make. First he wished me to get for him the letter of recommendation from the Political Agent which I had promised—and he also wanted a similar letter from me as well.

I shook my head. I would do nothing more, I said, until I returned; he would have to be patient—and now we would get on with the lesson.

We did so, for a few minutes. Then he began again, clearing his throat and speaking in short, dry sentences as he patted and shuffled his papers.

'You see, you have failed, Mr. Ackerley. You have made a recommendation—a *strong* recommendation—but nothing has come of it. You have been defeated by the Dewan, and it is an insult to you—and to the whole English people! You see?'

He glanced up, with a sly smile, for his effect. I laughed.

'Look here, Abdul,' I said, 'as a matter of fact, it's my doing that you haven't got the managership of the Guest House'; and I explained what had happened.

But he did not seem able to get this quite straight.

'Why have you not told me?' he asked, bewildered. 'You have not opened your heart to me.'

'Well, you know now, anyway; and I think it's time for you to go.'

'Mr. Narayan asked you to do this,' he said thoughtfully, as he put his books together. 'Is it not? I think so.'

I gave him ten rupees over his salary.

'Thank you, Mr. Ackerley; and I shall come to-morrow at the same time for a last lesson.'

'No, Abdul,' I said, 'this must be the last till I return; I shall be too busy to-morrow to see you.'

But this was not at all in accordance with his plans. He had not yet got any of his requests granted.

PART ONE

'Then I shall prepare some work for you to study while you are away. I will bring it to-night at nine o'clock.' I shook my head. 'Ah, you do not want? Then I will come at five, and take you for a walk. You walk often with Mr. Narayan at five o'clock, so it is a good time.'

'No, Abdul,' I said; 'I don't want to see you again before my return.'

'Ah, Mr. Ackerley, and what will happen to me while you are away? Will you not grant me a few minutes more of your valuable time and write for me a letter of recommendation—now—before my eyes? I shall dictate it to you, and so it will be a very good letter—the best.'

'*No*, Abdul,' I said.

He picked up his books.

'Very well, Mr. Ackerley. I do not wish to bore upon your time. You will write to me from your travels?'

'Perhaps,' I said.

'Only "perhaps"? Ah, Mr. Ackerley, that is not good, gentleman. . . .'

'Very well,' I said weakly, 'I'll write to you.'

'Ah, thank you, Mr. Ackerley. How many times will you write? Twice a week?'

'At least twice a week,' I said, yawning.

'And you will write in your letters your future addresses so that I may answer if I wish? You will say "I am here"—then you will write your present address—"until"—then you will give the date—"and then I shall proceed to"——'

He really is the most tiresome person I ever met.

Captain Drood and his wife left here yesterday morning.

On the previous evening His Highness paid them a farewell visit at the Guest House, and presented Mrs. Drood with a very beautiful piece of muslin worked with green and gold thread. He had quite recovered his health and spirits, and told us that if he had gone upon his tour he would have had to shave his head and moustache—everything except his eyebrows.

'If I did not do so,' he said, 'I should have had to pay double fees to the priests!'

'Oh, I should have loved to have seen you, Maharajah Sahib!' cried Mrs. Drood mischievously. He tittered into his sleeve and waved a protesting hand.

'I should not have come before you,' he said.

She was delighted with her piece of muslin, and when he said he had a state coat rather like it—of green and gold brocade—she begged to be allowed to see his finery and jewels, and he at once sent Hashim off in the car to fetch some of his wardrobe from the Palace. They were certainly lovely things: necklaces and brooches of precious stones; beautiful skirted coats of rich brocade, and turbans to match them, jewelled and plumed. The jewellery was all Indian work; but the robes, he said, were made in Paris. Mrs. Drood went into raptures over them, and her husband too expressed the greatest admiration. When they had finished examining and ejaculating, His Highness, who had been looking on in silence, waved the things away with a slight movement of his hand.

'I do not like them,' he said gently; 'I like *people*.'

It was full moon this evening when I left my house and walked over to the Guest House for dinner. On the steps of the verandah I saw Narayan and Sharma sitting together, but at my approach the latter rose and, going towards the pantry near which Hashim was standing, hid behind his back. Narayan rose also, but did not run away.

'Sharma!' I said, when I had reached the steps. There was no reply, and neither Narayan nor Hashim made any sign.

'Sharma!' I repeated; and this time both the others echoed me. Sharma came out from behind Hashim's back and stood still in the moonlight.

'Salaam!' I said, greeting him.

'Salaam!' said the boy touching his head.

I went in to dinner.

PART II

PART TWO

March 9th

I GOT back this evening at about five o'clock. Having delayed too long in warning Babaji Rao of the time of my arrival at Dipra, I found no car there to meet me; but there was a lorry at the station bound for Chhokrapur, and I got my luggage and myself on to that.

The driver of the lorry, which was already full of sleepy Indians with their little brass bowls and baggage, offered me the front seat next to him, and there I sat, very limp after a hot and stuffy journey, and waited for the lorry to start.

This occurred an hour later. A lean man in a yellow turban and threadbare European suit came and addressed me, having paved the way to conversation by a display of large teeth as yellow as his turban, to which I had not responded. He spoke English.

'Sir, excuse me; you are going to Chhokrapur?'

I nodded feebly, already bored by what I knew would follow.

'You have employment there?'

'Yes.'

'You are Dewan of the State, perhaps?'

'No.'

'Ah; then what is your business?'

'Private.'

A bead of perspiration trickled down my nose and fell on to the attaché-case I was nursing on my knees. The brown eyes examined me and my luggage again, and then gazed dreamily at the railway station.

'You are a soldier?'

'No.'

'In the political department, perhaps?'

'No.'

'Ah, then no doubt a civil servant?'

'No.'

He smiled faintly. This was certainly extremely interesting. Who *could* this Englishman be? After an interval he tried again. He felt sure he had met me, or at any rate seen me, before.

'Where?' I asked, watching the lorry-driver, who was arguing with some of the passengers and spectators over the crank-handle to which the engine had failed to respond.

'In Benares?' hazarded the man in the yellow turban.

I glanced at him, wondering whether I actually had seen him in Benares, and no doubt this decided him that he had made a good shot. Yes, in Benares, he felt sure, and he distinctly remembered that we had met and talked, and I had told him of the business upon which I was engaged, but the nature of which he had now unhappily forgotten.

'When was this?' I asked sleepily.

Somewhere between 1927 and 1929, he conjectured with a smile, and was confounded when I said that I had only been in Benares once, and then only for three days, and that only three weeks ago. Then, to show that I bore him no ill-will, I asked him whither *he* was bound, what his business was, what salary he was getting, whether he was married, and how many children he possessed; and having elicited, without the least difficulty, all this information, I said I wished to sleep, and he said he wished to make water, and we parted on good terms. Shortly afterwards the owner of the lorry, whose eyes were more vertical than horizontal, came to collect the fares himself, for no one would be so simple as to expect money to pass unchanged through the hands of employés. I asked for a ticket as far as Rajgarh, thinking that the Maharajah's car might meet me on the way, and was told that it cost three rupees. I smiled scornfully. As a matter of fact, I had no idea at all what the fare was, but one is always overcharged as a matter of course. It is the custom. The person in the yellow turban had re-appeared by this time, and was able to inform me that one and a half rupees was the correct price; so I requested him to ask the lorry-owner why I was being charged double.

'The Sahib is occupying double seat space,' was the naïve reply.

'The Sahib did not ask for double seat space,' I said smiling, and handed him one and a half rupees. The owner and the driver, who accompanied him, smiled calmly in return; they had failed to rob me, but were not cross with me on that account. After this there was a general agree-ment that no one had anything more to do or say and that we might as well start; it was 2.45 P.M., and there seemed to me to be no reason why we should not have started three-quarters of an hour earlier. Then the driver said that he was hot and wished to go round the corner to get a drink of water from the pump. This announcement was greeted with general disfavour; people who had been dozing when the remark was made stiffened into life and added their protest to the general outcry; and for about ten minutes there was a discussion as to whether or not there was time for the lorry-driver to go and get a drink of water from the pump. The man in the yellow turban, who explained to me what was happening, also voted. Eventually the driver gave in; the engine was flogged into motion, and we drove off. Five minutes later one of the Maharajah's cars appeared in a cloud of dust. I stopped the lorry and got out, and spent a few vain minutes trying, with the chauffeur's help, to get my one and a half rupees refunded. I didn't much care; but it was the right thing to do.

The lorry then proceeded upon its way.

There was a note for me from His Highness.

'DEAR FRIEND,—Delighted to hear you come to-day. Sending car. Napoleon the 3rd is also to reach Dipra at the same hour. If not inconvenient can you bring them with you too—and oblige.'

We drove back through the torrid heat to the station and made inquiries. Yes, the party His Highness was expecting had arrived; they were in the lorry I had just left.

The chauffeur was quite unmoved by this news, and I was, by this time, in a state of Indian resignation; so we set back without a word in pursuit of the lorry, which we found not very far from the place where we had left it. It had broken down.

Napoleon the Third was seated on a pile of dusty blankets inside it, wedged between the knees of his uncle and aunt.

He was wearing a yellow coat, pink cotton trousers, and some silver bracelets and rings; but he was very grubby, and had sore eyes which were lavishly smeared with a thick black paste. We rescued him and his uncle from the lorry and stuffed them and their baggage into the back of the car. The aunt, who kept her face carefully concealed, we left where she was.

When I had washed and changed my clothes, Babaji Rao came to see me. After talking for some time about my holiday and His Highness's pilgrimage, which is now dated to begin on the 17th, he said he was thirsty and called across to the kitchen for a *lota* of water. This was brought by Narayan, who handed it to Babaji Rao and then left.

Babaji Rao went out on to the verandah to drink it, and when he came back explained that there were many people in Chhokrapur who might have *talked* if he had drunk water in my house. He said he did not mind much about it himself, and had, indeed, often eaten and drunk in the presence of Europeans when he was at St. John's College, Agra; but it was better to be careful nevertheless. Of course it was only on these extreme points, he said, that he found himself personally tolerant; he would not receive food from lower castes, nor eat with them; nor would he allow his food to be cooked by any one except a Brahman or one of his own caste. I asked how it was that in the Palace His Highness employed a Mohammedan cook; but, Babaji Rao explained, he did

166

not actually *cook*, he only showed the Hindoo cooks *how* to cook; he was not even allowed in the kitchen, but sat outside and gave instructions through a hole in the wall.

After dinner His Highness sent up the carriage with its piebald steeds to bring me down to the Palace.

It was a warm, still evening; vapoury clouds trailed across a crescent moon, and the air was sickly with the scent of *sajna*. His Highness was curled up outside the Palace on a *charpai*. A dilapidated canvas fence had been erected round him, forming a private enclosure. My chair and the usual tables were set beside him; charcoal glowed through its soft grey ash in a bowl on the ground. Apparently the weather was not yet warm enough for him; but my shirt was sticking to my back. We chatted about one thing and another, while white-clad servants were visible now and then behind him, pale shapes floating in the gloom. One brought a hookah. I said I had heard he was intending to start very soon upon his pilgrimage, and after rather sharply inquiring who had informed me of this, as though a breach of confidence had been committed, he sighed that he was afraid that this time there was no avoiding it.

'They all say that I must go, and so——' He made a gesture of resignation. But he was very sorry to have to do so, he said, for the annual festival of *Holi* was beginning soon, and there would be a great fair, lasting for about a fortnight, at Garha, to which he had intended to take me. He went there every year, he said, during the *Holi* season, staying with his court in Garha Palace, while the visitors and friends he invited lived under canvas. It was a very important festival; people came to it from all over the Province and even from the big cities of India, to sell and buy; and there was always much interest and amusement of every kind.

But this year, owing to his pilgrimage, he would not be able to go, which was a great nuisance, and though Babaji Rao would no doubt take me there for a day's expedition, it would be a very half-hearted affair without his personal patronage.

Moreover he had already invited, he said, two very old and dear friends of his, Captain Daly and Miss Trend, to keep *Holi* with him; and now he must write and put them off.

I agreed with him that this was very disappointing and a great misfortune to us both, and asked whether he could not postpone his tour for another month. He struck his hands together as much as to say that the matter was beyond hope.

'If I do not go now, I cannot go until next year; it will be too hot, and then the rains will come.'

'Then put it off till next year,' I said, 'and let us go and enjoy ourselves at Garha.'

'Ah, I would like it very much.'

'Then it's done. For you are King and can do as you like.'

But he shook his head mournfully.

'I must go,' he said.

Then he changed the subject. He told me that Mr. Bramble had paid him another visit during my absence, but that his estimate of the cost of the Greek Villa had been too heavy, and so the Villa, on which he had really set his heart, had had to be reduced to a two-room Greek Pavilion which would cost a thousand pounds and was to be built more or less on the spot where we were sitting. I looked about me to take in the position.

'Then it will be just between the rear portico of your Palace and this unfinished building behind me?' I said, looking up at a dark mass of stone encased in scaffolding. 'What is it, by the way? Is it a temple?'

'Yes, a temple.'

'What kind of temple?' I asked.

His Highness slipped his feet out of his sandals, and dangling his legs over the side of the bed, trailed his toes in the thick warm dust.

'Oh—just a—just an ordinary temple,' he said.

'But this is bigger than any I've seen in the city; is it going to be the cathedral?'

'You are *quite* right,' he replied with a touch of importance; 'it is my cathedral—and also my private chapel,' he added.

'How long has it been building?' I asked.

He did not answer for some time, and peering through gloom, I perceived that he was shaking with merriment.

'Thirty years!' he at last spluttered, and was again convulsed.

March 11*th*

NARAYAN tells me that when I went away he was very unhappy, and sorrowed whenever he looked at my empty house. He could not eat any food that day, and when Sharma asked:

'Why do you not eat? Is it because the Sahib has gone away?' he replied:

'No; I have a pain in my belly.'

'Yet you seldom came to see me when I was here,' I said doubtfully.

'But Mr. Babaji Rao was always with you, or the doors were closed, and I was afraid you would be angry with me.'

He told me this yesterday and stayed three hours with me, taking both my hands in his as he left.

'Sharma a shy boy,' he said; 'but I do not know why he is shy of you.'

I asked him how it was that he, a Brahman, could have a friend of the barber caste.

'It does not matter,' he said.

'Can you take food from him?'

'No, I cannot.'

'Betel?'

'Yes, I can take.'

'Why did you choose him for your friend?'

But he only laughed softly at this, and when I repeated it the third time said:

'He was my class-fellow.'

Babaji Rao wrote to me while I was away that Abdul had been sent to Sarwar, a station just outside Chhokrapur, on

State business, and hoped to be back before my return, but that if he was delayed ('which alternative,' wrote Babaji Rao, 'I believe you will prefer'), he wished to be excused for a few days. Babaji Rao was quite right; my desire never to see Abdul again made it easy to leave him permanently in Sarwar, so I was not altogether agreeably surprised when he was announced to-day as I was finishing lunch. Hashim showed him in. He was all in white, very spick and span, but low-spirited.

'Good afternoon, Mr. Ackerley.'

'Good afternoon, Abdul.'

'Do I bore upon your time?'

'Please sit down.'

He placed his umbrella against the wall and sat down.

'You have had an enjoyable travel?' he asked abruptly.

'Very, thank you.'

'And you returned the day before yesterday, is it not?' I nodded. 'But you did not inform me of your return? I think you did not wish me to know of it, is it not? Am I right? I think so.'

'I thought you were in Sarwar,' I said.

'But you did not ask any man? Mr. Babaji Rao would have told you, or Mr. Narayan. But I think you did not wish to see me?' He dropped his head a little to one side, and drew up the corners of his mouth into a subtle smile. 'And *thank* you, Mr. Ackerley—thank you *very* much—for the *many letters* you *promised* to write to me while you were away.'

He cleared his throat, which was getting husky, and drawing in his chin, gazed into his lap. Then he cast a rapid glance at me and found me smiling. At once his lips began to tremble.

'Are you pleased, Mr. Ackerley? I think so. You are pleased at my misfortunes. I see. I understand. Every man hates me and wishes to ruin me, but I say to myself, "Mr. Ackerley will not forget me; he has given me his promises, and loves me in his heart." But I was wrong, yes? I think you do not wish to help me. You promise many things, and when nothing is done you mock at me and are pleased. I think so. Is it not?'

'Look here, Abdul,' I said, 'let's understand that I didn't write to you because I didn't think about you, but that I don't hate you or wish you any harm. I did my best for you before I went away, and I said I'd try again when I came back; so don't let's have any more of that nonsense.'

He brightened up at once.

'Ah, Mr. Ackerley, then you do not hate me and want to leave me? Ah, Mr. Ackerley, I am happy. But what must I do? For they hate me and will send me to Sarwar. . . .'

'I thought you'd been to Sarwar,' I said.

'Yes, I have been; but that was nothing. Now they say I shall be transferred there to work in the office. They are very angry with me, and so they send me away.'

'But that's absurd,' I said, vexed. 'You're my tutor. They can't send you away without my permission.'

'It is what I think; but they say *so*,' said Abdul shrewdly.

I asked him whether he had received his salary during my absence, and he said he had—the usual twelve rupees, without increment; but he did not wish me to do any more about that, he said; nothing mattered so long as I did not hate him and send him away. The Dewan hated him, and his officer hated him; that was all that my strong recommendation and His Highness's promises had done, but——

'Do not talk of it! Let it be! What about it? I am a poor man and cannot provide my family members; but what about it? Every one hates me, and wishes to injure me; but what about it? Let it be. . . .'

I said it was all nonsense to talk about people hating him and wishing to injure him; but he contradicted this, in a confused, trembling voice. Two pleaders had died suddenly while I was away, he said, and he had twice visited the Dewan to ask to be appointed to their places—for which he must have found a good deal of courage, I thought. And this was not like asking for an increment, he explained; for a pleader's life is a precarious one and depends entirely upon

personal ability. But the Dewan had practically told him
that if there was no one else in Chhokrapur to fill a vacant
post he would not give it to him. This, apart from anything
else, seemed to me stupidity in the Dewan, for Abdul would
surely make an excellent pleader, if he 'bored upon' the
judge's time as much as he has 'bored upon' mine.

But perhaps the Dewan is the judge.

I sat on my verandah this afternoon and watched the
squirrels play. They are small and of a light tan colour, with
four dark-brown stripes running down their backs from
head to tail. Every tree seems full of them, and what a com-
motion they make, bickering and flying about the branches
and up and down the trunks!

Whimsical, electric creatures! Two of them had a fight—
malicious, I think—one leaping upon the other from behind
whilst he was enjoying a peaceful tea of bullock-dung.
What a scuffle ensued! They whirled round and round like
a Catherine-wheel, so that one could not tell where one
squirrel began and the other left off. Then having produced,
I dare say, acute indigestion in his indignant victim, the
attacker beat a hasty retreat, fleeing in long, curving leaps
to an adjacent tree-trunk. Pretty, restless, mischievous little
people; gluttonous and incontinent; neglectful parents, I feel
sure, and saucy, perverse children.

Abdul called on me again this afternoon in great distress.
The blow had fallen; his officer had ordered him to make
ready to proceed to Sarwar to-morrow for a month.

What was he to do? I told him to go away and not to
worry, for I would see to it that he was not sent to Sarwar.
But I myself was worried—and rather angry. Later on
Babaji Rao arrived, and I unloaded my annoyance on to
him.

I said that if this ill-treatment to which Abdul was being
subjected was still part of 'the little scene' that had been got
up between him and his officer, it had gone far enough.

PART TWO

Although I did not expect the officer to consult me before giving orders to his subordinate, I felt I was entitled, at the very least, to notification before being deprived of my tutor, and since Abdul's visit to me was not official this had not been done. Also the promise of increment, from which I had not withdrawn my support, had not been made good. I said I was sorry I had ever interfered on Abdul's behalf, but that having done so I must now go on, and suggested that I had better call on the Dewan myself.

'Perhaps that would be best,' said Babaji Rao, gazing at the carpet, and promised, meanwhile, to write a letter to the officer requesting that, if convenient, Abdul should not be sent away. After this we spoke for a few moments of His Highness's pilgrimage, which was regrettable, I said, coming at this particular time. Might not His Highness be persuaded to postpone it again, I suggested tentatively, so that we could all go and enjoy ourselves at Garha?

But now it was Babaji Rao's turn to be angry.

He retorted, with some heat, against my selfishness, and said that His Highness's religious duties were not to be compared in importance with such things as Garha festivals—indeed with anything else in his life; that they should have been performed years ago, but that His Highness was not a strong man, and owing to his ill-health they had had unfortunately (he coughed) to be postponed more than once; but that now His Highness was determined to delay no longer, and would not, of course, consider putting off a matter of such vital importance for such comparatively trivial reasons.

When he had finished I took his photograph with a camera I had borrowed from a Rajgarh lady.

His Highness has a sore throat, and I found him this evening looking a little dejected with a piece of white muslin wrapped round it. I saw in this a good omen, better than any mongoose, and told him of my remarks to Babaji Rao and of the latter's heated reply.

'He bullies *me*, too,' said the little man, chuckling; 'I am quite afraid of him.'

But, he added, suddenly assuming a grave expression, although his inclinations were to go with me to Garha, his conscience pointed him the other way. It was his duty to go, and besides, all the arrangements for accommodation and transport had been made, for there had to be special trains to carry him and his suite.

I asked how many people accompanied him. Seventy-five, he said; which included guards, pundits, cooks, water-carriers, washermen, servants and barbers, etc., and they were all quite indispensable.

March 12*th*

PROMPTLY at his appointed time to-day Abdul arrived to give me a lesson. The order to remove to Sarwar had been cancelled, so he was in excellent spirits, and wished to show me his gratitude by feasting me. Would I grant his feast? I said I wouldn't. Never mind then, he would come and take me for walks in the evenings when I had leisure from my writings, and we would go wherever I wished and talk nothing but Urdu so that I should come to speak the language *very* well.

'No, Abdul,' I said, 'one hour a day is quite enough.'

'Very well,' he replied; 'I do not want to bore upon your time. So I will come to you whenever I wish in the evenings and we will not talk a word of Urdu.'

'What I *meant*,' I said, 'was that one hour a day of *you* was quite enough.'

This seemed to amuse him, and he tittered into the pages of his book.

I sallied forth to call on the Dewan in the later afternoon. He lives in a big bungalow surrounded by the pleasant garden which was one of the first things I was shown when I arrived in Chhokrapur. It is situated just beyond the tennis-courts on the outskirts of the 'city.' The Dewan frequently plays tennis himself, sometimes in brown leather slippers and *dhoti*, with his shirt hanging outside; sometimes in European flannels, when he tucks his shirt in. He is excessively fat, and hopes to decrease it in this way; but at the same time he is nervous about his heart and fears to overtax it, so that if he cannot get the doctor (who lives close by) to join in, he likes to have him among the spectators. They all play a very flabby game.

There were some servants sitting on the verandah of the house when I arrived, and I sent one of them in to ask the Dewan if he would speak to me.

Some little time afterwards he came waddling out, excusing the delay on account of massage treatment he had been receiving.

'So kind of you to call,' he said, in a voice that bubbled with politeness. 'Very kind. Delighted. Please to seat yourself.'

I did so, and he sat beside me on a large heavy chair, rubbing his knees with his small brown hands, and uttering breathless, merry, exclamatory sounds. A servant came forward to put on his sandals.

We talked for some time of trivialities, and then I brought out the real object of my visit—the treatment of Abdul. No doubt he was expecting it, for as soon as I said that I should like to know more or less what the position was, he laid it unhesitatingly before me in a high-pitched, excitable voice. Of course, he said, he would be very pleased to do what I wished and instruct Abdul's officer to give him an increment of eight rupees monthly; but the result would be very bad for Abdul, for as soon as I left he would lose his job, his officer would dismiss him, and no other officer would take him on. He (the Dewan) had told all this to His Highness, he said, and His Highness had replied, 'But you must do this for Abdul. What will Mr. Ackerley say to me if you do not?' Well, he was perfectly ready to do it; it made no difference to him; he had merely to sign a paper, any one could do that; I had only to say the word, and Abdul would at once receive twenty rupees a month salary, but it would be the ultimate ruin of him. What was my wish? Please to instruct him.

But, I said with dismay, this would be a grave injustice to Abdul, and surely he, as Dewan, would prevent it.

But he was perfectly clear about what he would do; perfectly clear and outspoken. How he talked! It is quite impossible to reproduce it, his vigorous volubility, rising to shrillness as he emphasised his definite, unswerving policy, and accompanied by abrupt gestures of his small hands.

He would *not* prevent it. Perhaps he could, but he would not. He never interfered with his officers. They were good men; he had chosen them all carefully, without favouritism, with only one end in view—the efficient working of the State; and so long as that went forward smoothly and well, he was satisfied and asked no questions.

Efficiency—that was all that concerned him: the efficiency of each department combining for the efficiency of the whole. His officers were answerable to him personally for that; they had full powers to organise and work their separate departments as they thought fit; so long as they produced efficiency it was his policy never to interfere. Sometimes he himself would recommend men to them; but if they said they did not want them, he would at once reply, 'Very well, then; do not have them.'

But, I said, the recommendation this time came from the King himself, and so, apart from questions of obedience, it must also be part of a Dewan's policy, in governing a State which was a monarchy, to see to it that the King's wishes were upheld and his promises fulfilled. But he denied this with amusement. His Highness, he said, had given him the power to run the State as he wished, so long as he reported on everything he did, and these orders he faithfully and loyally carried out. For nine years now he had been Dewan, and not even His Highness knew more about the administration of the State and its difficulties than he did; no man now could show him his business, and so he took orders from no man. If His Highness was displeased with him he could always get a new Dewan; but this would not occur. Once he had resigned his office, but he had been recalled almost immediately; he was indispensable to His Highness. But where would the State be now if he had listened to His Highness's recommendations? Dozens of times a day men came to him with promises from His Highness; but all he said to them was, 'My good boy—go avay.'

'Then,' I said, 'the upshot of all this is, that His Highness's promises and my patronage are not only to prove of no benefit to Abdul, but will, if persisted in, cause his ruin?'

With this the Dewan imperturbably agreed.

But things could hardly be worse for Abdul than they were at present, I said; for even without his increment he seemed already to have forfeited the goodwill of his officer and was being persecuted by him. But the Dewan denied this; naturally his officer was displeased with Abdul for going behind his back, but this would soon be forgotten—unless the increment were granted.

I listened to him with amazement, astonished by the audacity, the cleverness of all this, with its flavour of insolence. Accustomed as I was to my unique, dignified position as 'The Sahib,' it was quite the last reception I had expected, and I began to understand something of Abdul's fear, Babaji Rao's admiration, and the Political Agent's dislike for this man, and why I had been practically ignored by him. Like all Europeans, I had been expected to interfere; I *had* interfered, and there was a feeling of personal animosity behind the Dewan's words for which I was sorry, since I did not wish to make enemies.

He went on to say that though he himself had sometimes been tempted to make favourites of people, it was a thing he had never practised; but I asked him to believe that neither had I been actuated by quite that feeling, and that I did not care for Abdul more than for any one else I had met in the State. I had only put myself in his position. He had quite reasonably looked upon me as a unique opportunity of securing benefits for himself, and I had allowed myself to be used by him. I was very sorry, I said, that I had done so; but it was the kind of error of judgement that most of us committed at some time or other in our lives, causing annoyance and unhappiness to other people and often to ourselves. Once one was involved it was difficult to withdraw. Just as Abdul had tried to make the most of me, I might exploit His Highness, I said, on the strength of the relationship between us, and perhaps would be considered a fool for not doing so. But I had not undertaken Abdul's cause quite stupidly; if I had thought him a fool I should never have interfered; but he seemed to me to be an industrious and able man, poorly paid, and worthy of a rise. Apart, therefore, from promises and petitions, could not his officer quite honestly, without feeling himself under pressure or in any awkward position, raise Abdul's salary, on account of industry and merit, if not to twenty rupees, at any rate by so much as he thought fit?

But the Dewan would not budge. Abdul was not worth a rise in salary, he said; but he would nevertheless instruct the officer to raise it if that were my wish.

I got up to go. I had been with him for an hour and a half, and it seemed clear that I might stay with him for the rest of my life without getting any further. I said I was sorry, but the matter had better be left where it was, and could I come one day to take his photo with my borrowed camera?

The effect of this request was quite remarkable. From being intractable, politely dictatorial, and rather unfriendly, he became suddenly bashful and shy, and began simpering and smoothing his belly.

'Very pleased. Thank you, thank you; yes, any time; thank you.'

And a little later on Babaji Rao came up to see me in my house, and brought word from the Dewan that he had thought the matter over and was prepared to raise Abdul's salary (on account of merit) by three rupees with his blessing, but that any greater increment would be given without his blessing.

178

PART TWO

His Highness has been informed that there is plague in Gaya; which is a *great misfortune*, for it may mean another postponement of his pilgrimage. He has sent a messenger to find out the extent and gravity of the outbreak. Meanwhile his sore throat is better. But Babaji Rao, when he brought me this news with the Dewan's message, rubbed his forehead a little impatiently; there is always a slight outbreak of plague in Gaya at this time of year, he said, but His Highness's itinerary will not take him near the infected area.

March 14th

NARAYAN spent most of yesterday evening with me, and gave me betel to chew. He carries it with him, wrapped up in a piece of muslin, in a metal snuff-box. I chewed betel a good deal while I was away, accepting it from the various merchants in Benares, Agra, and Delhi from whom I bought things, and soon came to like it.

I asked Narayan which God in the Hindoo pantheon he worshipped, and he named Krishna, the dark hero-god.

He is the most popular of the Hindoo gods, he said, though all the others also have their adherents. I asked him how and when he worshipped, and he said that at twelve o'clock, before taking his food, he poured oblations of rice, sandal, and *dhal* (pulse) before an image of Krishna which he had in his house.

'What are the prayers that you pray?' I asked.

'Poetry,' he said.

'And do you make special requests of him?'

'Yes, for a better brain and a healthy body.'

Later on Sharma came up the hill to seek him, and we induced the boy to come and sit with us in my house. He seemed very nervous and kept his eyes fixed upon his friend.

I said it was a pity that they did not eat European food, for we might all have had dinner together, but Narayan said that as a matter of fact Sharma ate and drank in secret all manner of forbidden things, such as meat and eggs, cake, crystallised fruit, and invalid port. He would never admit to this, of course, but it was true nevertheless.

'He is a fool-boy!' he observed, expressing his disgust at the thought. But then all low-caste Hindoos were the same, he said; they ate meat or anything else they could get hold of—all of them, and he dismissed equally, with a contemptuous sweep of the hand, his friend beside him, the beautiful Sharma, favourite of the King, and the rude peasant workmen who were building the garage outside.

Sharma had no idea, of course, what was being said about him. They both came and sat with me while I ate my dinner, and though I tempted Sharma with chocolate and crystallised fruits, much to the amusement of Narayan and Hashim, he refused to accept them. After dinner the carriage came to take me to the Palace, and both the boys drove down with me into the city.

'What is sin?' His Highness greeted me with as I entered the enclosure and bowed to him. I wasn't very good at this, not understanding what lay behind the question, and produced some excessively dull observations on transgression of the principles of Christian morality which must have bored him considerably.

'Why, anyway?' I asked, suddenly realising that life was beginning to sag and that it was my fault.

'It is this tour of mine,' he said. 'I have had such a day! They say that if I do not go it will be a sin.'

'Who say?' I asked.

'My priests—and Babaji Rao.'

'But I thought there was plague in Gaya?'

'I think so, too,' he said, popping a betel-leaf into his mouth; 'but my messenger cannot get definite information.'

'Well,' I said, 'since you have good health and good weather and a gay fair at Garha and a desire to enjoy it and good friends to enjoy it with, I think it will be a sin if you *do* go on your pilgrimage to Gaya.'

This was much more the kind of thing he was wanting, and, with his arms clasped round his knees, he began to rock on his rump. Such a queer, unearthly little figure he looked, bareheaded and wrapped in a dark-red toga, rocking on his rump in the moonlight.

'All day long,' he said, 'it has been a struggle between my conscience and my inclination. But I must go.'

There had been a kind of conference held during the day, he told me, to decide finally whether the pilgrimage was to be undertaken or not, for if it were undertaken, the rituals, the shaving and purifications, would have to be begun by midday to-morrow, and from that moment there would be no getting out of it. The conference had decided nothing; but it had been very exhausting. The priests had quite rent him, he said, when he had shown a mild disposition to waver. They had been unanimous in their displeasure, and as for Babaji Rao—Babaji had been *formidable*. Chiefly moved, I expect, by acute nervousness at the idea of having to cancel at the last moment, for the second time in one month, all his arrangements for special rail-transport and accommodation, he had quite domineered over the little man, lecturing him on duty, expatiating on sin and eternal punishment (which had not impressed him much), and rebuking him for an infirmity of purpose which would bring down ridicule and contempt upon them both.

This last warning had certainly had its effect; but on top of it had come the Dewan, practical, sceptical, and scornful, who had told the King to do just as he wished, and not to take the least notice of any of them.

'They are all mad!' he had cried, waving a contemptuous hand at the opposition; 'and as for Babaji Rao—he is the maddest of them all!'

His Highness wheezed with husky laughter as he repeated it to me; and so, he said, suddenly grave again, the conflict had continued all day—and I could very well picture his small thin figure sitting, crumpled but alert, in the midst of them, chewing betel and expressing, every now and then, a feeble determination to do his duty whilst egging on the Dewan with the same breath.

'But of course I *must* go,' he remarked, as though the whole city were bent on hindering him, and expectorated a bright-red stream into the spittoon beneath him.

I didn't understand the reason for the resignation in his words, for there was none in his voice, and made my second mistake that evening. I urged him again to postpone.

'The Dewan,' I said, 'is certainly the only sensible man among them, and as for ridicule—no one will dare to laugh at you. What is the good of being a king if you can't indulge every whim that comes into your head?'

But he shook his finger at me sadly.

'You should not be saying these things,' he said; 'for to-day is a Friday, and advice given on a Friday should never be taken, for it is sure to have bad results. So you must say "Go, Maharajah! Go! You *must* go!"—and then, perhaps, to-morrow——?' he turned his hands.

However, I was not quite happy about it when I left him. Babaji Rao might still manage to commit him to the rituals from which there was no retreat, so when I returned from my ride this morning before breakfast I sent this letter to the Palace:

'I saw a mongoose this morning, King. It was slinking in the direction of Garha, was obviously in a great hurry, and appeared to be smiling to itself. What does this mean?'

The reply was disappointing:

'I can't explain, except that the whole day has passed to-day in anxiety and worries. I do not know if I go now or not . . .'

However, later on Babaji Rao came up to see me, looking as if *his* day also had passed in anxiety and worries.

'You have got your wish,' he said in a distant voice; 'His Highness's tour has been postponed.'

'That's a good thing!' I replied.

'I thought you would think so,' he remarked rather coldly; 'we have not the same point of view.'

And, later still, came another note from the Palace:

'DEAR FRIEND,—It has been decided. I do not go upon my tour. I am very tired.'

March 17*th*

NARAYAN and Sharma sat with me this evening before dinner. I asked Narayan what he thought of the Mohammedans here who look after the Guest House, and he said that Hashim was the only good man among them. The cook was a thief, and as for Munshi, he was old and very crafty. But Hashim was a good man.

'Why is Hashim a good man?' I asked.

'If he hear secret talk he say nothing. Other people hear and tell all, all. I do not like that. That is bad.'

I smiled, but he remained quite grave.

'Not good,' he repeated; 'I do not like.'

They had some business, the two of them, in the city, so could not sit with me while I had dinner; but they said they would return later on and drive down to the Palace with me. When I had finished I found them waiting for me on the verandah of my house, and with them a young man named Prasad.

I met him first some months ago, when His Highness sent him up to me as a companion on approval. But I did not like him at all. He was vain, and his manners were as bad as the English he was alleged to speak; he didn't remove his shoes on entering my house, nor wait to be offered a chair or a cigarette; and since he was ugly as well, I told His Highness that I never wanted to see Prasad again.

I was surprised, therefore, to find him on my verandah with Narayan and Sharma. He had driven up in the carriage, he said, and wished to drive back in it again. He thereupon seated himself in front, next to the coachman. But it seeemed to me that there was an air of uneasiness about the three of them, and though on the way down Prasad became playful, and suddenly twitching Narayan's

183

hat from his head, tried it on himself and then pretended to throw it into a tank, this jocularity was not well received; Narayan was annoyed, and Sharma alarmed and vigilant. When Prasad left us in the precincts of the Palace, I asked Narayan what he thought of him.

'He a very bad man!' he pronounced with great severity. 'He steal your cigarettes to-night. Nine cigarettes. I tell him he very bad man—if he ask, you give. I tell him put them back, but he say No, I will not; so I tell him I tell you, so you not think *we* take them.'

The Hindoo never builds an arch; he prefers the rectangular form, the straight stone beam resting on uprights; for then there is pressure in only one direction, downwards.

The Mohammedan builds arches, but the Hindoo despises them. There is pressure in two directions, downwards and outwards, and the Hindoo considers this self-destructive.

'The arch never sleeps,' he says.

I was thinking of this, this evening, as I sat with His Highness and looked at the entrance to his unfinished 'Cathedral.' Then I turned my attention to the massive back porch of his Palace.

'What sort of thing would you call that?' he asked me, seeing the direction of my gaze.

'Architecturally, do you mean?'

'Yes,' he said, and there was an expectant pause while I surveyed the ugly stuccoed projection, clearly a recent addition, supported by two fat pinkwashed Georgic columns.

'Well,' I said, 'I should say it was—Heaven knows what!'

He gave a crow of joy.

'Yes, yes,' he said, 'you are *quite* right; it is a "Heaven knows what." '

He explained that he had had it built over the Palace steps at the request of two old men who used to sleep there. There had been no shelter there before, and the rain used to pour down on them as they lay, so they had come to him one day and said: 'Can we have a roof to sleep under?'

That was why he had had the 'Heaven knows what' built, and as it was nearing completion—he struck his hands together—both the old men had died.

'One was eighty,' he concluded, 'and the other was eighty-five.'

This story amused him so much that he almost choked.

'Who were they?' I asked.

He became serious again, and replied with an air of importance:

'One was my court painter, and the other was the Poet Lockrit.'

' "Laureate"?' I suggested. We got that straight. 'And why, in any case, did they choose to sleep on the Palace steps where the rain was likely to pour down on them?'

'They did not choose,' he replied; 'I told them to. Did you not know I like old men, and always keep some near me to crack jokes with them when I wake up at night? And this is where they sleep. Old men and boys—I like them very much.'

March 20th

WE drove to Garha last night. I sat in the back of the car between Narayan and Sharma: Hashim and Habib sat in front with the chauffeur. On the plains it was chilly, but when the road dipped between hills the air was warm. A strange, wild country, I thought . . . and strange, wild companions. I put my arm round Sharma's shoulders, and he at once became alarmed and nervous; but when he saw that my other arm was round Narayan's shoulders he did not mind, and allowed me, later on, to clasp his hand. We arrived late, driving round the great tank with the Queen's palace on its rim, and through the market-place which stretched away on our left to the seven famous temples. It was already filled with booths and stalls, but they were dark and silent now, their owners asleep round their charcoal fires.

About a mile further on a newly made path to the right took us off the main road to where our encampment lay among the trees.

This morning Sharma wasn't well; he had a slight chill, and an abrasion on his heel where his new shoes had rubbed it.

'His body very great trouble; very . . . lazy,' Narayan tried to explain, and I gathered that his friend was feeling a little stiff. He told me this during breakfast, having hesitated shyly in the entrance to the marquee, awaiting my invitation to join me, as though none of the invitations and permissions that had gone before could have any bearing on this or any future occasion. This hesitancy is due, no doubt, partly to the sensitiveness of a gentle, timid nature, and partly to the rigid observances of his own kitchen-rituals. I have asked him, on two or three occasions, to sit with me whilst I had my dinner, but that established no precedent in his mind, and certainly gave him little guidance to my views about breakfast. Also there are his own sensibilities to consider; it can hardly fail to disgust him to see me eating the things which he has been brought up to regard as inedible, and as I poked poached egg into my mouth, I wondered what he was thinking and what his father would say if he knew his son had been present at such an exhibition o depravity. Later the sick Sharma arrived bare-headed upon the scene, and Habib, when I had finished eating, handed round some cigarettes; but Narayan did not like this—the Sahib's servant handing cigarettes to a low-caste creature like Sharma; he was vexed into a sharp 'No!' and taking a cigarette from the tin gave it himself to his friend.

Sharma complained a little about his sore heel, and I told him, through Narayan, that if he came with me to my tent I would give him some iodine to put on it. When he had looked to Narayan for advice on this point, he agreed, and crossed the gravelled place with me, shambling beside me like an animal with his toes turned in. He doesn't move like Narayan with grace and dignity, but shambles along head

186

first, drawing his long loose legs after him. When we reached the tent, I took up my attaché-case to get the iodine, but it was unfastened, the lid dropped open, and all the contents were scattered on the floor. I gazed for a moment with mock consternation at the scene, and then at Sharma.

He was watching me with awe—a kind of fearful sympathy. How would the Sahib act in the face of such a disaster? his expression seemed to say. Treacherous attaché-case! The Sahib would surely be very angry! His dismay was so evident that I laughed aloud, and at once he laughed too, childishly relieved, and went down on his knees to collect the scattered things. Among them he found various objects to interest him—a postcard of a stone image of Buddha, and a small red packet of razor blades. The latter he found very mysterious and attractive. What was it? I told him; we both laughed again, and I pulled the wispy topknot that hung like a short piece of string from the crown of his bullet head. Later on, I heard, he recounted to the kitchen how the Sahib had dropped everything out of his bag on to the floor and had only roared with laughter.

I walked through the fair with Narayan later in the morning and examined the wares. There was nothing there of much interest, except some rough local brass-work, and a few pieces, more elaborate and finished, from Ahmedabad and Benares. Otherwise there was the usual assortment of stuff: Indian sweetmeats and foods, haberdashery, cloth, and cheap trinkets, mostly of Japanese or European manufacture. There were also some primitive merry-go-rounds and a performing bear.

One of the general stores had a few gramophones for sale, and the storekeeper played an Indian record for us, which we did not much like.

Although the fair was not quite at its height, there was a great surge of people up and down the narrow passages between the stalls, and among them one or two Europeans, whom I did not know, probably up for the day from

Rajgarh. It was very hot, and after a little we got tired of
the market itself and wandered around the outskirts. We
peered into the courtyard of His Highness's grandfather's
tomb, against the entrance to which grows the pretty plant
which I have already mentioned. It is the oleander (*kanel*),
a poisonous evergreen shrub with bright red or white flowers
and leathery spear-like leaves. I remembered what was
alleged to have happened to His Highness's grandfather, and
wondered whether this plant, which was the only vegetation
growing there, had been deliberately selected to keep this
particular memory green. The tomb, Babaji Rao tells me,
contains nothing but an oil-painting of the deceased, his bed,
pillow, and sandals, and a few of his ashes.

Then we walked round the Palace and saw a man playing
with a little boy, who, Narayan said, was the Raja Bahadur,
His Highness's son. He was a pretty little chap, dressed in a
silk coat and trousers and a round black hat embroidered
in blue; but he was very shy and would not speak to me
or shake hands. In fact, he seemed very frightened of my
strange appearance, my queer white skin and my queer white
hat, and hid his face against the man's chest as though he
were going to cry. Sharma was given a detailed account of
our adventures when we returned, and grieved very much
that he had not been with us when we had heard the
gramophone play.

His Highness paid a call this afternoon, and hobbled
about with Babaji Rao and me among the tents. He was
very smartly dressed in a new skirted coat of white silk,
beautifully embroidered with blue and silver thread.

The encampment was completed and ready for the
reception of Captain Daly and Miss Trend, who are due to
arrive to-morrow; it included five or six doubled-sided bell
tents and a dining-marquee. His Highness surveyed the scene
in silence, and then asked first me and then Babaji Rao what
we thought of it. I said I was very comfortable and thought
it very nice indeed, and Babaji Rao echoed my satisfaction.

PART TWO

'Well, I am *not* satisfied; I am *far* from satisfied,' announced
His Highness promptly, and began to scold Babaji Rao
with heartless glee. As for me, he said, I was not expected to
know any better, for I had no 'political knowledge'; but
Babaji Rao—was this really all he had learnt in all these
years? Could he possibly stand there and look at these
things and say that he was satisfied? Then he was a fool!
What did he think he was doing? Had he no eyes? For some
people this accommodation might do, but not for such important, influential people as Captain Daly and Miss Trend.

'What will my guests say,' he cried, 'when they see such
. . . such . . . Swiss cottages? Miss Trend will go away at
once. She will say to me, "Maharajah, is it for *this* you have
called me here?" She will be very angry. She will eat me up!
She will eat us all up!'

He prodded the unhappy Babaji Rao with his stick, and
said that bigger tents must be put up at once.

I did not like having the poor man ragged in front of me,
so I said that if the new guests were so particular His Highness had better build a palace for them, for nothing short of
that would do; and this broke his tirade.

Then he summoned Hashim, and told him that if he did
not attend well to the needs of the new guests, if there was
one complaint, he would cut off his nose.

Then he summoned the cook, and threatening him with
his stick, said that if he did not cook better than he had ever
cooked before he would cut off his head and place it on a
table in his Palace bedroom. In fact, he was in a very good
humour indeed, and when he had spread consternation
throughout the whole camp, he stumped off with one hand
in the small of his back, to call on a Miss Potter, a missionary,
who it appeared had just arrived from nowhere in particular
and pitched her tent close behind our encampment. A
weedy-looking Indian boy, a proselyte no doubt, seated on
a folded harmonium outside the tent, observed our approach
and called his mistress, who at once appeared. She was a tall,
placid-faced woman. She told the proselyte to bring out

some chairs for us, and then came forward to greet us. But His Highness was in no mood for preliminaries. He opened fire at once.

'Miss Potter—where is God?'

'He is everywhere,' replied Miss Potter with dignity.

'But, my dear Maiden,' exclaimed His Highness, planting himself firmly on one of the chairs, 'what good is that to *me*?'

March 22nd

'ONLY fools care about caste!' observed the Dewan yesterday afternoon: a remark which caused his disciple Babaji Rao to look down his nose. They had both come up to the encampment to call on Captain Daly and Miss Trend, to whom the Dewan appears to have a particular attachment, and we were all sitting in a circle in front of the marquee.

Conversation had turned on marriage in India, and Miss Trend had said that, considering the huge dowries that high-caste Hindoos had to give to marry their daughters, it was hardly to be wondered at that so many female infants did not long survive birth. But the Dewan argued that this particular practice of infanticide had been due not so much to financial difficulties as to caste pride. High-caste Hindoo families had had the greatest difficulty in marrying their female offspring to persons considered suitable; and by suitability was meant their suitability as sons-in-law or, to a less extent, as brothers-in-law; their suitability as husbands was unimportant. How was it possible to find any man quite good enough to be given the freedom of the terms *susra* and *sala* (father-in-law and brother-in-law)? Indeed, so vexed had been this question, that the words had now become expressions of contempt and abuse. But Hindoos, intelligent Hindoos, cared less about caste now.

'Only fools care about caste!' he said.

But with the fools the difficulties remained, and, he admitted, he experienced them himself.

'I have the misfortune to be of the very highest family of

Brahmans,' he said, 'and because I send my nephews to England for their education, my people say to me, "You are not a good Brahman. You send your nephews to England, and then you eat with them. We do not care for you." "Very well, my good fellows," I say, "then go avay. If you do not care for me I do not care for you. Go avay!" '

But now, he said, the time has come for him to marry his nieces, and he is having the greatest difficulties. His own words are being turned against him. 'You did not care for us before,' his old acquaintances say; 'why do you care now?'

It is a great problem, and though, he confessed, he does not much like the idea, he fears he will have to marry them outside his own caste.

'Only fools care about caste!' murmured slow-witted Babaji Rao with a snigger: but the Dewan was already proceeding. Over his nephews, he was saying, he anticipated no difficulties; one of them, in fact, was already married to a Nepalese girl.

'The Nepal girls,' he observed, 'are very good; they are white and do not live long. Very rarely after fifty.'

Later on in the conversation, apropos of something or other, the Dewan said that he held very strong convictions, but that they were always founded on fact. He liked facts. So, if he had been told twenty years ago that men would fly, he would have said, 'Go avay, my good fellow. You are a fool.'

But now that it is a fact, he would say, 'Very well; that is all right. You have convinced me.'

Now he is troubled about the soul. He used to suppose that there was one soul in each living creature; it wasn't a conviction, but he tended to that belief. But now Babaji Rao has told him about the earthworm—that when it is cut in half, both halves live. Is the soul then divisible? Or are there two souls? Or more than two? No one has been able to convince him on this subject, and so he refuses to hold an opinion, for he does not like to have to change his mind.

When he has an opinion he sticks to it, and so he never holds an opinion which it may be necessary to abandon. Once in his life, when he was a young man interested in politics and had a seat on the council at Delhi, he was forced to alter his mind three times in twenty minutes, and he thought to himself, 'Who then are you? You are a very small thing in this world.' But since that shock to his amour-propre he had never once had to alter his mind over any conviction.

He has no hatred, he says. Hatred is weakness. Miss Trend said she considered it right to hate bad people; but the Dewan said that if he were told that X was a bad man, he would say:

'Very well, let him be bad. That is his affair. It is nothing to me. What do I care if he is bad? Why should I hate him? Why should I trouble myself? If I hate him, I hate myself, for I destroy myself. Hatred is heat. It consumes and wastes. Why should I consume and waste my body and burn my blood because X is bad?'

'But,' said Miss Trend, 'whether you hate him or not, it is your duty as a citizen to do something about him. You will have to tell him that he is bad and try to correct him.'

'Why?' inquired the Dewan sharply. 'If I tell him that he is bad, then perhaps I shall make an enemy of him, and he will hate me and injure me. That is senseless. If I am walking in the jungle, and I see a big lion coming for me, why should I hate him, poor brute? It is his habit to prey upon people and eat them. He must have blood, and here' (he indicated his enormous bulk) 'is a store of blood. If he does not eat me perhaps he will not live. It is necessary that he shall eat me. Also if I do not want to be eaten it is necessary that I should shoot the lion. But I shall not hate him. And if I have no gun I shall be eaten—without malice. But I do not want to be eaten by him, so I shall do what I can to help myself. I shall not say "You are a bad man to want to tear and injure me"; but I shall say, "My good fellow, why do you come to me? I am not the only person in this world."

And if I have any one with me I shall point to him and say.
"Go to that man over there; do not come to me." '

'Suppose the other person is your wife?' asked Captain
Daly. 'Will you offer her first?'

'Certainly,' cried the Dewan, on a shrill note. 'I would
hold her in front of me.'

'You clearly aren't a philanthropist,' said Miss Trend,
laughing.

'Certainly I am a philanthropist,' retorted the Dewan
without the least hesitation, 'for I have helped one person
in this world—even though he does happen to be myself.'

Narayan comes to me to-day looking very sad and untidy,
his hair dishevelled and his shirt dirty.

'How are you?' I asked.

'Very bad,' he said, keeping his gaze fixed on the ground.

'What is the matter?'

'Maharajah Sahib very angry with me. Send me here.
Say me I no sleep in New *Bakhri* any more with Sharma.'

I asked what had happened, but he only subsided into a
chair, and looked down at the tablecloth. Then he asked
me please not to repeat anything to His Highness, and
started off.

'Sharma have no bed in *Bakhri* for him and me to sleep,
so he say *Tahsildar* (the departmental officer) to give him bed,
and *Tahsildar* say *Jama'dar* (the captain of the guard). But
Jama'dar no give; so Sharma say Maharajah Sahib *Jama'dar*
no give bed; so Maharajah Sahib very angry and say punish
him, so he punished.'

I asked how the *Jama'dar* had been punished, and was
told that he had received two slaps, one on each cheek,
administered by a superior official. Slapping is a recognised
form of punishment here; it is carried out in public by
authorities or their delegates, and is intended rather to
shame than to hurt. But as a result of his slapping the
Jama'dar had gone crying to the Dewan whose servant he
was. Thereupon the Dewan wrote to the Maharajah saying

193

that Sharma was a bad man and had punished his *Jama'dar*, that Sharma was a proud and arrogant man, and that it was time he was suppressed.

This letter the Maharajah read out to Sharma, who said 'You told me to have *Jama'dar* punished, and this I have done.' So the Maharajah sent for the Dewan, who came and abused Sharma in front of him, saying that he was a wicked man, that he was always spreading false tales, and that he (the Dewan) would 'give him the shoe.' And Sharma wept after the Dewan had gone, and would not eat; he had done as he was told, he said, so where was his offence? The Maharajah said to him 'You must eat'; but he would not. 'So Maharajah call Dewan again and say "Love Sharma!" So Dewan say him, "You are a boy, and I am your Dewan. I am your father and your mother. If I say hard to you, excuse me." '

So Sharma was pacified and ate his food. But later on he went out, and foolishly, in front of other men, told Narayan that the Dewan had apologised and said 'Excuse me.' Narayan had beaten Sharma for this indiscretion. He had slapped him many times, in many places, so that Sharma had wept again. I expressed regret at this hard treatment, but Narayan said, 'He is a fool-boy.' It was his duty to slap him, he said, just as it would be my duty to slap *him* (Narayan) if he were in fault. But anyway the mischief had been done.

In the evening one of the men who had overheard Sharma's speech went in to the Maharajah and informed him that Narayan was 'telling a report' that the Dewan had apologised to Sharma, the barber's son; that the Dewan had fallen down at Sharma's feet and begged to be forgiven. This man was His Highness's 'Kindness man' and an enemy of Narayan's, and he was supported in this story by two confederates, and had other tales to whisper as well, such as that Narayan was a thief and furnished his house with things stolen from the Guest House, and that his influence over Sharma was perverted and bad.

So in the night His Highness sent a servant to the New

Bakhri to spy upon Narayan and Sharma as they lay in bed together, to learn how they acted together and of what they talked. Two or three times during the night he came and stood in the shadows and watched; but Narayan was asleep, and only Sharma saw him. And in the morning His Highness, having received a disappointing report from his servant, sent for Narayan and accused him of the other story, which Narayan denied.

'I did not say such things,' he answered, and told the story as it had really happened. But His Highness refused to believe him, and said that he was a liar and should have his tongue cut out; that his father and his brother were good men, but that he was a bad man, that he must leave the New *Bakhri* at once, and that he would be punished when they returned to Chhokrapur.

Narayan urged his innocence again, and said:

'I have not said this thing, but *if* I have said this thing, you are my Lord and I am a poor boy—please excuse me.'

But His Highness sent him away.

And Sharma had gone to the Palace to plead for him; but His Highness had said:

'For every good thing you say of him I will do him ill. Tell him to go away from me, and give him two slaps.'

But Sharma had said:

'He is my friend.'

So Narayan had left the New *Bakhri*, and on his way here had met his enemy and accused him; but his enemy had replied:

'I did not say.'

So Narayan had left him and gone among the tents and wept.

'Why are you weeping?' Hashim had asked.

'Because I have a little fever,' he replied.

And then he had come to me.

'I am so ashamed,' he said; 'I want to die.'

While we were talking, a servant came bringing Narayan some food from Sharma, but Narayan sent it away.

'Why don't you eat?' I asked.

'My stomach is full of uneasy,' he replied.

Sharma had promised to come and visit him, if he could do so without being seen, and presently he arrived, slouching into the tent with an air of guilt and apprehension. He shook hands limply with me, and then, sinking heavily on to a chair behind Narayan, stared childishly about him. For some time no word or sign passed between them; then Narayan addressed some question to him in a low voice without turning his head, and after a short conversation Sharma slouched out again.

'What is my defect?' Narayan asked me.

'Perhaps you are too honest,' I said, smiling.

'It is a good policy?'

'The best, they say.'

'Then what is this matter?'

After a pause, he said:

'I have no flattery. I say the truth always, always. If you say me, "He is a good man?" I say you what I think. I say you, "*You* a good man." So I think. But if I think you a bad man then I say you it.'

Before he left he asked me again to say nothing of what had passed between us.

'To-day,' I said, 'you don't trust any one, do you?'

'Ah, excuse me!' he murmured.

March 24th

WHEN I returned from my daily ride this morning at about 7.30, Habib met me as usual in the encampment to take possession of my switch and gloves, in order to place them on the table in the tent which I was myself about to enter. As soon as they are restored to their accustomed place he departs. It is one of the many important services he unfailingly performs, and I did not take any particular notice of him.

'Sahib!' he said, without moving. Conversation was not part of his routine, and I looked down at him with surprise.

Tears were streaming down his cheeks.

'Whatever's the matter with you?' I asked.

He made no reply, and thinking that he had probably only been scrapping with the other Mohammedan boy, I went on into my tent.

Later on Hashim came in to say that breakfast was ready, and I asked what had happened to Habib.

'He is a very bad boy,' said Hashim severely. 'He has broken your camera.'

This was indeed bad news, for it isn't my camera; it was very kindly lent to me by a lady in Rajgarh. Perhaps a camera has never been seen in Chhokrapur before; at any rate, since it came into my possession I have become very popular and have had quite a number of new visitors. Babaji Rao's servant, the Dewan's coachman, His Highness's cook—all sorts of quaint young men have 'called'—that is to say, have hung bashfully about the vicinity of my tent, displaying red or white teeth, and on being asked their business, have expressed a polite desire to be photographed. But foreseeing damage to it at the hands of Habib, I had forbidden him to touch it.

I examined it, and his activities were at once apparent. I had made only one exposure on the film, and had turned it on to number '2'; but now it was turned on to 'Finish,' and the screw was bent and jammed. What had happened was obvious enough.

While I was out riding he must have picked it up and seen the number '2' through the little red window at the back. He had turned the screw, and '2' had vanished. A few more turns, and there was '3.'

This was great fun. After '3,' '4' '5' and '6' had been made to pass the little red window; but '7' had been a long time in coming and then had been found not to exist; instead there was this word 'Finish,' which, no doubt, he had not understood. Then, either because he wanted to see the little numbers pass again, or because he thought he had better leave the camera as he found it, he had tried to reverse the spool, and found, to his dismay, that the screw would not turn that way. He had forced it until it bent; but behind the little red window nothing had moved. Then in terror he had dropped the camera and run to tell the cook, who had boxed his ears.

In a very short time the story of Habib's wickedness was all over the encampment, and fearful and sympathetic advisers crowded about my tent.

'He must be punished,' chanted the cook.

'Shall I slap him?' asked Hashim.

'I told you he was half-made,' said Narayan.

But I said I would not have him slapped, only warned never, in any circumstances, to enter my tent again on penalty of such a slapping as his infant mind had never dreamed of. For the rest of the day he sulked, like Achilles, in his tent; but in the evening, as I went down to the Palace to visit His Highness, I saw him with a friend among the bushes. He was hurling stones at a troop of 'disgraced' monkeys.

His Highness complained of not feeling very well.

'Narayan doesn't seem to be very well either,' I said.

'Narayan! What is the matter with him?'

'He has been crying a lot and seems to be rather unhappy.'

'He is a very bad man,' said His Highness. 'I have sent him away from my Palace. Did he not tell you?'

'He said you were very angry with him, Prince.'

'What else did he say?' he asked quickly, fixing his protuberant eyes upon me.

'I didn't question him further.'

'He has been very bad,' pursued His Highness, with a nod. 'I had to punish him. He is a liar. He has told many lies, and made mischief with the barber's son.'

'I'm very surprised to hear that,' I said.

'So am I. He is the grandson of my old physician, whom I loved very much, and for his sake I wished to be kind to

Narayan, but I cannot overlook these bad reports I have of
him.'

'Personally I always find him a remarkably honest boy,'
I said. 'In fact I can't believe he has lied to you, Prince. I
should have thought you could have told how truthful he
was merely by looking at him. Don't you think he's got
rather a fine face?'

His Highness raised his brows politely.

'I have never looked closely at him,' he said.

The Dewan to-day, in conversation with us, warmly
denied having said that he would sacrifice his wife's life to
preserve his own. He must, of course, he said, do his best to
save her. He must die for her or for any other member of his
family: it was quite impossible that he should have thought
or spoken otherwise. Miss Trend said she did not wish to
disbelieve him; she was only too glad to hear that women
had eventually some value in the Hindoo's scheme of life,
and he agreed with her that the lack of interest with
which female babies were received into the world was very
sad.

But he denied that these first feelings of disappointment
and indifference continued.

'We worship our daughters,' he said. 'We touch their feet.
They do not touch ours. We cannot ask them to—it would
be a scandal, a disgraceful request. Nor can we ask them to
do any menial labour.'

Narayan said to me this evening:

'I like you very much; give me fifteen rupees a month, and
I will come and live with you for always. I will be your
servant instead of friend.'

I asked him what difference this would make in his conduct towards me, and he said he would not sit in my
presence, nor smile and laugh with me. He asked if he
might have a photo of me, and I gave him one. It was very
beautiful, he thought, and he would like to kiss it.

'Your face is good and some beautiful,' he said. 'You are thin, with no belly and the chest of a fight-man.'

When I went back to England, he said, he did not know what he would do; he would take my photo and speak to it; but it would not answer.

I had no cigarette to give him, so I offered him the one I was smoking myself; but he said he could not accept it, because it had been in my mouth.

March 25*th*

TO-DAY was *Holi* day, the chief day of the festival of *Holi*, which, as far as I could gather from Babaji Rao, is named after a girl, Holikar, who was a devotee of the devil Madhu. Being herself insensible to fire, she conspired with her father to carry her brother into the flames and burn him up because he worshipped Krishna.

This was not the first time that they had tried to destroy the young man, but Krishna had always contrived to out-wit Madhu whose instruments they were; and he was not at a loss on this occasion either, but managed to transfer the protective virtue from sister to brother, so that the wicked Holikar was consumed instead.

Holi, then, is in honour of Krishna. It is held under the full moon, and used to be an occasion for the wildest excesses. The merrymakers would work themselves up with music, dancing, and *bhung* (the intoxicating juice of hemp) into such a frenzy that they would tear off their clothes and dance naked about the streets, singing improper songs, exhibiting improper images, and ending up indiscriminately in each other's arms. But the British Raj did not encourage such high spirits, and much of the interest has now died out. It is still, however, a queer affair. Babaji Rao told me that the inspiring idea was 'Fellowship.' On *Holi* day, Hindoos go out to meet their friends and enemies and embrace them all, old disputes are patched up, and grievances forgiven. Moreover, social differences, as distinct from caste observances, disappear; all men are equal and may be treated so in the name of Friendship.

This gives opportunity, of course, for a good deal of licence which on any other day would be termed disrespectful and punished. A clerk may pinch or slap his employer in a jocular manner, and the latter may not take offence. He may, however, retaliate; and though the attacker is entitled to only one pinch or slap, the attacked may have as many as he chooses; but good-humour must prevail, and pincher and pinched must part in peace. The only way to avoid this Brotherly Love is not to venture out, and Captain Daly, Miss Trend, and His Highness who was sitting in the marquee examining beautiful Kashmir shawls and silken muslins which a Benares merchant was spreading before him, warned me not to go down to the Fair. But I was curious to see the festival, and asked Babaji Rao to accompany me.

'Certainly,' he said, beaming through his spectacles; 'but I cannot take responsibility for what may happen to you.'

'What *may* happen to me?' I asked, and he said they would probably throw coloured powder at me.

'They will make you like the rainbow,' wheezed His Highness; 'you should not take him, Babaji Rao.'

'Let him go! Let him go if he wishes!' cried the Dewan, who is now very friendly with me. 'They will not do him any harm.'

'Do you dare to come?' asked Babaji Rao.

'When I've changed into my oldest suit,' I said.

We drove down in the Dewan's car, which was greeted with loud cheers and held up by a mob of Hindoos outside the Palace, where the festivities were taking place.

The three-sided courtyard was crammed with people; boys perched upon the walls and roof, and clung like monkeys to the minarets, and a kind of dance was taking place in the centre.

'Shall we get out?' I asked Babaji Rao, gazing rather nervously through the window at the yelling mob; but the answer came from outside. A Hindoo, whom I recognised with difficulty as the Dewan's chief accountant, had already pushed his way through the crowd towards us, and opened the door of the car. His face was smeared with red powder, as were all the other faces round us. He was the Master of Ceremonies, I learnt, and was followed by an assistant bearing a brass tray on which were two huge heaps of powder, one bright red and the other silvery, like the scales of a small fish.

'Come out of the car,' cried the M.C., 'or we shall drag you out!'

It wasn't difficult to make a choice between these alternatives, and Babaji Rao and I got out. The Dewan remained seated.

'Come out, Dewan Sahib!' called the M.C., but the Dewan refused to budge.

'You have two victims,' he said, laughing shrilly, 'and that is quite enough.'

I wasn't altogether surprised that no one insisted. Although one may not harbour malice for liberties taken at *Holi*, I doubt whether I should have tried to get equal with the Dewan for one day if I was to be unequal to him for the rest of the year. At any rate nobody molested him, and after a few moments he disappeared. So too, in a manner of speaking, did we. No sooner had we got out than the M.C. stuck his thumb in the red powder, which is called *gulal*, and pressed it firmly against our foreheads. This was the mark of friendship, and courtesy demanded that we should return the compliment, though there was no room on his face for any more. Other thumbs were dug into the stuff and pressed upon us, and I dug and dabbed wildly in return; then the M.C. took a handful and threw it in my face, and, apparently liking the effect, finally emptied the tray over our heads. The crowd closed in on us after this; daubed, laughing faces were pressed towards me; brown arms embraced me, drew me along, propelled me from behind, and rubbed more powder into my hair and clothes.

PART TWO

'He is a very good man,' said a voice; 'give the Sahib more.'

Babaji Rao, his spectacles like bright-red saucers, was holding on to my sleeve, and in front of us a thin, naked man with a purple wig, a cod-piece, and bells on his ankles, was dancing and hooting. Remembering the spirit of the occasion, I smiled rather dimly through the red mist of powder, till a handful of water struck me in the face.

'No, no; no water!' cried Babaji Rao, with an ingratiating snigger; but his voice was lost in cheers and laughter, and when we had been squeezed to the centre of the courtyard where a space had been left, a hose of violet-tinted water was turned on us both.

This made the colours run nicely, and when we were stained and soaked from head to foot and could not be made any wetter, we were abandoned for other victims. We stood for some time and watched them receiving similar treatment; then a rather spiritless game was played, in which a body of men armed with staves attacked a body of women, also armed with staves, who were defending a mysterious bundle hanging from a cross-beam. I intended to ask Babaji Rao whether this had anything to do with the legend of Holikar, and whether *gulal* represented fire; but my curiosity was a little damped. When we returned to the encampment His Highness was still there examining silks and brocades, and thinking he would be amused to see me, I went in to him before changing and said I too was a piece of brocade and would he care to purchase me.

He gave a shrill cry of horrified laughter and hid his face in his hands.

'Go away!' he cried. 'Go away! Go away!'

In the evening Miss Trend told me that she had paid a call on the Maharani. European ladies are permitted to visit Indian ladies, it seems, and are often invited to do so. She said that the Maharani was a charmingly pretty girl, not yet twenty years old, and that it was dreadful to think of the

203

loneliness and monotony of her life, shut up in that Palace with only her women for company, and seldom visited, even by the Maharajah, who in any case could hardly be considered romantic. Her pleasure, after a few moments of shyness, at Miss Trend's visit had been touchingly childish, and she had brought out all her fine dresses and jewels, which she seldom had a chance to display except to her women.

March 26th

WE were due to leave here to-day. His Highness was to have departed very early in the morning, during the only auspicious hour, but a postponement had to be made and we are to stay on for another four or five days.

I am not very pleased about this, for it is getting uncomfortably hot for canvas, and in the dining-marquee, which has only a single roof, I have to wear my hat during lunch.

The reason for the postponement is that the young Prince has smallpox.

At least, that is what the Dewan told me yesterday afternoon. But in the evening His Highness contradicted it.

'It is measles,' he said.

'Oh, well, that's better, isn't it?' I said.

'They say it is the same thing,' he replied fretfully. 'It is a great nuisance, for after this evening I shall not be able to see you for some days.'

'Because of infection?' I asked.

He began to shake with amusement.

'No, no,' he said. 'But I must not shave, or put on my hat or shoes.'

This is ritual, apparently; for smallpox, of which there are said to be three kinds, is presided over by a Goddess named Devi who has a thousand arms. The remedy for the disease lies in her thousand hands. Certain ignorant country-people believe that she causes the disease; others think that she actually *is* the disease, and will not allow the bodies of those who succumb to it to be burnt in case Devi is burnt too, though this would seem, in the circumstances, to be the very best thing for her; but more enlightened people, such as those that surround His Highness, are of the opinion that her power is purely remedial. For this reason doctors are not allowed to touch the patient, for that would be a declaration of scepticism as well, perhaps, as a breach of professional etiquette. It would also be sacrilegious; for the body of the patient is considered holy, a house ready for the Goddess to enter; so only the mother and nurses may touch the patient, preparing it for the divine visitation, while the father, bareheaded, unshaved and unshod, makes pilgrimages to all the Goddess's temples in the neighbourhood to entreat her assistance.

I was sitting by myself on a chair in the Palace courtyard this afternoon, waiting for Babaji Rao who had gone in on some business, when the stout Hindoo doctor came waddling out of the Queen's apartments.

'How is the child?' I asked, as he came over to me.

'Much better,' he said. 'It is only a heat-rash and there is no fever.'

'How do you know there is no fever?' I asked slyly.

'I do it this way,' he explained. 'I make the nurse place her hand on the child's body and keep it there; then I feel the nurse's hand and so discover how much heat has been transmitted by the patient.'

Later in the afternoon the Political Agent arrived in Garha, and the Dewan made excuses for the Maharajah's absence, saying that the little Prince had smallpox and so His Highness could not, on that account, personally receive his guest.

'It is thought to be measles, not smallpox,' said Babaji Rao.

'Smallpox,' repeated the Dewan firmly.

'It is a heat-rash,' piped the stout doctor from the background.

'Anyway,' observed the Dewan with finality, 'we are taking it to be smallpox, and Their Highnesses are observing the rites.'

An Englishman who sat at my hotel table in Delhi, I remember, told me that he had contracted smallpox within twenty-four hours of arriving in India, from dirty sheets in the —— Hotel, Bombay. I expressed surprise at his unblemished appearance, and he said he shared my surprise; he had expected to look like a gruyère cheese for the rest of his life.

I visited the —— Hotel myself on a number of occasions when I was in Bombay, but without ill consequences. The only note I have about it is of an Indian soldier, in khaki, wearing puttees but no boots or socks, whom I noticed one day chatting to the clerk at the reception desk. His slight claim upon my interest was that he dropped a pencil on the floor, but instead of bending down to pick it up, he merely glanced at it, seized it deftly between his toes and, without interrupting his conversation or altering the indolent attitude in which he leant against the desk, lifted his foot and restored the pencil to his dangling hand.

Captain Daly and Miss Trend have gone, and as the Dewan did not make his usual visit to the encampment, where I now reign alone, I went down to his house in the evening to call on him. He was not in, but I soon espied him a little distance away, perched on a high wooden platform. The platform was reached by steps, and a large canvas umbrella shaded the Dewan from the heat of the sun. In front of him was a rough table bearing a black tin box, some books and papers.

But he was not reading or writing; he was sitting quite motionless with a string of beads in his hands. Directly he saw me, however, he heaved his enormous bulk out of the chair and came waddling to the top of the steps to welcome me.

'Come up, Mr. Ackerley, come up! How kind of you! Very pleased!'

He seemed delighted. We talked a little of the Prince's illness, and the Dewan said that Devi was his family Goddess, but that his private God was Mahadeo (the Great God) or Siva.

Siva has numerous forms, but is chiefly worshipped in one shape, the phallic symbol of generative and creative power—plain upright stones called *lingams* which are scattered all over India. But the Dewan said he did not worship the *lingam,* because he did not believe in Mahadeo or in any God, only in an idea of Duty and doing good to others. He saw me looking at his beads on the table and said yes, that might appear to be an inconsistency, but that when he told them, as he frequently did when he was worried or had nothing to do, he was not thinking of God, but repeating a familiar formula which he found soothing and tranquillizing. His Highness, he said, also carried beads which he told, usually when he was returning from a journey, and it displeased him to be interrupted whilst doing so. We passed from that to talk of friendship, which, he thought, was essentially a youthful affair. There had to be passion in friendship—though not necessarily sexual: and only boys were capable of that passion and enthusiasm. He himself had had that passion in his youth, and the friend he had then made was a staunch friend still.

'I was quite attractive when I was a boy,' he said, 'but no one could find anything attractive in me now.'

But his greatest alliance was and always had been with his brother.

'We are as one,' he said, 'and if he dies I do not care to live.'

But he was slow now to make friends, slow and shy. He had wanted to be friends with me, but had perceived a similar reserve in myself. That was why we had not got on well together, and perhaps never would.

I said I feared that there had been other reasons that had kept us apart—that he had looked upon me as an intruder and a busybody; and he agreed that he had been afraid that I would interfere, but that it was clear now that I had no inclination to do so, and he thanked me for that.

'What can I do for you, Mr. Ackerley? I am anxious to do something for you, here or in Chhokrapur.'

He was glad that we were now friends. He had always felt that we should be; that he had more in common with me than with Captain Daly, but:

'I am like a maiden,' he said shyly, 'I have to be wooed.'

March 28th

IT is getting appreciably warmer every day. After returning at about eight o'clock from my morning's ride I seldom go out again until five in the afternoon, but sit in my tent and write or read in a state of continual perspiration. Yesterday the sky became heavily overcast, and a strong warm wind began to blow. It has been blowing ever since, and brings with it occasional tornadoes, miniature no doubt, but of a very exasperating disposition. While I sit and sweat, a sudden boisterous swishing is heard in the surrounding jungle, and like a wild thing, a whirling funnel of wind arrives in the encampment and gyrates furiously in front of my tent.

It does this in order to suck into itself all the dust and dead leaves in the vicinity, and when it has got as much as it can hold, it makes a dash for my tent and whirls explosively through it, taking all my personal belongings out through the opposite flap and leaving all its dust and dead leaves behind. Wishing that I had a thousand arms like the Goddess Devi, I snatch at my vanishing possessions, trying to save something out of the wreck.

This has happened three times in the last few hours, and I am beginning to read purpose into the way in which these whirlwinds make again and again for my tent, and find myself agreeing with the villagers, who believe them to be devils and stand in great awe of them.

Yesterday evening I saw as much of the Queen as I suppose I shall ever see. She was on her way, in procession and on foot, to one of the temples to pray for her son's recovery. But she was not visible, of course. She was walking within a canopy of red curtains, carried on poles on the shoulders of four men, preceded by musicians and followed by her women attendants.

If a temple has been desecrated one may enter it without taking off one's shoes. But the Dewan says he never removes his shoes whether temples have been desecrated or not. He says, 'My good fellow, if you wish me to take off my shoes, I shall not enter your temple.' Then they admit him, for they like having their temples visited. But of course if a temple is actually being used, he added, he does not try to enter it at all.

I told Narayan that I did not think his moustache suited him very well, and that he should cut it off; but he said that it was an Indian rule that a Hindoo boy must not shave his upper lip until after his father's death.

This afternoon I was again sitting outside the Palace waiting for Babaji Rao, who had gone in to speak to the Dewan. He eventually reappeared, accompanied by the Dewan, the doctor, and an aged priest.

'Has the Raja been given his medicine and a bath?' I heard the Dewan ask the doctor.

'No,' said the doctor.

'Why not?'

'Her Highness and the priests did not wish these things to be done.'

'But they must be done!' cried the Dewan. 'I *told* you to do them. Let them be done at once!' He then turned to the priest. 'The child has not got smallpox.' The old man shook his head mournfully. 'I say it has *not* got smallpox. We have taken it to be smallpox for the sake of convenience, but it has *not* got smallpox and it must be given medicine and a bath!'

He threatened the doctor with mock severity with his stick.

'If you do not obey my orders I shall beat you!' he said.

'Does your authority extend even to the medical department, Dewan Sahib?' I asked, amused.

'It extends everywhere,' he replied briefly.

Continuing about himself, as he accompanied Babaji Rao and me towards the officers' quarters, the Dewan said that he has a great ability to dismiss things from his mind. He can give an order and, turning to other business, forget all about it until the moment for its operation arrives. Then he remembers it. Even personal troubles can be treated in this way.

'If they can be solved, then solve them and forget about them; but if they cannot be solved, then—forget about them.

So at the end of a day he puts everything out of his mind and plays bridge. He loves bridge and never misses his evening's rubber—with the doctor as partner, of course.

'On only one occasion have I missed my game, and that was when twelve prisoners escaped from the jail. I did not play cards that evening. I wanted to play, but I thought it was my duty not to at such a serious moment.'

So he pulls along very well with himself. And he pulls along very well with His Highness too.

Before doing the smallest thing he always asks His Highness's permission, and His Highness always gives it.

'My orders are seldom interfered with; but if His Highness says to me: "I am thinking of upsetting this order of yours, Dewan. What do you think?" Then I look at the order and say, "Of course, upset it by all means." '

He said that His Highness was a very clever man; that he set great store on truth and frankness, so that one must always speak one's mind to him and never carry tales to him about other people, for he had an uncomfortable habit of confronting one with the subject of one's story. I thought this statement difficult to reconcile with the treatment of Narayan; but I did not say so.

'He often makes himself appear to be a fool,' concluded the Dewan; 'it is a policy of his; but do not be taken in by it. He knows everything that happens. You may be sure, for instance, that he knows very well that you are walking with Babaji Rao and me at this moment.'

I was amused at his self-confidence, for His Highness has recently been considering his dismissal from the Dewanship and has been discussing the matter with me.

It appears that the Dewan is demanding an increase in salary, and His Highness is put out over it and wants to be rid of him.

'He talks too much,' observed the little man peevishly.

But almost as though he perceived what was passing

through my mind, the Dewan began himself to discuss this very question. He said he was not a rich man; that besides his salary of a thousand rupees a month, he had a private income of only four thousand rupees a year; but that it was, nevertheless, more money than he needed.

'I have so much money that I do not know what to do with it. What to do? What to do? I do not know. Yet I want more and more.'

He likened himself, unconvincingly I thought, to the mendicant who did not rise to his feet when Alexander the Great rode past.

'Why do you not rise when the Emperor passes?' asked Alexander, more amused than angry.

'Why should I rise? I am an Emperor myself.'

'An Emperor, eh? Then where is your army?'

'Where, on the other hand, are my enemies?'

'Well, your treasury—where is that?'

'Where are my needs?'

Similarly, the Dewan said, he had few needs, and the salary he drew was far more than he required. For his first six years as Dewan he had drawn only half that—five hundred rupees—and even that with his private income had been more than he could use. But at the end of the six years, his contract expiring, he had felt that he was entitled to more although he did not require it, and had demanded an increase to a thousand rupees, which had been refused. So he had tendered his resignation, which had been accepted.

His Highness had then submitted to him a list of names, and asked him to nominate his own successor, and he had complied honestly with this request, but had prophesied at the same time that the nominee would not give as much satisfaction as he himself had given, and that sooner or later he would be recalled.

He had then returned to his Lucknow home and reverted to his literary work.

And nine months later His Highness had recalled him as he had foretold. Then, unhappily, he had not wanted to move; he takes root easily and does not like being disturbed, and he had expressed this disinclination to His Highness, but had added that should His Highness *command* him to return he should consider himself as having no choice in the matter. The command had been given, and he had returned to Chhokrapur to resume his duties as Dewan, on a three years' contract at a thousand rupees a month. But now the three years have passed, and he has told His Highness that if he is required to contract for another term of office he must have fifteen hundred rupees a month.

'I do not need it,' he cried, 'but I am worth it, and therefore I must have it.'

Again he has been refused; again he has sent in his resignation; again about ten new candidates for the Dewanship have been called, and again the Dewan has been asked to nominate his successor.

But this time he has replied: 'They are none of them of any use; no one can replace me. If Your Highness calls God himself I shall advise you against Him. He cannot serve you as well as I can, for He has not had the nine years' *special* experience that I have had of the difficulties of this State and the difficulties of your complex nature. I am the only successor to myself that I can honestly recommend, and I am worth fifteen hundred rupees a month to you, and the State can easily afford to pay it—I, as Dewan, am the best judge of that.'

He has not got it yet: His Highness has not made up his mind; but I do not think there can be any doubt as to what will happen.

March 29th

I ASKED Babaji Rao to-day whether it was true, as Narayan had told me, that a Hindoo boy may not shave off his moustache during his father's lifetime. It was quite true, he said.

'Does that give rise to jesting or bitter retorts in family

disputes?' I asked. 'I mean, might an angry son say to his
father, "Well, the sooner I have a clean upper lip the
better!" '

Babaji Rao rather uneasily agreed that such a thing
might possibly be said, but that as a rule children did not
dispute with their parents.

He was sitting with me in the encampment, and I asked
him if he would like a drink of iced water.

'But I suppose you won't be able to take it, will you?' I
added, remembering.

'Perhaps *you* have some there?' he inquired of Narayan,
who is a Brahman. Narayan nodded.

Shortly afterwards one of the kitchen staff brought a jar
of water, from which Babaji Rao drank.

'But from whose hands are you taking water?' I asked.
'That man wasn't a Brahman. Was he of your caste?'

'No,' said Babaji Rao, 'but I know him, and he is of a
caste from whose hands I may receive water.'

'Oh dear,' I sighed, 'what a muddle you've made of life!'

But he said, smiling, that it was I who had made a muddle
of his life—that was to say that I was indirectly responsible
for a very grave occurrence in his house. His Mohammedan
tonga-wallah, with whom I converse in grins, had snatched
a brass *lota* (a small vessel for water) from the hands of his
Hindoo servant. Such a thing was unheard of. The touch
was defiling, and if the thing touched was brass it had to be
cleansed with fire; but if it was *phul*, or some other substance
that could not stand heat, it had to be thrown away. He
himself had not witnessed the disgraceful incident, but his
wife had been present and had been very angry indeed. And
what did I think the tonga-wallah had said in self-defence?
He had said that his master Babaji Rao would not mind,
since he was himself so lax in principles as to drink water in
the house of a European!

When we had both agreed that of course the boy's statement was not true, for Babaji Rao always takes his water on

to the verandah to drink, we allowed ourselves to be amused
at this little scene, and I asked him how long he thought
the paralysing state of affairs which gave rise to it would
continue. He said that every intelligent Indian naturally
desired peace, solidarity, and social reform, and that progress *was* being made; but it was inevitably difficult and
slow. I asked him for instances of this progress—any evidence
to show the least sign of reconciliation between Mohammedans and Hindoos, and he replied that a Hindoo was
now able to receive betel from the hands of a Mohammedan.
That was certainly something, I said, but that it seemed to
me that he, as an intelligent man in pursuit of truth, should
be giving active support to the movement, not necessarily
in public, but quietly at home, where charity begins. He
might, for instance, in this very affair of his tonga-wallah,
have given a lead, by drinking himself, let us say, from the
contaminated vessel? Had not the Dewan eaten an egg?

But Babaji Rao replied that such a course had not been
open to him, for where his kitchen was concerned other
people besides himself were involved. When his father and
mother came to visit him, for example, they ate with him on
the tacit understanding that his utensils had been used in
the orthodox manner. One could not possibly abuse this
confidence; it would be deceitful and unfair.

'But I wasn't suggesting that you should deceive any one,'
I said. 'I meant rather that you should then write to your
parents and say that your utensils had *not* been used in an
orthodox manner, and that in future, therefore, if they felt
disinclined to use them, they had better bring their own.'

Babaji Rao smiled deprecatingly.

'I would not dare to do such a thing,' he said.

We went down to find the Dewan in the later afternoon,
and were just in time to see him returning from his evening's
exercise, a run. He was wearing his small pink hat, a collarless shirt hanging outside his *dhoti*, a waistcoat, and leather
slippers on his bare feet, and he came waddling along

215

towards us with an energetic movement that never quite turned into a run, brandishing his stick and chattering to himself. He said that he did not much like taking strenuous exercise, but that it was good for him; he had a lazy disposition, and that was why he stayed on as Dewan of the State. Some part of him was contented to remain, but he did not really care for the work, it meant nothing to him, and being a person of independent means he could discontinue it if he wished. But he was too lazy to break away, though if any circumstance should forcibly deprive him of his position he would be very grateful.

His real wish—his dream—was to be an actor, and though this was not looked upon as a serious or respectable profession in India, that was not the reason that withheld him from following it. He would particularly like, he said, to act in his own dramas, of which he had written several.

Here Babaji Rao, usually deferentially silent when the Dewan is with us, chimed in. He also expressed dissatisfaction with his life; he, too, would welcome more leisure to continue his philosophical writings; but he had not the Dewan's independence, and moreover, they both agreed, their affection for His Highness put another obstacle in the way of their leaving him. But they both managed to find a little leisure for their private interests.

'He is writing my biography,' said the Dewan, indicating his friend. But his own duties, he continued, though not arduous, were as much as the doctor would allow him to undertake at present.

He suffered greatly from nerves. Once he had over-worked; he had written three books in one year, and it had affected his nerves so badly that his doctor had ordered him to lead 'a fool's life.' This he had done ever since.

'In fact, for the first six weeks I did not even *think*!' he said.

I asked him what his symptoms had been, and he replied:

'First of all, if I bent forward like this, I felt I should fall over on to my face. I never did actually fall, but the feeling was there. Secondly, I had a kind of drowsiness in my eyes,

a kind of . . . bitterness. There is a little still, but it has
practically all gone.

'Thirdly . . . What was my third symptom?' he asked his
biographer. They pondered this together for a moment.

'I have forgotten now,' said the Dewan. 'But anyway
there were three.'

'You must look it up in your diary,' murmured Babaji
Rao.

To-day is Saturday, which, with Tuesday, is especially
sacred to Hanuman, the monkey-headed God of Physical
Power. One of his shrines is built near the encampment, and
had many visitors throughout the day, among them Narayan.
As they approached to worship they shuffled off their shoes,
walked barefooted once round the shrine, bowed, or knelt
and touched their foreheads to the ground. Some of them
brought cocoanuts and broke them before the image, a
hideous figure painted with vermilion and armed with a
club. I was very surprised to see our Mohammedan cook
taking part in this idolatry, which the Koran strictly forbids.
He carried a cocoanut, which he broke before the image,
and having sacrificed the milk, took back the pieces with
him to the kitchen to make puddings and toffee. Narayan
said it was not at all an uncommon sight; many of the
Mohammedans resident in the State had adopted the
Hindoo customs—a topknot, for example, was being culti-
vated by Hashim on the head of his baby—and I thought
this a much better sign for the future than Babaji Rao's
alleged neutrality of the betel-leaf.

When I returned to the encampment in the dusk,
Narayan came down the path to meet me. I thought how
graceful he looked in his white muslin clothes, the sleeves of
his loose vest widening out at the wrist, the long streamers of
his turban floating behind him. The breeze puffed at his
dhoti as he approached. moulding the soft stuff to the shape of
his thigh; then as he turned a bend in the path another

gentle gust took the garment from behind and blew it aside, momentarily baring a slim brown leg. I took his hand and led him into my tent, and he told me that His Highness had invited him to return to the New *Bakhri*, but that he feared to do so lest he should be treated with disrespect, and anyway it did not matter much because he liked being with me.

'I want to love you very much,' he said.

'You mean you do love me very much.'

'I want to.'

'Then why not?'

'You will go to England and I shall be sorry. But you will not be sorry. I am only a boy and I shall be sorry.'

When he got up to go, he asked me not to accompany him as usual to the fair-ground where he meets Sharma, but to let him go back alone this evening; then before I had time to reply, he suddenly laughed softly and drew me after him. And in the dark roadway, overshadowed by trees, he put up his face and kissed me on the cheek. I returned his kiss; but he at once drew back, crying out:

'Not the mouth! You eat meat! You eat meat!'

'Yes, and I will eat you in a minute,' I said, and kissed him on the lips again, and this time he did not draw away.

March 30th

OUR second attempt to leave Garha occurred to-day, and by three o'clock we were all packed and ready to move when the *Tahsildar* arrived on a pale-green bicycle to say that His Highness had a boil on his shoulder-blade and we were to stay on for another two days.

We all unpacked again. Later on Babaji Rao came up to the encampment and read peevishness in my face.

'You are not very pleased?' he suggested.

'No one could possibly feel pleased,' I replied, 'after packing and unpacking a large portmanteau in 103 degrees in the shade.'

He said nothing, the decent, gentle fellow—for I suddenly

remembered that earlier occasion when it was *he* who had been put out by His Highness's postponements and I had shown complete heartlessness at his discomfiture.

In the evening we sat with the Dewan, and I asked him how the complicated network of rules and regulations with regard to eating and drinking had originated. From the earliest days, he said, when through fear of poison it was written that 'an Aryan must take food and drink from the hands of an Aryan, and *may* from any other man he trusts.' Out of that feeling had been evolved the intricate caste laws of the present day, by which, one might roughly state, Hindoos were permitted to take water from any Hindoo except from a sweeper, fruit and dry food from any Hindoo, but cooked food only from their own or higher castes. As for Mohammedans, he said, their touch of course defiled, and one could take nothing from them at all. ' Except betel,' I put in brightly, quoting Babaji Rao's single instance of the reconciling of the two races. But the Dewan promptly rejected this. One could not take even betel from a Mohammedan, he said. Babaji Rao murmured apologetically that there was a difference between betel *prepared* and betel *handed* by a Mohammedan.

'There is no difference,' said the Dewan flatly, and Babaji Rao sank back into the silence from which he had so rashly emerged.

I asked why the touch of a Mohammedan and a European was so contaminating, and the Dewan said it was due to their meat-eating habits and to their lack of scrupulosity in washing. If his wife left the kitchen for a moment, he said, to fetch him something, for instance, she would wash her hands carefully before returning; but Mohammedans and Europeans had dirty habits: they used paper instead of water in their lavatories, they did not take off their leather shoes in the kitchen, they smoked in the kitchen and ate BEEF, and when they did wash they washed with soap which is made of animal fat.

Europeans touched their lips or the wet ends of their cigarettes, and cooked their food or shook hands with other people afterwards without having washed. Smoking was a filthy habit, he considered, and when I remarked that many high-class Hindoos had contracted it, he agreed that this was unhappily true, but at any rate they *washed*. But Europeans had no care over such important matters; look, for example, at their disgusting custom of afternoon tea! The strainer they used! On account of it, though he had sometimes consented to drink tea with Europeans, he had never once accepted a second cup. What happened? When the cups were refilled, frequently without having been emptied of their dregs and rinsed with clean water, the mixture composed of new tea, dregs, and sputum would rise and touch the strainer, which would then be transferred to the next person's cup, and so on! Ice too! This was often put into a glass from which a man had already drunk, and so carelessly that the spoon was permitted to touch the polluted liquid and then the same spoon was used again for somebody else's glass! Or even if it did not actually *touch* the liquid, the falling ice might splash up drops on to it! Disgusting! He had sent ice away in these circumstances, And the custom of the 'loving-cup' of which he had heard, he thought unspeakably revolting; nothing could induce him to drink from another person's glass. He spoke very forcibly; but I said that although when I considered it I understood the danger of germs and disease, it seemed to me that only by ceasing to breathe could one escape from it, and that I did not think about people's mouths in such a way.

What about kissing? I asked. With such ultra-hygienic notions as he held, how could he bring himself to kiss his wife? He replied that a man and his wife were one. . . . Well, I said, passing this over with the silence it deserved, what about the other members of his family—his parents, sisters, and children? Did he kiss them? Certainly not, he said, that was to say not on the lips; one kissed one's children, and perhaps one's mother, on the cheeks or brow, but one never kissed any other members of the family after they had passed the age of puberty.

'For a man to kiss his elder sister would be an *enormity!*' cried the Dewan; 'to kiss her *anywhere*,' he added. Europeans did not seem to attach much importance to a kiss; they kissed the mouth passionately or dispassionately according to their feelings. 'But in India,' he said, 'a kiss on the mouth is a very big thing; it is a completed sexual act.'

This evoked another mild protest from Babaji Rao. One had, he murmured with a deferential cough, to take into consideration the states of mind of the kisser and the kissed. But the Dewan rejected this, and in answer to a further question from me, declared that although he could not say that a good deal of illicit love-making did *not* go on in the State, there was *no* kissing upon the lips.

'Why should there be?' he inquired ingenuously. 'A man can kiss upon the cheeks and upon the eyes, and that is good enough.'

I felt that I was not getting accurate information from him, and forbore questioning him further on the subject.

March 31*st*

WHEN I was riding in the jungle this morning I saw a tree in the near distance more beautiful, I thought, than any other tree I had seen. Its feathery foliage was so light that it seemed more like a soft green cloud drifting a little in the breeze. It was a mango tree.

I rode up with a desire to touch it, but reined in my horse when I saw a blue jay sitting in the branches. I watched it for a little until suddenly, for no reason, it flew away.

'Yes,' I called after it, 'and if I had wings like yours I would spread them too.'

The blue jay is sacred to Siva, the destroyer and re-creator; not, as I was told, because blue is Siva's colour, but because both the bird and the God are called *Nil-Kanth*

(Blue Throat). Siva has a blue throat because, out of com-
passion for the human race, he swallowed a deadly poison
which would otherwise have destroyed the world. He kept
this poison in his throat and would not let it go further,
'for,' said he, 'I have the Lord Vishnu in my heart.'

But Siva's colour is white. The bull Nandi on which he
rides is white, his hair and face are white, and his body is
covered with pale ashes. And the commonest distinguishing
mark used by his followers is three horizontal white lines,
representing the God's trident, which are painted across the
forehead.

As Babaji Rao and I were walking in the outskirts of the
village this evening, two old peasants, a man and a woman,
begged of me. The woman was ill, it seemed; she squatted
on the ground at my feet and moaned and rocked herself,
holding out clawlike hands, while the old man, who was thin
and hairy and almost entirely naked, begged for medicine for
her. '*Good* medicine,' he kept saying, ' "Rodgers" medicine.'

Babaji Rao was very amused and explained to me that
there were some steel articles of recognised excellence,
marked 'Rodgers,' being sold at the fair, and the old man
wanted some medicine as good as this steel.

'Of course he thinks you are a doctor,' he said; 'these poor
people think that all white men are doctors.'

I asked him to explain that I was unfortunately not a
doctor, and I gave the old man a rupee to buy some
'Rodgers' medicine.

The Dewan took me with him to see a bridge being built
in the neighbourhood, and I remarked on the poor physique
of the builders—lean, under-nourished men with little round
bellies—and asked what wages they were getting.

'Twopence-halfpenny a day,' said the Dewan. They had
recently mutinied, he said, and had been given a rise.

I asked what their wages had been before the rise.

'Twopence a day,' said the Dewan.

He remarked, too, that this was a great advance upon the past, for fairly recent statistics showed that the average wage of a labourer in Garha used to be one and a half rupees (two shillings) a month. Chhokrapur does even better. No labourer there gets less than fourpence a day.

I asked whether they did not find it a little problematical to live on even fourpence a day, and he said abruptly: 'Not at all! It is exactly twice as much as they require.' A labourer's expenses were twopence a day, he said—two pounds of grain (barley) which cost him a penny-ha'penny, and a ha'porth of vegetables. He could live on this on his present wages and treat himself every now and then, out of his savings, to rice, which, at its lowest quality, costs two-pence-ha'penny a *seer*. The better quality rice, such as Narayan, for instance, eats, costs fourpence a *seer*.

For a little time I watched these poor emaciated creatures carrying blocks of stone—eight men to each block, which was suspended on chains from a long pole. The Dewan said that there were sculptures on the Garha temples showing that the labourers a thousand years ago had handled stone in exactly the same way.

'If I am introduced to an Englishman, and he says "How d'you do?" to me, what do I reply?' he asked, as we drove back. 'Shall I say, "I am very well, thank you, how are you?" What is the rule, please?'

I said I did not think there was any rule, but that the best thing was to say 'How d'you do?' too, and to try to get it in first and to say it with as little fuss as possible.

His question reminded me of a young man who got into conversation with me in the train from Benares. Having questioned me closely about myself, he said that he hoped soon to travel, too, and to visit England. I remarked how difficult I thought it must be for Hindoos to go about outside their own country, considering their religious and caste restrictions.

'But I know how to use the spoon and fork,' said he; 'I have learnt.'

He then enquired whether it would be all right for him to wear in England the clothes in which he was now dressed— a round brown hat, cotton pyjamas and a Condy's Fluid coloured coat.

'Will they make fun at me?' he asked.

April 2nd

WE returned to Chhokrapur yesterday. It is oppressively warm, and I have not gone back to the little house I used to occupy, but live alone in the spacious rooms of the Guest House, which has hot-weather facilities. During meals the *punkah* waves ceaselessly over my head, pulled by an unseen hand or foot in the kitchen, and all the doorways are being fitted with *khus-khus tattis*. These are bamboo screens thickly plaited with the sweet-smelling *khus-khus* grass, and made to fit into the frames of the doors; and the water-carrier, visiting them at intervals throughout the day, slings water against them from the verandah outside, so that not only do they shade the blinding light, but the hot air, beating against them, is cooled and perfumed as it enters the room.

His Highness is still reported to be ill.

I asked Narayan if he took the five products of the cow. He did not understand what I meant by products, so I recited them.

'Yes,' he said, 'when I get mistake.'

It was now my turn to require an explanation; he meant when he had done anything wrong—eaten, for instance, something he should not have eaten. Then he would have to go to the pundits, and they would give him a mixture of the five products—a purifying dose.

His father is a pundit, so I dare say the old man doses his son himself, for he is a very holy man and reads the *Puranas* aloud from eleven till one o'clock every day, and tells his beads for an hour in the morning, which practices amuse Narayan very much, though he does not show his amusement, of course, for he is frightened of his father.

'But now I do not take it,' he said, referring back to the cow, 'it is much dirty.'

'Then how do you purify yourself now after getting mistakes?' I asked.

'I do not get mistakes now,' he replied with a sly smile.

He then told me, in confidence, that after the Maharajah had recalled him to Garha Palace the other day and forgiven him his alleged faults, His Highness had beckoned him nearer the royal *charpai*. Narayan had asked respectfully why he was required to come closer, and His Highness had spoken flatteringly to him, had said he had always loved him and wished to see him naked. It was not the first time that the Maharajah had made such advances, Narayan said, and not the first time he had refused. His Highness had then threatened to punish him and send him out of the State, but Narayan had remained inflexible.

'Why did you refuse?' I asked.

'It is a sin!' he cried vehemently. I smiled at the warmth of his tone. 'It is!' he repeated, with the same force. 'It say so in the *Purān*.'

'And why do you tell me these secret things?' I asked him mischievously. 'I thought you did not care to hear secret things repeated?'

'But you are my friend,' he said, looking at me in surprise; 'so I must say you everything, everything. Is that not good?'

'That is very good,' I replied quickly, for I wanted to hear everything, everything.

Abdul came to-day. He had done his best to persuade me to take him to Garha, but I was sick of him and left him behind. However, he turned up to-day, unsummoned, to give me a lesson. It was of the usual kind—the only slight variation being that this time it was a *friend* of his, to whom he would introduce me, who wished to feast me.

I am polite and diffident by nature, and it is owing to this weakness that I am still suffering from Abdul's requests. Driven by his egoistic persistence, and unable to speak my mind bluntly and rudely, which would have been the best thing to do, I have usually dodged and evaded, temporised and prevaricated, and so got deeper and deeper into difficulties. But I am better at it now.

Hindoo food is divided into *kuchcha* and *pukka*. *Pukka* food is cooked food; *kuchcha* food is raw, that is to say it comprises all the things like rice, pulse, bread, curry, etc., which are not cooked in clarified butter. These latter foods are the ones which receive the strictest care; they can only be taken, Babaji Rao says, from his own caste or from orthodox Brahmans; over *pukka* food, I seemed to gather, a certain laxity is permitted.

Once, he said, he had accepted an invitation to dinner, which really he should not have accepted at all, on the understanding that he would be given *pukka* food to eat; but he was served with *kuchcha* food instead and felt obliged to eat it. It is one of the worst heterodoxies he has ever committed. But, he went on to say, he would not greatly mind eating *pukka* food in even my presence, provided that I too was eating *pukka* food and no meat, and had a separate table at some distance from his.

'What sort of distance would you consider safe?' I asked.

'Just out of touch would be sufficient.'

Some people insisted, he said, that there should be no connection even *beneath* the tables; that is to say that they should not be placed, for instance, upon the same strip of carpet; but he felt this to be a little extreme.

'Would you really be upset,' I asked, 'if I happened to touch your table?'

'No,' he replied with a smile.

'Of course not; or you would not shake hands with me.'

'The fact is,' he explained, 'we have made such a fetish of

eating that we believe ourselves to be in a state of holiness when we are doing so.'

The Dewan is a meat-eating Brahman, so Babaji Rao ought not to eat with him at all; but he does so, nevertheless.

Cooks are usually relatives, because they have to be of the same caste as the household, and so a man like the Dewan, who is of the very highest caste, would no doubt be hard put to it if he were single, strictly orthodox, and had no poor relations.

Cooks are usually female; otherwise difficulties arise. If Babaji Rao had a male cook, Mrs. Babaji Rao would not be able to appear before him, which would be highly inconvenient. He had a female cook recently, but when she grew old she contracted asthma and coughed a lot, so he got rid of her and is now looking for a new one. Meanwhile his wife cooks for him; but she does not eat with him; a Hindoo woman never eats with her husband.

I asked why not, and was informed by the Dewan that it wasn't considered proper; it was her business to wait upon her husband, or at any rate to see that he was looked after.

I asked him if his wife had ever seen me. 'She must have,' he said, meaning, I suppose, that she had had so many opportunities to peep at me out of the window that it was most improbable that she had not done so. Then he clearly felt uneasy about this, and added that though, theoretically, she was not supposed to look, few people nowadays insisted upon such extreme *purdah*.

The European dresses, but the Hindoo undresses, for dinner. When a Hindoo feeds he wears nothing but his nether garment, his *dhoti*, his shirt being under various disqualifications. It is not washed as frequently as the *dhoti*, which one bathes in every day, and for other reasons, too, it cannot be considered so clean an article of clothing.

For one thing, being only an adopted garment, it is

seldom of Indian manufacture and is usually sewn, and Heaven knows what fingers have sewn it; whereas the *dhoti* is a single piece of cloth, and is not sewn anywhere. Moreover, the shirt, unlike the *dhoti*, is always sent to the washerwoman, and the washerwoman starches it, and starch is often made out of rice, and rice is *kuchcha* food. So, altogether, the shirt is under grave suspicion. Babaji Rao's brother, who is rather lax, eats in his shirt, but Babaji Rao has never done such an improper thing in his life.

April 4th

NARAYAN invited me to his house the other day. If I stood outside it on its western side and called his name he would come, he said. I did so, and a tiny door high up in the bright wall popped open, and he beckoned me up the flight of dung-washed brick steps that led to it. Hindoos do all their charing with cow-dung. Narayan had nothing on but his *dhoti*, and showed a poor physique. A roll of two of fat, seen above the waistline of the *dhoti*, suggested that his belly would probably bulge if released from the constriction of that garment.

His room, though small, was larger than Abdul's, and was furnished chiefly with European furniture, easy-chairs, a dressing-table with a mirror, and a mosquito curtain over the *charpai*.

Pinned or nailed to the walls were two photographs of His Highness, one of His Highness's grandfather, a cheap highly-coloured print of an Indian hero about to embrace an Indian heroine, and my drawing of Sharma, now thickly outlined with ink and subscribed 'Drawn by Narayan.' On the floor was a carpet, and on the carpet was the subject of our drawing, squatting in front of a betel-leaf chest, on the top of which he was smearing and preparing the leaves with various ingredients from various little drawers. I was invited to sit down and was shown many treasures—safety razors, a cigarette-case, and a broken watch—produced from locked boxes under the bed. Scents and oils were handed round,

and then a harmonium was brought out of a corner, and
Narayan and Sharma tinkled on it by turns. I was not feeling very well, so I refused the betel, cigarettes, and Marsala
that were offered.

'How can I do respect?' asked Narayan rather unhappily;
and I said that just to be where I was was pleasure enough
for me. We talked a little about the things in the room, and
then Narayan said:

'When I go to the lavatory I do like this,' and, laughing,
he twisted the sacred thread, which was round his neck,
over one of his ears. But it was a very short thread and had
to be strained to get it over the ear.

'Why do you do that?' I asked.

'I do not know,' he said.

'Aha!' I exclaimed, 'I thought not.'

At this they both burst out laughing together, and
Narayan clapped his hands.

'When you do that, then you make me happy,' he said.

'When I do what?' I asked, mystified.

'Aha!' he mimicked, and they both laughed merrily again
and touched each other and tried the sound over and over
again in their own throats. My facial expressions and the
sounds I sometimes make have always been a source of
interest and amusement to them, and Sharma, who understands nothing that is being said, sits and watches me with
round eyes, ready to laugh at any moment should Narayan
lead the way.

When they had got over that, I told Narayan that the
reason why a Hindoo hung his sacred thread over his ear
when going to the lavatory was to prevent it from touching
and being defiled by the unholy parts of his body as he
squatted down; but that since his own thread was so short
that it obviously could not possibly hang down that far, it
was entirely unnecessary to go on taking that precaution.

'But I cannot make water if I do not do it,' he said.

He asked to be allowed to accompany me back to the
Guest House, and as we were leaving, a slight, pretty girl

came out of the house and stood on the verandah with her face uncovered watching us pass. Narayan said that she was one of his sisters, and that she was a widow.

'Does she always go out uncovered?' I asked.

'She does not go out at all,' he said, without interest, and then added that she cooked for him and brought him his meals. I asked for more information about her, and learnt that she was twenty-one years old, and had been a widow, childless, for four years. She could not, of course, marry again, but divided her life between the houses of her father and her father-in-law, doing a little work in each. This rule against remarriage was only among high castes, he said; lower castes could and did remarry as often as they pleased.

I asked whether he was not sorry for his sister, and did not think the rule cruel that forbade her another mate, and he agreed that it was a very bad rule indeed and particularly hard when the widow was so young.

'What would happen to your sister if she married again?' I asked.

'No man will speak to her any more,' he said.

'And you?'

'I will send her away. I will not speak to her.'

'Do you love her?'

'Very much.'

'Yet you would send her away?'

'Indian rule,' he said. 'If she lay down with any man and have a baby in her belly—just the same. Every man will send her away. And if any man give her shelter all will hate him.'

'But if there was no baby in her belly, and only you knew that she had had a lover? What then?'

'If I know she lay down with any man I send her away. But worse if she have a baby, for then every man know.'

He could not do otherwise, he said; his father, his relatives, and spiritual leader would treat him in the same way if he gave her sympathy in such circumstances; and so strong was his fear of being outcaste that he would let his sister kill herself sooner than stretch out a hand to her in her disgrace. Of his father, he said, he was very frightened indeed; so frightened that he never even dared to raise his eyes to the old man's face (unless he was looking another way) nor to eat in front of him; but remained always with lowered gaze, very timid and abashed.

If his father knew, for instance that he smoked, he would be very angry and would probably slap him—a thing he had not done for years.

'What would you do if your father slapped you?' I asked.

'I will cry. But many boys beat their fathers if their fathers beat them, and give anger for anger. Very bad boys.'

Very bad boys, I agreed, and expressed the hope that there were a lot of them about, since I could not see how anything was ever to move in India unless very good fathers were constantly slapped by very bad sons—a remark which Narayan received with silent disapproval.

April 5th

THE difference between marriage and concubinage is money, says Babaji Rao. That is why it is considered more seemly that the bridegroom should go empty-handed to the house of the bride on his wedding-day; any gift from him to the bride's father might be misconstrued. The feeling about this is so strong that until recently it was most compromising and unwise for the bride's father to enter the bridegroom's village, and even now one does not stay in the house of one's married daughter or sister, for this would be to accept something from her husband. So Babaji Rao's father has never stayed with his daughter, and Babaji Rao himself, when visiting her, used to put up with friends in the village; but he did not find the cuisine to his taste, and was at last compelled to transfer to the house of his sister, who understood from experience his gastronomic peculiarities.

But he is always considered as a paying guest in her house, and leaves behind him a nominal sum of four or five rupees at the end of each visit.

Younger brothers may stay with their married sisters without fear of comment, for they never had the right to dispose of them.

He explained this as I accompanied him to the hospital to-day. He was not feeling very well, and wanted to have his throat painted. The hospital is a dingy one-storeyed building, with a colonnaded verandah, forming three sides of a square. It is a hundred years old, Babaji Rao told me, but I do not know whether it was civic pride or astonishment that prompted this information. In the centre of the court was a short black lamppost, rather like a stage 'prop,' stuck on a white stone platform, and just behind this a small *jaman* tree was growing.

The tree had begun to collapse, I noticed as we passed; it was supported by a piece of stick, and a coil of torn and soiled surgical bandage.

I told the doctor I was pleased to see that the trees also received medical attention; but he did not seem to find amusement in this little joke, and merely remarked that the *jaman* tree produces a pleasant fruit, like a plum, which is good for constipation.

The doctor is a Bengali from Calcutta, and he eats meat. But meat is said to be eaten generally in Bengal, even by Brahmans. He is a very stout man with protuberant pale green eyes. Once he had eight per cent. of diabetes, but he has reduced it. His children, on the other hand, have been allowed to accumulate; he now has eight sons and one daughter. While Babaji Rao was having his throat painted in the dispensary, the doctor showed me his operating theatre. It was a small dark room containing two cases of instruments, a tin washstand, and a blood-stained table. On the wall was a snake-bite chart, giving diagrams of the physical characteristics of the various poisonous snakes, and information of what to do when bitten by each. I have seen these charts before, but have always refrained from studying them, feeling that I should certainly get it all wrong if I ever had need to remember it, and that a quick death would be preferable to the awful dual anxiety of trying to recognise one's snake and recall its particular antidote.

From a cabinet in the wall the doctor brought out two large yellowish lumps of chalky material to show me. They were gall-stones, he said, which he himself had removed. But he had not removed a gall-stone for some considerable time; he followed a different system now, he crushed the stones inside the bladder. I diverted him from this painful topic by asking him what he thought of the Indian system of medicine, and he said it was very good, indeed many men had returned to it after qualifying in the European system. What were his views as a doctor, I asked, on the medicinal value of cow's urine, internally administered? Also of the semen of the bear, which I had seen advertised in a Delhi newspaper named *The Rajasthan*?

'In olden days,' the advertisement had run, 'these Rajbansi pills were used by many Badushas of Delhi who owned many wives. This is prepared according to the old Urdu Sastras with very great cost, risk, and valuable ingredients and herbs, along with the *essence of the well-grown generative organs of the male bears as to cure impotency*. The above pills have to be taken in . . . This is a heavenly nectar for impotents. A trial will give you conviction to its effect. . . . All correspondence treated as confidential.'

After a moment's thought the doctor replied that semen contained albumen like an egg and was therefore strengthening; but the Dewan, who is seldom far from the doctor and joined us at this moment, pooh-poohed the efficacy of this remedy. We then passed on to artificial insemination, and the Dewan remarked that if a man were impotent and heirless he would be quite justified in purchasing the semen of a friend—so long, of course, as the friend were a Brahman or of the purchaser's caste.

'Urine,' said the doctor, 'contains bile, which is good for constipation and lassitude.'

He added that of course I knew of the veneration in which Hindoos held the cow.

'We look upon it as our mother,' he said, 'because it gives us milk.'

In the evening after dinner I went for a walk in the city, and since it was very dark, took the punkah-wallah, a poor, thin boy of about sixteen, to light me down the hill. He lives in the town, and not wishing to drag him all the way back, I took the lamp from him at the city gate and gave him fourpence. He dropped down on his knees before me and laid his forehead on my feet.

April 6th

I HAD a letter from His Highness this morning, my first direct news of him for several days. It ran:

'D.F. (Dear Friend),—I am very much ashamed of my be-haviour really—but what could I do—my illness of the abscess —or boil what it may be termed—was so nasty this time that I couldn't do anything in the least. . . .

However, I am little better since yesterday—and if Almighty *wills*—I shall see you this afternoon anyhow and it will cover up all my shameful behaviour to you. I can't write more. Ta-ta till 4 o'clock.'

However, like the termination of his letter, he looked sprightly enough when he arrived, dressed in a new coat of French brocaded silk—small gold flowers upon a dark-blue ground. But I, on the other hand, was not feeling at all well, or inclined for this drive in the hot sun.

'How are you, Prince?' I asked gloomily, as I clambered into the car and sat down beside him.

'A *little* better. A *little* better,' he replied, without con-viction; and since I knew that he would never inquire after *my* state of health, I informed him of it.

'I'm not feeling at all well myself,' I said.

He clapped his hands together once.

'So!' he exclaimed bitterly. 'Here is another! Since Garha *every one* is ill. My secretary, my wife, my son, my servants—every one, every one. And they are all very angry with me. They say it is all my fault. They say I should have gone on my pilgrimage, and that I have angered the Gods. They are all very angry indeed.'

I felt too crushed by this to say anything, and after a few moments of sombre silence, he asked rather crossly:

'What is the matter with you?'

'Oh, nothing much,' I said hurriedly, sorry now that I had mentioned it; 'only a slight headache and general feeling of slackness. I dare say it's the heat.'

'But, my dear sir, this is not heat! Have you been to the doctor?'

'Oh no,' I said, 'I'm not bad enough for that. Besides, if it's the wrath of God it's not much use consulting a doctor, is it?'

But he was taking now, when it was no longer welcome, a serious interest in my health, and was not to be diverted.

'But you must do so, Mr. Ackerley.'

'Very well,' I said feebly. 'If I'm not better to-morrow I'll go and call on him.'

After that we drove along for some time in silence through the torrid atmosphere, and then he said he wanted my advice, and began a long rambling story about an American lady named Murdock who wishes to set up here a discreet dispensary for timid Indian ladies—too timid to visit the hospital where there is insufficient protection for the sensibilities of their sex and caste.

Nearly a year ago Miss Murdock introduced her philanthropic scheme to His Highness: she would build the dispensary with her own money if His Highness would give her a site; she would also procure the services of an American lady doctor to take charge. His Highness, always childishly pleased with any new idea, shared her enthusiasm without her practicalness.

He loves Miss Murdock. She shall have her dispensary. They will build at once. She must choose her site and secure the lady doctor without delay. She does so. There is an ideal site—the site of a demolished building—just outside the

walls of the city; it has a well of its own, and more important still, a natural gully at the back which, with very little
trouble, can be converted into a private passage down which
timid Indian ladies will be able to steal unperceived from
the city to the dispensary.

Miss Murdock thinks of everything. She has been thirty
years in the Province. She knows it stone by stone. But
apparently she does not know His Highness. He approves
the site; he expects it will be all right, but he must consult
with his ministers. He has the power to decide, but prefers
not to do so. No doubt he has already consulted with his
ministers and found them suspicious and unfavourable;
and no doubt he does not care whether there is a dispensary
for timid Indian ladies or not; but he loves Miss Murdock
and cannot bear to take the blame for disappointing her.
Others must shoulder that. His Ministers must shoulder
that. They do not like the idea of the dispensary. Undeniably it is necessary, undeniably it would be nice to have
one without paying for it, without taxing for it, without
reducing the labourers' wage from tuppence-ha'penny to
tuppence again—but they are suspicious of it; it is the thin
end of the wedge; a European dispensary for timid Indian
ladies invariably turns into a kindergarten, and a kindergarten into a mission-house.

But neither do the ministers want the blame for thwarting
Miss Murdock, so they call in public opinion. Public
opinion, they say, objects to a European dispensary inside
the city, so they regret Miss Murdock may not have the site
she has chosen, but she may have that one over there, about
five hundred yards further away, or indeed any other site
she wishes on or outside that radius.

But Miss Murdock wants the site she has chosen. Five
hundred yards make a considerable difference to her, and
that site over there has none of the natural advantages of
her site; it has no well, and no gully for timid Indian ladies
to creep along; also the amount of excavation and levelling
that would be needed to prepare it makes it impracticable.

Besides, she points out, her own site fulfils the requirements of public opinion, for it too is outside the city. But this is disputed. True, her site is outside the walls, but the walls are very old, and the city itself has spread outside them; her site is *not* outside the city.

A long and wearisome argument ensues, throughout which His Highness, by professing complete helplessness and pretending that her disappointment is also his, tries to preserve the friendship he so deeply values.

But in vain. The lady doctor, her grip packed, is waiting impatiently on the quay in America for her call, and Miss Murdock, vexed and irritable, has taken refuge in Rajgarh, where she stirs up against His Highness the displeasure of the British Cantonment.

'How does one make a decision? How does one make up one's mind?' sighed His Highness.

One doesn't. The business of the dispensary has been dragging on for months.

April 7th

I DID not feel any better this morning, so very early, before breakfast, I went down to find the doctor. He was sitting on the verandah of his house, smoking a hubble-bubble and contemplating the scenery, which comprised the back premises of his hospital and the back premises of a goat which was rooting about among the weeds and refuse of which his garden consisted.

'Very kind of you to come,' he said amiably, struggling out of an armchair which was rather too small for him and offering it to me.

'Yes, it's partly friendliness,' I said; 'but also because I want some castor-oil.'

'May I see your tongue?' he asked politely.

I protruded it. He gazed at it in silence, and then, returning the stem of his pipe to his mouth, fell to contemplating the scenery again in a thoughtful manner.

'Very dirty!' he remarked, eyeing the goat, which had given a little skip and drawn nearer. Then he stretched out a plump brown hand and felt my pulse.

'You must fast for two days,' he said, 'and then you must take only light things like milk pudding, vermicelli, and fish. You will be all right in a day or two.'

He bubbled for a moment into his pipe and then said:

'You are to leave us soon?'

'Yes, in about a month's time.'

'I am sorry. His Highness will be sorry. Have you enjoyed it here?'

'Oh yes, very much indeed. But I find it a little too warm for me now.'

'Of course, of course,' he said, 'I understand. And is it not a little lonely for you sometimes—up at the Guest House by yourself?'

'Yes, it is sometimes.'

'It is natural. We are not made to be alone. If there is anything that I can do for you, please to tell me. The society of girls, it is not difficult to arrange. . . . If you speak to your sweeper, she will find you some one.'

'Thank you, Doctor Sahib,' I said, 'but I can get along without.'

He nodded.

'His Highness says that you will come back again?'

'I hope so,' I said.

'Will you come alone?'

'Alone?'

'You should marry in England and bring out your wife to Chhokrapur with you.'

I smiled.

'If I come again,' I said, 'I shall come alone.'

'It is a pity,' he replied. 'For then you will not stay.'

With another little skip the goat mounted the steps of the verandah and entered the house.

'If you will come with me to the hospital,' said the doctor, 'I will give you some castor-oil.'

PART TWO

April 10*th*

WHEN I return from my early morning rides I find flowers on my dressing-table. Sometimes there is a single blossom of scented *chaman*; sometimes a handful of petals, usually jasmine, scattered upon the marble. I thought, for some time, that these gifts came from Narayan; but now I learn that they are from Hashim, the waiter.

Abdul has gone off to Deogarh for a day or two in search of a new job. He was afraid, he said, of what would happen to him after my departure, so wished to take measures for his defence while I was still here. After all, I had done nothing for him except make his life more difficult; but if I would now give him a certificate—a good certificate—to the district Commissioner, he might yet retrieve the fortunes I had jeopardised. Yes, I had done my best for him; he knew that; but nothing had come of my promises, nothing—three rupees! I had failed.

I gave him an excellent certificate, feeling that if it was going to rid me of Abdul praise could not be too extravagant, and told him it was the last work I would do on his behalf. Eventually a reply to his application came—a telegram telling him to present himself at once to the Deogarh Collector for examination.

His diplomacy was admirable at this point. After expressing his gratitude for the success of my certificate, he said that he could not however take the journey, for that would interrupt my studies with him. I said they would not suffer much by the interruption, and advised him to go. He consented—it would be only for a few days.

'Very well, Mr. Ackerley, I will go, since you wish it.'

But one other thing—he distrusted the wording of the telegram; it said nothing about 'expenses paid,' and his railway fare would be twelve rupees, which he could ill afford. Since Mr. Ackerley wished him to go and apply for the job . . .

I shook my head.

239

'Nothing more, Abdul.'

He received the refusal with perfect composure and left, exhorting me to study hard while he was away so that we should be able to make great progress when he returned. I watched his retreating figure, stiff, self-conscious, humourless, and knew that I had had my last lesson.

There is a golden mohur tree near the Guest House, and I sat on the verandah to-day looking at its beautiful cascading orange flowers. A mina bird perched on its branches, looking very inquisitorial and making a variety of inquisitorial noises. The mina is a kind of starling, and is said to be as intelligent as the parrot in learning to talk. Maybe it is; and its harsh voice is no less unpleasant to listen to. Bird noises are seldom pleasant, however. The peacock's voice is as ugly as his nature, but then he is beautiful to look at, so perhaps nothing more should be expected of him.

In a *neem* tree close by a family of doves was disputing, peevish and spiteful; and a tree-pie gurgled somewhere overhead, like an air-locked water-pipe. Then a bulbul, the Eastern song-thrush, arrived; but he did not contribute to the concert; he only turned up his tail at me to show me that his bottom was decorated with a tuft of red feathers, and then flew away.

April 14th

BABAJI RAO left Chhokrapur for two months' holiday yesterday, so I shall not see him again. He said he would give me a call for farewells at five o'clock this morning as he passed the foot of the Guest House hill on his way to Rajgarh; but as he had not come by half-past five I walked down to his house, fearing I had missed him. But he had not started. A fantastic green wooden coach, to which two lean horses were harnessed, was standing outside his gate; some tin trunks and a bundle in a blanket were stacked on the roof, and three children were clambering over it like monkeys.

Eight people were to travel in this, and a plank had been placed across the two benches inside to afford more seating room. I asked one of the children where Babaji Rao was, and a grubby hand pointed in the direction of the Palace; so I sat on the wall and waited. At a quarter to seven he came, carrying papers and smoothing his scant, disordered hair.

'How late you are!' I said.

'What could I do?' he replied. 'His Highness called me at four-thirty, but when I got there he had fallen asleep again and slept until six o'clock. When he had dictated some letters I came away.'

That was all he said, and without the least suggestion of impatience or reproach or any sign of bitterness.

'Will you catch your train?' I asked.

'I do not think so; but we must try.'

I said good-bye to him at once so as not to delay him further, and returned to the Guest House thinking what a kind, generous man he was and how sadly I should miss him.

Babaji Rao departing, Abdul returns, very brisk, very self-possessed, very punctilious. After perfunctory inquiries about my 'homework,' we turned to more important matters. His visit to Deogarh had been most unsatisfactory, the Collector had offered him the job at forty-five rupees—but only on a month's probation. Abdul had not trusted the Collector. He was a Hindoo. Moreover he had not refunded Abdul's train fare.

If only there were some one to write again to the Commissioner to put the case before him, to ask for protection for Abdul—and to request the refunding of his money. If only Mr. Ackerley would do this for him—the last request he would ever make—for consider the effect Mr. Ackerley's certificate had already had on the Commissioner.

'Very well, Abdul,' I said, 'get me some notepaper.'

He was quite astonished—astonished and delighted. Pen and paper were brought.

'By the way,' I said, as I signed it, 'I'm dismissing you to-day—this is our last lesson.'

He could scarcely believe his ears.

'What, Mr. Ackerley? No more lessons? But Mr. Ackerley, that is very bad. It cannot be. You will never learn to speak in this way, and you are much improved. Oh, my Lord! You are joking, I think. Is it not so?'

I shook my head.

'But why will you not go on with your lessons? What is the matter?'

I said the weather was too hot.

'Oh, my Lord! But what of your promises, Mr. Ackerley, that you will keep me with you till the last? Oh, my Lord! Do not forsake me also, gentleman, at this moment! Never mind, then, I will come without payment to teach you for nothing. Ah, Mr. Ackerley, do not send me away from you.'

There was a lot more of this; but I was firm.

'But I shall come to visit you, Mr. Ackerley?' he cried. 'I shall come to visit you—from time to time—when I wish?'

I wanted to refuse even this, but of course I hadn't the courage. So I said that he might come, but not too often, and never again with any hope of assistance from me. Then I made him a present of his railway fare to Deogarh, and with this and the letter he departed slightly consoled.

April 18th

HIS HIGHNESS told me the Hindoo's poetic conception of male beauty the other day as we drove out together. The hair, he said, should be like scorpions' stings; the nose like the parrot's beak; the eyebrows drawn bows meeting above it, and the eyes the eyes of a fawn. The cheeks should seem like looking-glasses; the chin a lemon; the teeth pomegranate seeds; the lips coral, and the ears mother-of-pearl. The neck should be like a shell; the arms like serpents; the torso like the leaf of the sacred *peepal* tree, and the thighs plantains. I had never noticed the leaf of the *peepal* tree, so he stopped the car and sent his grey-bearded cousin to pick one for me. It was a beautiful bright leaf, and His Highness illustrated with it the poet's fancy. From the stalk (the human neck) the edges of the leaf ran squarely out on either side (the shoulders) and then curved round and inwards to terminate in a finely-pointed tail, some two inches long (the waist), so that the suggestion was of a square, broad torso upon a very narrow waist, like the Minoan Vase-bearer. From the spine of the leaf, running from stalk to tip, the ribs curved out to join and form a fine tracery just within the outer edges, and from these ribs radiated a scarcely perceptible network of small and large veins.

On our way back, a bird flew across the road. His Highness called my attention to it, but I was too late to see it. He said it was a bird he had never seen before. 'Not that rare blue bird of yours?' I asked. No, this one was red.

'It flashes like a jewel!' he exclaimed. 'It must be the robin red-breast!'

Narayan says that he has no physical love for Sharma or for any man. This is wrong, he thinks.

But he kisses him sometimes in praise, as he beats him in blame. When Sharma does a good act Narayan kisses his hand, and when he makes a good speech Narayan kisses his cheek; but publicly, never in private.

'Not his mouth?' I asked.

'He eats meat,' said Narayan.

One night, he told me, when they were lying together on a *charpai*, Sharma whispered:

'Narayan! Narayan! Kiss me.'

Narayan pretended to be asleep. But Sharma knew he shammed, and touched him. Narayan would not respond to this either, so Sharma leant over him and kissed his hand. And in the morning Narayan said that he had dreamed that some one had kissed him on the hand. But Sharma would not believe in this 'dream'; he said Narayan had been awake all the time and knew it was he who had kissed him.

Laughing, Narayan had denied this and asked why Sharma had kissed his hand; and Sharma had replied:

'I got much love.'

'He love me very much . . . very much,' said Narayan, recounting this story. 'I say to him one day. "If I die, what you do?" and he say, "I die too. I have no father, no mother, no God, no friend, only you. You are my God, my friend and brother. What can I do but die too?" And then he say in English, "My darling Narayan." '

But Narayan's feelings for Sharma are not so simple, so honest, or so beautiful.

His affection towards him, I feel, is based chiefly on possession; he is proud of the influence he has over this wild, handsome creature, of Sharma's unquestioning, unswerving devotion and respect. Sharma never does anything without Narayan's consent; his eyes seldom leave his friend's face; he reflects, like a mirror, all his moods and variations.

Narayan is not unkind to him, but he is clearly indifferent to the handsome body and contemptuous of the childish mind, and treats him usually as if he were a slave or a hopelessly backward pupil.

'He is a fool,' he said to me one day, 'so I do not tell him anything.'

And once, I remember, he sent Sharma to bring him some iced water, which he received and drank without a word of thanks.

'He is my bearer,' he observed, with faint amusement, when Sharma had taken away the empty glass.

I was walking with Narayan while we were talking of these things, and a hideous Indian pig came foraging and grunting towards us.

'Pretty creature,' I remarked playfully.

'Pretty?' said Narayan, looking at me in perplexity.

'Very beautiful animal.'

244

'Dirty!' replied Narayan loftily; 'it eat shit.'

'So do you,' I said.

For a moment he didn't understand what I meant; then he was very cross. Did I consider, then, he demanded, that there was no difference between the excrement of a cow and the excrement of a man? After deep thought I conceded a slight difference, and then, laughing, put my arm round his shoulders. Later he began idly kicking along in front of him some dry cowdung, so I laid a restraining hand on his arm.

'Don't kick good food about,' I said; ' "Waste not, want not," you know.'

But I don't think he quite liked this form of jesting.

April 23rd

EVERY morning at about five o'clock or even earlier, before the sun has risen, I go out riding into the jungle. This used to be rather fun, exploring the wild country and meeting peacocks, jays and parrots, jackals and wild deer. It was an adventure to see for the first time the *chilla* tree with its silver bark and thick clusters of little round leaves, like pale-green coins; or the bare, leafless *dhak*, apparently dead, burgeoning suddenly into flame-like flowers. It seemed, then, a good morning's work to have traced a sweet smell to the tree or bush that emitted it; to have associated a strange bird-call with its author. I remember how pleased I was when I connected a loud, clear, sharp note with, to my surprise, the smallest bird I had ever seen, which was hopping about from twig to twig in the dim interior of a thick hedge. It was a dark-green bird with a black ring round its neck, a long thin beak, and a tail that stood up almost vertical. And how satisfied I was when His Highness, to whom I always recounted my adventures, told me that it was, of course, the sun-bird.

'Why the sun-bird, Prince?' I had asked.

'Because it eats nothing but sunbeams,' was the prompt reply.

245

But now I have explored all the country within range, and am tired of revisiting it alone. My companionless state, of which I am now so conscious, causes in me petty irritations with whatever points it—my stallion's behaviour when he meets a mare upon the road; the unwanted flies that swarm about my head and cannot be left behind, however fast I canter, when I return at seven. After about that time the sun becomes so dangerous that even the pith helmet is insufficient protection against it, and I do not leave the Guest House again until the evening.

And the dust! the dust! It lies, this ash of a burnt-out season, over everything; I am caked and clogged with it when I return. I remember it vividly in Delhi and how active the sweepers were. Whenever I went out sight-seeing they seemed to spring up from nowhere in my path to lay about them with their bundles of twigs, valiantly attacking the unconquerable dust, so that it rose up in blinding, choking clouds, only to settle back again, partly where it was, partly upon me. Did it have to be disturbed at all, this dreadful, ubiquitous, deep grey powder, I wondered? Would not the winds shift it, the rains rinse it, in God's good time?

At any rate, I did not welcome it in my always moist face, or on my alternative white duck suiting which had to last a week; it got there fast enough in any case without being driven and directed, as many of those sweepers seemed purposely to drive and direct it, upon me as I passed. Perhaps they were revenging themselves upon the world they might not enter, or merely disporting in their own element—wretched untouchables, dregs themselves, whirling among the dregs.

What does my friend, the Dewan, think of all that, I wonder, with his squeamishness about dirt and germs, his disgust with other people's mouths, his dread of sputum in the tea-cup, his repugnance to the kiss upon the lips. With all his shrill prejudices against European customs, how does he fare in his own land? Indians are great expectorators.

Hawked-up phlegm, streams of red betel-juice saliva, are shot about incessantly as they walk. It was one of the first things I noticed when I landed in Bombay, the patches everywhere of bright red spit. I thought it must be blood, until I was forced to the conclusion that, in that case, everyone was bleeding. And there the sweepers were in Delhi churning it about, whirling it all up in one's face, the dried sputum in the dust, anonymous coughings; one could not help but have it in one's nose, in one's mouth. Give me the unhygienic customs of Europe! Give me the loving-cup! Give me the kiss!

The horses they send me are drawn from the State cavalry. I have never seen this body functioning—though the Dewan is said to inspect it at his house every Sunday morning— but considering the condition of the more carefully selected ungelded mounts with which I am supplied, it cannot be a very fearsome company.

The army, which is termed 'irregular,' comprises also the Royal Guard and an emergency militia, which together are computed at five hundred strong in round figures; so I do not suppose the State cavalry could amount to more than a score of horse.

His Highness has the greatest contempt for his military forces.

'If there was a battle,' he remarked, 'they would all fled away.'

'Have you seen the barber's son to-day?' he asked me, as we drove out yesterday afternoon.

'No, not since the day before yesterday.'

'He is a fool-*buchcha*!' remarked His Highness.

'What is a "*buchcha*"?' I asked.

'Has your tutor not taught you that word? "*Buchcha*" is Hindi for "baby." I call Sharma my "fool-*buchcha*." He is always asking for things. He asks for too much from me. I do not like that. His last request is for a gramophone.

247

"Maharajah Sahib, I want a gramophone"—just like a
baby. So I teased him. I said, "Why must I give you a
gramophone? You will break it. You are quite uneducated.
You cannot read or write. You are a fool-*buchcha*!" '

His Highness began to shake with laughter.

'Last night I sent for him to come and talk with me, and
what message do you think he sent back? "I am only a baby,
a fool-baby. I am only five years old. I do not know how to
talk or reason. Let me sleep!" '

He chuckled over this for some time, and then asked:

'Have you seen Narayan?'

'Yes, Prince.'

'When? When?'

'Almost every day.'

'What does he talk about?'

I laughed.

'Nothing much. Neither of them talks very much. Sometimes they will sit with me for an hour with scarcely a word
passing. They aren't very lively companions.'

'Have you been to Narayan's house?' asked His Highness.

'Yes, he invited me there only the other day.'

'What was it like? Was there furniture?'

I became a little vague.

'Yes,' I said, 'I think there was some furniture.'

'What furniture? What furniture?'

'Oh, there was a *charpai*, and a bit of carpet, and a
chair. . . .'

'What kind of chair? Was it like a Guest House chair?'

'I hardly remember. Perhaps it was like a Guest House
chair. Why, Prince?'

'The matter is that Sharma asked me for furniture from
the Guest House and I gave him these things. Now I hear
they are in Narayan's house.'

'Well, if you gave them to Sharma, can't he do with
them as he likes?'

'But, my good sir, he told me they were for himself.'

'I see,' I said.

'I have sent two men to Narayan's house to see what he has got there,' His Highness remarked.

'I don't believe Narayan would do anything dishonest,' I said. 'I think you make a mistake in suspecting him.'

'But I have very bad reports of him—all the time. They say he makes his widow sister lie down with Sharma. Is it true? Has he told you?'

'Of course it isn't true,' I said irritably, and told him of the conversation I had had with Narayan on the day that I visited his house. 'Perhaps it would be a good thing if it were true,' I added.

'It would be very bad,' said His Highness severely.

'Well, it's not true, anyway,' I replied.

'But what must I believe? I do not know what to do.'

I said I had always understood that the usual procedure was to start by cutting out the informers' tongues; but he didn't seem to think much of this suggestion.

When I got back to the Guest House I heard a call from above and saw the grinning faces of Narayan and Sharma peeping down at me from the roof. The roof is flat and protected by a low wall; I sleep on it every night under the open sky, and often sit there in the evenings to get the benefit of whatever breezes may be about. I climbed the wide stone staircase now and joined the two boys, who were in high spirits, chewing betel and laughing over some private joke.

'Well, you've done it this time, you two,' I said, as I sat down between them. 'His Highness is very angry with you.'

As soon as I had said this I regretted it; immediate gloom descended upon them both. In a scared voice Narayan asked me what I meant, and when I told him he passed it on to Sharma. Then silence fell upon them, and I realised that I had let myself in for a depressing evening. At last Sharma suggested that he should go off and see what was happening, and this being approved, he departed, leaving Narayan sombrely brooding. I did my best to encourage him, but without success. Soon Sharma returned and reported that their worst fears were realised; His Highness's spies had visited the house; they had been admitted to Narayan's room by his father and had seen the Guest House furniture there. When he had told us this news he wept.

'He say he is very much frightened,' said Narayan sympathetically.

I took Sharma's hand. He murmured something in a tearful voice.

'He say he wishes to die,' interpreted Narayan.

I pressed the bony hand; it returned my pressure, and again the unhappy voice mourned.

'He say he wishes you to say some comfort,' said Narayan.

I asked how the furniture had got into Narayan's room, and learnt that it had been taken there the day before my visit for my benefit. They had been intending to restore it to Sharma's house ever since, but had foolishly delayed doing so. At this point Narayan also began to weep, though less noisily than Sharma, so I took his hand too and said there was really no need for all this fuss, for His Highness was not a tyrant or an ogre, he believed that the furniture had been falsely obtained, and if they told him how it had come to be in Narayan's house he would not be angry any more. But Narayan rejected this simple solution; he said that it was not really a matter of furniture at all; His Highness hated him and was always seeking some excuse for disparaging him because he was friendly with Sharma and with me.

It was the first time I had ever heard any one speak disrespectfully of His Highness, and I said that it was nonsense.

April 25th

NARAYAN has intercourse with his wife once every two or three nights. She is fourteen years old and he twenty, and they have been married and together for three years. During the first two years he went with her too much; frequently they had intercourse two or three times a day and he found this bad for his health. She was then nearing twelve and he was seventeen. He had had many affairs with other girls

PART TWO

before her, during his sixteenth year, and has had many since. She is not beautiful and he does not love her much.

He was sitting with me in my room in the late morning when he told me these things.

A dim green light filtered through the grass door-screen against which, from the outside, water was flung at short intervals, and the sweet smell of the grass pervaded the air. I said I should have thought it injurious for a girl to begin sexual practices at the age of eleven, but he disagreed. Girls were ripe for the marriage bed, he said, when they grew their breasts.

'But has a child of eleven breasts?' I asked.

'Yes. Little, little. So big. Like a lemon.'

'How old is Sharma's wife?'

'Twelve years.'

'And she has her breasts?'

'Yes. Like a lemon.'

'Does he lie down with her?'

'I do not know.'

'Do you not know?'

'I have not ask. If I ask, he get much shame.'

'Why should he get much shame?'

'I do not know.'

'How would he show his shame?'

'He would turn away his face.'

'Ah, Sharma!' I said, smiling. 'He is certainly a shameful boy.'

'He Maharajah Sahib's lover-boy,' Narayan said.

'Does he like that?' I asked.

'No, he does not like.'

'Then why does he do it?'

'I do not know. He is half-made.'

'You don't approve either, do you?'

'No, I do not like. It is bad, wrong. But what can I do?'

Swish went the water against the screen, swish, swish. I closed my eyes drowsily.

251

'*You* get much love Sharma one time,' said Narayan, after a pause, smiling at me.

'What did he tell you?' I asked.

'He tell me "The sahib try to kiss me".'

'And what did you say?'

'I say he must kiss you if you want.'

'If I have a tent put in my Palace courtyard,' His Highness said to me, 'will you leave your house and come and live there? I will give you servants just the same, and you will be quite comfortable.'

This was rather difficult.

'Should I be of more use to you there, Prince, than I am at present?'

'Yes, for if I think of any questions in the night I can come to see you.'

Poor little king. If the invitation had been issued earlier in my stay I would have accepted it eagerly, but now in this heat I was not at all sure that I wished to live in a tent and be wakened up throughout the night, like the late Poet Lockrit and Court Painter, to discuss Pragmatism and Marie Corelli; indeed I was pretty sure that I didn't. I already knew, from various sources, himself included, that he was a light and capricious sleeper, and roamed the Palace a good deal in the small hours as the fancy took him, and had sometimes been observed trying to make out the time on the recently installed sun-dial in the courtyard by the light of the moon. So I excused myself as well as I could. At any rate, it did not hurt his feelings, for: 'I will not leave you, Mr. Ackerley,' he said; 'I will not leave you now. How can I keep you with me? Will it be possible for you to come back every year for six months? I will pay your passage money and give you a thousand rupees a month. Will it be enough?'

In the evening I walked with Sharma down to the caravanserai outside the city gate, where Narayan had

arranged to meet us, and there we came upon the largest
bullock we had either of us ever seen, harnessed to a wagon.
It came from Deogarh, we learnt, and was worth one hundred and sixty rupees as against the normal price of fifty or
sixty; and yet it was not a perfect specimen, its owner said;
it was over-fat and stood too high on its legs. But how magnificent it was!

I gazed in wonder and admiration at the huge white
marble form and calm, majestic face. How peaceful were
the long drooping ears! How beautiful the line of the heavy
dewlap and the gentle jowls! Above the wide rounded forehead two short black incurving horns rose; and the large
dark glowing eyes set far apart were finely marked with
black as though their heavy lids were rimmed with soot.
Over each a double wrinkle lent to the great white face
a grave wisdom and benignity of expression. A cord ran
through the dark nostrils. No wonder, I thought, these beasts
are venerated, and the females thought to be the seat of the
Generator. I glanced at Sharma. His attention also was
absorbed in the brute, and I noticed the expression of awe
in his great silly eyes, and beneath his vest and *dhoti* the
fugitive lines of his animal body.

'Ah, my fine young bullocks!' I thought.

April 27th

THE poor frogs are in a parlous state this weather. Most of
the lakes—or tanks, as they are called—have almost completely dried up, and one sees the heads of myriads of frogs
protruding like pebbles from the black shallow water. The
din they make is incessant, for they have frequent and un-
welcome visits from the heron, which have only to stand in
the water to gobble up as many frogs as they like without
moving an inch. The mere drying up of the water does not
cause the frogs to perish, for they are able, like the fish, to
bury themselves in the mud and remain there until the
rains bring them liberty again; but many of them are young

and inexperienced, no doubt, and perceive their danger too late when they find their home unaccountably contracting. There was a heron among them as I watched, sprouting on his long thin legs from the centre of the puddle, which is all that is now left of what was once a pretty little lake. He looked surfeited and bored, and seemed deaf to the hubbub of despairing croaks around him. But suddenly he plunged in his beak and brought out a frog by its hind leg. I clapped my hands, hoping to startle him into dropping it, but he only flew off, carrying the frog with him.

'Well, I hope it is hot enough for you now, Prince,' I said to His Highness as we drove out yesterday afternoon.

'It is very hot,' he replied.

'Does it get much hotter?' I asked.

'My dear sir, it gets *very* much hotter. *Very* much! Soon I shall sleep in a house built of *khus* grass, and when in the early morning I have to go out to attend to natural needs'—there was an impressive pause—'I shall get quite *exhausted!*'

He was not at all pleased. His theatrical manager, he said, had reported to him yesterday that Napoleon the Third had leprosy. The boy had been playing with some gunpowder and had burnt his leg, and the theatrical manager, who examined the wound, was very concerned because (he said) water came out of it instead of blood or pus. This could only mean one thing: Napoleon the Third had leprosy.

Naturally this had upset His Highness very much and had caused him a sleepless night; but in the morning the doctor had said that it was all nonsense—there was no leprosy at all.

It was not the first time, muttered His Highness, that his theatrical manager had made this mistake; once before he had reported a case of leprosy among the Palace servants, but this had turned out to be a boil.

'He talks at random!' said His Highness peevishly.

He relapsed into silence after this, and then asked:

PART TWO

'What must I say to God when I meet Him? What shall I say to Him for my sins?'

'I shouldn't mention the word,' I said. 'He'll be the best judge of your life. If you've got to say anything I should say, "You sent us forth into the world incomplete and therefore weak. With my own life, in these circumstances, and according to my own nature, I did what I could to secure happiness. But I did not even know what happiness was, or where to look for it, and it was whilst I was in search of it that I dare say I got a little muddled." '

This seemed to encourage him considerably, and he made me repeat it to him twice, which I did, not without misgivings.

Abdul called on me at two o'clock a few days ago whilst I was having a siesta. A slip of paper was brought bearing his name and the request that I should spare him a little of my 'valuable time.' The word 'valuable' had been written in above the line as an afterthought.

When one wants an excuse for anger anything will serve; I was feeling limp and disagreeable, and the addition of the word 'valuable' filled me with annoyance. I told them to send him away, adding that he could return in the cool of the evening if he wanted to. I said it roughly. He didn't return that day; but this afternoon he called again and did not this time risk announcement. I was ploughing, with the aid of a dictionary, through a French novel, when suddenly he appeared at my sitting-room door, for it was slightly cooler and I had dispensed for once with my grass screen.

'Good afternoon, Mr. Ackerley. May I come in?'

I was too surprised to protest, and pointed to a chair.

'I do not come to talk about my affairs,' he assured me. 'I came the other day to visit you, but you sent me away, you refused me—but no matter—in a very bad way—but no matter. But—ahem—I do not wish to talk about myself.'

I did not wish to talk about him either, but needless to say, that was the subject we eventually arrived at—by a process of elimination of the rest of his family.

The main object of his visit, it appeared, was to make a small request—nothing to do with his own affairs—would I take a photo of his son? The little boy wished me to do so. He frequently spoke of 'the Sahib.'

I said I was awfully sorry but the camera had only been lent to me and had now been returned to its owner in Raj-garh. But I could borrow it again, he said, just to take a photo of his little son. I said I couldn't; I had reason to believe that the owner would not lend it to me a second time.

'Ah, sorry, sorry,' murmured Abdul, and concentrating his attention on the carpet, reconstructed his plans after this unexpected reverse.

'Mr. Ackerley, next week, in a few days' time, there is a great Mohammedan festival, and I carry an invitation from my *mother* to you to come to our house on that day, so that we may feast you.'

He looked at me with an engaging smile.

'Thank you,' I said. 'Please give my compliments to your mother and ask her to excuse me.'

He was amazed! He was shocked!

'But my *mother* invites you, Mr. Ackerley! You cannot refuse. In India that is very bad. She will be much disap-pointed, for she has set her heart on it.'

I shook my head. But how could he carry back such a message, he demanded. He could not do so. He could not bring himself to disappoint his mother. I *must* come—just for a little, for ten minutes, any time of the day. I need not eat much—only a sweetmeat or two. He would bring for me a horse, a carriage, at his own expense; indeed he had in-tended to do so. I must not refuse. And not only his mother, but his wife and his little son also. They all expected me. The little boy asked often after 'the Sahib,' and looked lovingly at 'the Sahib's' photo. I could not disappoint them all. . . .

I continued to shake my head.

'Do not ask. Do not ask.' I repeated. 'Never make your requests twice.'

'But, Mr. Ackerley, why will you never honour us or

256

grant my feasts? You are bad to me. You do not love me. But you must love me, for I love you and keep you always in my heart.'

'It's no use, Abdul,' I said. 'You never did love me.'

'By God I did and I do.'

'It isn't true.'

'Ah,' he said, 'you are English and do not know about love.'

After this he took up my French novel and began to read it aloud with an unintelligible pronunciation, and to examine me on my knowledge.

'Now go, Abdul,' I said.

He almost dropped the book.

'Go? Mr. Ackerley, what does this mean? You are very bad to me. You cannot speak in this way, "Go!" In India it is thought very bad. You say I may come to visit you, and I have not stayed for ten minutes when you tell me to go!'

'How much longer did you intend to stay?' I asked.

'As long as I wish,' he replied, with an insolent smile. 'It is for me.'

'You have said all you had to say.'

'But I have not. I wish to ask you if you will recommend me to the Political Agent—or any other man—trouble yourself—great benefit to me, and God will reward you, and I will remember you all my lifetime. . . .'

'Go! Go!' I cried angrily.

He moved hurriedly to the door, and from that strategic position, with his way of escape open behind him, inquired:

'Why must I go?'

'Because I say so.'

'But I may come again? You said I may visit you from time to time—every three or four days. . . .'

'Have yourself announced and I will send word.'

'Very well, Mr. Ackerley. And thank you—*very* much.'

He stiffened, and raising a hand to his tarbush jerked a little bow.

I swatted a persistent fly during breakfast this morning,

and it fell with a broken wing, and some internal rupture no doubt, and lay on the ground on its back, desperately moving its little black legs. I gazed down at it with something of an Indian conscience, or at any rate with that fearful fellow-feeling with which we are likely to regard even our worst enemy at the approach of the common foe.

Nearby, a colony of ants had its home, and there was a great coming and going round the entrance, where the colonists were taking in stores of the crumbs that had fallen from my table. Running hither and thither in their spas-modic spurting way, sometimes quite erratically it seemed, as though they relied upon some other sense than sight, they hurried off with their burdens into their mysterious underworld, the entrance to which was a narrow cleft be-tween the flagstones of my verandah pavement, or emerged, often as many as a dozen at a time, suddenly, like a puff of dark smoke, or as though shot up in a lift.

The fall of the wounded fly, almost into their midst, with a pretty deafening thud one would have thought, did not seem to discompose them in the least, and one or two of them, unburdened, passed and repassed quite close to it on their indefatigable journeyings without appearing even to notice it, though above their own small noises, scuffle and patter of ant feet, shrill of ant voices, it must surely have been kicking up the most infernal rumpus.

At length, however, a solitary ant approached the fallen giant, and was at once repelled by a convulsive movement of the struggling legs. But he was not deterred. With remark-able courage, I thought, he returned and, single-handed so to speak, leapt boldly upon the fly. A fearful battle ensued, the details of which I could not clearly see, but the ant seemed to fasten himself upon the fly's head, perhaps with the object of putting out its eyes. He was again repulsed and again returned to the assault, making for the same part of the fly's anatomy, and was then flung off so far—a dist-ance of quite two inches—that he apparently came to the conclusion that this was not a one-ant job and went off in search of help. Soon he returned (though I confess I could not swear the identification) with some comrades, and in a business-like manner they divided their small force, some climbing nimbly on to the fly, whose struggles, weakened no doubt by its recent exertions, were growing feebler and feebler, others crawling beneath it to loosen it from the paving stone to which its own blood was causing it to adhere. This done, a single member of the band began to drag the fly off by one wing—a notable feat of strength—while its legs continued to wave and twitch.

Looking down on this gruesome scene, I was suddenly back in the dawn of May 3rd, 1917, advancing under fire with my orderly against the German position in the village of Cérisy in France. It was twilight, and we were following our barrage up the slope of a hill, darting from shell-hole to shell-hole in short spurts as the curtain of fire lifted and moved forward. Resting in one of these shell-holes in this inferno with my orderly, of whom I was both proud and fond, I noticed a strange movement on the crepuscular skyline of the hill, some fifty yards ahead, and regarding it intently for some time, made it out to be the moving arms of a man, presumably a wounded German, who must be lying on his back. I could not see his body, only the arms, which rose high in the air and fell, rose and fell, in the most strange and desolate rhythm, like a man trying to keep warm in slow motion, or the last wing-beats of a dying bird—or the weak wavings of this fly's legs. Then I noticed that my orderly had left me and was rushing up the slope ahead. I was astonished and angry; his strict duty was at my side. I yelled at him, but he paid no heed—if, indeed, in that appalling racket, he ever heard. What on earth could he be doing? It was soon and shockingly evident. Quite careless, apparently, of danger, which, as he approached our barrage, became doubly grave, I saw him, silhouetted against the flashing explosions, reach and stoop over the wounded German, poke the muzzle of his rifle into the man's body and pull the trigger. The rising arms hovered for a moment, then finally fell. Even then I did not entirely twig, until my orderly came leisurely back to rejoin me, a smile of deep satisfaction on his handsome face, and held out to my inspection a German officer's revolver, field-glasses, wristwatch and cigarette case. He had murdered the wounded man in order to rob him. 'Souvenir!' he said, smiling at me.

When the ant had dragged the fly close to the entrance to its subterranean abode, other ants came forward to help carry it in. But the fly was too bulky for the narrow crevice, and after some attempts had been made to squeeze it through, it was rapidly dismembered outside, while it still lived, and carted down in sections to the underworld.

April 29th

I DO not know whether clothes are ever mended in Chhokrapur; at any rate European garments seem to be worn until, like the waistcoat of Babaji Rao's tonga-driver, they gradually disappear in decay. The court tailor, a lean man with steel spectacles, certainly has no experience of socks. Finding my own supply *in extremis* the other day I sent him four pairs to be mended, and it was quite a week before he brought them back, and laying them appropriately at my feet, murmured:

'Huzoor! It was very difficult.'

When I had inspected them I showed them to Babaji Rao, who was then still with us.

'What in the world does he think is the good of that?' I asked.

The holes in the socks had not been drawn together. Instead, with infinite care and patience, the finest cobweb of thread had been laid over them, so that when I pulled the socks over my hand the colour of my flesh was plainly visible.

'He says he has done his best,' interpreted Babaji Rao, 'and does not wish to be paid unless you are satisfied.'

'And if I *am* satisfied?'

'As much as you care to give. But your satisfaction is what he will value most.'

This was altogether too delicate, I thought, for the application of truth; I gave satisfaction and money, and left correction to my successors. And I now observe that such Chhokrapurians as wear socks and stockings do not have them mended. A hole merely serves to remind them that a new pair will soon be needed, and when the hole has so spread that most of the sole and heel are worn away, the new pair is purchased and put on under the old pair to prolong the former's life. Shoes, too, are never mended. The peasant wears a shoe peculiar to the Province, with an upturned toe and a large leather shield in front to protect him from snakes and scorpions when working in the fields; it is very cheap, and to mend it would cost far more, no doubt, than to buy another pair. But Narayan and Sharma, who are always shod though seldom hosed, would not wear such clogs, of course; they now favour an American shoe, obtainable in Bombay at sixteen shillings a pair, because it has a roomy toe for broad Indian feet. It is styled 'Derby,' and these two boys wear their 'Derbys' until they are absolute wreckage under their feet, and then they buy another pair.

Hindoos require no furniture; even the bed (the *charpai*) is only a luxury for the well-to-do, and can be dispensed with, and its place supplied with straw and a blanket. But chairs, and therefore tables, are rarely used in Chhokrapur, and then uneasily. When a man is tired of standing up he squats on his heels, like Habib in his portrait.

In this position he can remain for hours, and take his food or write his letters on the floor. It is very economic, and it seems a pity that Europeans have lost this simple use of their legs and burdened themselves instead with property

261

and the class distinctions of property—special seats for special bottoms. Clothes, no doubt, make a difference; but now that trousers are so much baggier, there seems no reason why we should not, with a little practice, reacquire the habit of dropping down upon our heels, which would be very useful when we are waiting in queues or are fatigued in the street; and in course of time, perhaps, we should gradually rid ourselves of much of the property which we now consider indispensable.

Narayan, when he comes to visit me, sits on a chair at my side, but it is never very long before he grows uncomfortable, and he always ends by drawing up his feet on to the seat of the chair. He did this this morning, and I noticed that a piece of common string was twined round each of his big toes.

'What is that for?' I asked, pointing.

'I have a pain in my testicle,' he said.

He explained that his father, who is a physician, had told him that this was a good remedy, since the testicles and the big toes were connected. Apropos of this, he remarked, after a pause:

'There was semen in your water this morning.'

'Was there indeed? And how do you know?'

'The sweeper, she show the pot to Hashim and me before she empty,' he replied gravely.

'I see,' I said. 'And what do you make of that?'

'They say here that you are a *sannyasi*.'

'What is that?'

'He is a man who give up all worldly things, everything, everything.'

'Well, I assure you I'm not,' I replied.

'I think yes,' he said.

No one would think, to look at them, that squirrels are sacred animals, but they are.

Krishna loved them, Narayan says, and used to take them from the trees into his arms and stroke them.

PART TWO

That is why they have four dark lines down their backs from head to tail; for Krishna, as the name implies, was very dark-skinned, and these are the marks of his fingers. His Highness, however, with whom I drove this afternoon, had never heard of this legend and appeared to discredit it. The squirrel was certainly sacred, he said, but because Hanuman, the Monkey-headed, once took on its guise when he went on a journey to rescue Rama's wife from the demon Ravana.

'Why has the bulbul got a red bottom?' I asked.

'They are *clerks*,' replied His Highness promptly. 'They are of the Kayastha or Clerk caste, who are all rogues, and so God cursed them in this way and gave them red bottoms so that all other birds poke fun at them.'

Narayan had never heard of this legend and appeared to discredit it.

It was recently full moon, and I used to go every night before sleeping to gaze at the Palace buildings from the Raj Ghat. The serene surface of the lake, still unappreciably diminished when the smaller tanks were drying up, reflected the short line of low white buildings on its opposite shore, with their domes, *chhatris* and minarets overhung by heavy-foliaged trees—but reflected it mistily, as though the sharp contrast between moonlight and shade above had run together in the water below. Everything was so peaceful and so still. The air was heavy with the sweet scent of the *sajna* trees around me, in the shadows of which cows lay placidly in the dust. Fireflies glimmered above them, frogs and crickets filled the night with small sounds, and only the great radiant moon gave light, overflowing and spilling upon the world. On the gleaming face of the water not a ripple moved to disturb that other city below its brink, hardly less real, it sometimes seemed to me, than the one above.

'Four days of moonlight—then darkness,' say the Hindoos, sadly contemplating life.

May 1*st*

'WHAT does it mean?' asked His Highness gloomily, throwing a long envelope on to my knees.

The letter I found inside was headed 'The Universal Astrological & Statistical Bureau of Indore,' and professed to be His Highness's health chart up to the end of his present (fifty-eighth) year, with forecasts up to the end of his sixty-first year. It was a remarkable document, illiterate and badly typed, in blue and red inks, on a special trade paper with advertisements down the margin.

'May it please your Gracious Highness . . .' it started, and then proceeded in a manner which was scarcely likely to do any such thing.

From the beginning of the Maharajah's fifty-eighth year he was to suffer a gradual decline in health and strength, which would continue unabated for some years and culminate, probably in death, at the end of his sixty-first year. At that time, observed the prognosticator, there would be such a 'choking up,' from one cause or another, of all his organs—heart, lungs, kidneys, liver, brain, etc.—as to render them functionless. Much might be done to postpone the fatal date by dieting, by propitiating evil spirits, and by keeping the system clear 'with the help of a perge or enema.'

But, said the writer, during his fifty-eighth year he need not alarm himself—which, since His Highness is already nearly fifty-nine, was small comfort to him.

During it he would be afflicted indeed with sundry minor ailments, such as slight fevers, coughs, colds, and boils; but these were only the first symptoms of the great decline; nothing grave would happen to him in his fifty-eighth year.

And so that he might know when to expect these boils and chills, the writer had approximately dated them, dividing up into periods of sickness and health the whole of His Highness's fifty-eighth year, from last August.

Thus he would ail between August 12th and September

PART TWO

27th; enjoy health between September 27th and October 9th; ail again between October 9th and November 6th, and so on. Most of the periods of health were short, I noticed—one comprising only four days; and by a rapid arithmetical calculation we discovered that he was condemned to sickness for eight months in the year.

'How much did you pay for this information?' I asked.

'Three hundred rupees (£20),' he said bitterly. 'And I had to pay it before they would send the letter. What does it all mean?'

I explained it to him. He had, of course, already read it numerous times and had underlined the word 'boils'; but he wanted to be comforted. So we went carefully through it and found that in only one case—the recent boil—could the writer be said to have hit the bull's-eye.

Of course His Highness would not admit to having enjoyed *really* good health at any time in his fifty-eighth year; but there had been little specific.

'What do they mean?' he exclaimed vexedly. 'In the last letter they sent me they said that I must have three months' serious illness in my fifty-eighth year, and I thought that that was this boil of mine I had just now—but it only lasted a fortnight. And now they make no mention of that illness at all! Also they said that if I recovered from my serious illness at the end of my sixty-first year, I should live on till my sixty-eighth or seventieth—but they make no mention of *that* here either! What does it mean?'

'It doesn't mean anything,' I said. 'It's just rubbish.'

'You are quite right,' he replied. 'They are all rogues—rogues and rascals!'

Narayan did not come to see me this morning because he had a *pooja*, a religious ceremony. His father had had trouble he said, and had prayed successfully for relief; he had therefore been obliged to hold a thanksgiving feast. It was the custom. Twenty-five Brahmans had attended, and the cost of the entertainment had been thirty-seven rupees.

He and Sharma walked with me in the evening, and on the whitewashed wall of a house we saw some figures roughly designed in wet cow-dung round the doorway. On the right side were two suns, on the left a very crude pea-cock, and above it a pattern of lines which, Narayan told me, represented a stool for the God to sit on. These designs meant, he said, that a child had just been born there, and any one seeing them would understand their glad import and keep clear of the house. I thought they were the work of unedu-cated peasants, but he said that the custom was quite general, and that if his own wife had a child these same designs would be scratched on the walls of his house. While we were looking at these things the barber who cuts my hair passed by. He smiled at me and salaamed, and then held out his hand towards me, palm down, with the fingers extended upwards. This was all done on the move.

'He asks after your health,' said Narayan.

So I nodded my head reassuringly. There were many other provincial signs, Narayan told me, used instead of speech when one was in a hurry or for some other reason did not wish to stop. He showed me some more—mostly obvious —while Sharma, finding this a huge joke, imitated him like a monkey. A cupped hand under the lower lip meant 'I am thirsty and going to drink'; joined finger-tips popped in and out of the mouth, 'I am hungry and going to eat'; the head rested against the right forearm, 'I am tired and going to bed.' To make imaginary rings with a finger round the right ear meant 'I am going to make water,' and there were also definite signals for 'Go on' and 'Come on,' but these were such slight movements of the hand that it is difficult to describe them.

We went on into His Highness's private garden to look at the trees and plants, and saw the lemon with its young fruit like small jade marbles, and the sweet lemon, the leaves of which smell so nice when crushed.

The *chandan* or sandalwood tree was there, from which is extracted the white paste used in so many religious ceremonies; and the *hari shringar* (God's adornment) with its small aromatic pink flower.

The *mahwa* tree has a large pale leaf, and a yellow flower and berry from which the peasants brew an intoxicating drink. Bears, too, are partial to its juice. They clamber up the tree after its flowers and, it is said, sometimes fall out of its branches completely sozzled—and perhaps it is whilst they are in this predicament that the manufacturers of the *Rajbansi* Pill take liberties with them. The banana, too, was there, but stunted and unproductive; and the pomegranate, most boring of fruits. The gardener presented me with two buds of double-jasmine—beautiful little things that looked more like exquisitely carved ivory than living flowers, and we argued for a little over the pretty, poisonous oleander. His Highness had once told me that there were only two true varieties of this shrub, one bearing pink and the other white blossoms. But the gardener showed me five varieties, including the two already familiar, and maintained that they were all true. Of the remaining three flowers, one was ruby, another yellow and bell-shaped, and the last like the English pink wild-rose. The leaves of all of them certainly had a very strong family resemblance; so eventually I sent him to His Highness with the five flowers, and a note to say that since the honourable gardener asserted that each of these blossoms was the true oleander, perhaps the best way of settling the dispute would be to feed him with them.

May 6th

At about eight o'clock last night, while I was sitting in a long chair in the dining-room reading a newspaper before climbing up to my bed on the roof, Abdul appeared in the doorway.

'Good evening, Mr. Ackerley. May I come in?'

'Why don't you have yourself announced in the proper way?'

'Ah, sorry, sorry: I did not know. Are you displeased with

me, Mr. Ackerley? I will know another time. I will not do it again. Please accept my apologies—for this time. May I come in now, Mr. Ackerley?'

'Yes, yes,' I said feebly. 'Come in.'

He stayed half an hour, and spoke throughout, with very little assistance from me, in subdued, mournful tones, his hands clasped in his lap, his eyes downcast, his head a little sideways, and his chin drawn in.

The entire interview was, no doubt, already planned in his head. I always had from him, on every occasion, this impression of previous rehearsal; point by point he had considered it and worked it out, arranging it so that all his requests were nicely graduated and all the transitions carefully oiled. Here and there in his monologue he broke off to make polite inquiry:

'Is that your newspaper you are holding, or are you engaged in important work? I do not want to bore upon your time. A newspaper? Then I shall remain a little longer and converse with you. Ahem. May I remain a little longer?'

And with such diplomatic interruptions breaking the sequence of his petitions neatly up, he brought every card he had into play.

The Deogarh Collector had written to say that the post was no longer vacant, so he was just as badly off as before, a poor struggling man, preyed upon by his enemies. He was now trying to get a job in Africa as a stationmaster. Then the requests began and, with the production of each, he looked full at me and sniggered, his lips tightly compressed. He looked very horrid, I thought, with the rag of a beard he had just begun to grow for his religious festival, and his squat tarbush, very greasy round the edge, pushed down to his ears.

Once more, he said, he wished to request me to honour his feast—it was to-morrow—even for only a few minutes. His mother had renewed her invitation. She had been rendered disconsolate by my former refusal, and begged me to reconsider my decision. Had I the heart to disappoint her? I said I had.

'Send along some food as you did before.'

'*Very* well, Mr. Ackerley. I shall send you some sweet-meats—very good sweetmeats.'

The head sank down again, with a faint smile on its lips, while he connected his next move.

'You know, Mr. Ackerley,' he tittered, 'I told my friends you had promised to honour my feast. I shall be much ashamed before them.' He paused expectantly. I had nothing to say. 'They will laugh at me—and mock me. What can I do? I was a fool. But how could I know you would refuse me?' There was another pause. Another silence. 'I also told to them that you were paying me twenty-five rupees a month—for your lessons.'

He watched alertly the effect of this.

'And why did you do that?' I asked.

'All Europeans pay so much for their lessons—thirty, forty, fifty rupees a month. Never less than twenty-five. Every man knows this. So I said *so*. I said you were paying me twenty-five, though you only paid me ten, for I was much ashamed before them. I was a fool!'

'You were indeed,' I said.

Again the spinster-like titter and the effect of sinking, of disappearance, of abrupt withdrawal down into his own mind to select and reappear with a new card up his sleeve, blandly, as though confident that no one could have missed him. It was like an elaborate conjuring trick.

'Oh, Mr. Ackerley—I have a request to make of you. Can you—will you be so kind as to grant me a little black polish? Only a small piece. I shall be very grateful.'

He fished a Nugget Boot Polish tin out of his pocket.

'Blacking?' I said, astonished. 'Whatever for?'

'For my shoes. To-morrow we must all have clean shoes for the festival, and I have no blacking in my house and cannot afford to buy some. But I only want very little. Just enough for one shoe.'

Concealing my amusement, I told him that Hashim would no doubt supply him with what he wanted.

'Thank you, Mr. Ackerley, thank you *very* much.'

The tin was restored to the pocket, and again, so to speak, he sank, but for so long this time that I felt that he must be played out, that he had got to the end of the suit, that nothing, except perhaps the ace, remained. Eventually he came up with it, and in spite of my dislike for him I could not help feeling a certain admiration for his perseverance. Having failed to get what he wanted by putting me under a new obligation or playing for my pity, he now asked for it direct.

'Mr. Ackerley, if I make a request will you grant it?'

'No.'

He sniggered.

'Oh! You will not? You say "No" before you have heard me speak.'

'I know quite well what you are going to say,' I said.

But he could not allow that.

'It is a very *simple* request—a request you are able to grant very easily, with no trouble or inconvenience to yourself. May I make my request and will you promise to grant it?'

'I think it's time you went,' I said.

'We have our festival to-morrow which I spoke of, and there is much expense—we have to buy food and sweetmeats and invite our friends to our house and—I am a poor man, Mr. Ackerley. Will you be so kind as to grant me a little money? You will do me the greatest service, and I shall thank you from my heart, and remember you all my lifetime and——'

'Good-bye, Abdul,' I said, 'I won't do anything more for you.'

'Ah, Mr. Ackerley, only three or four rupees—if you will be so kind—my family members . . .'

'Run along, Abdul.'

He got up without any sign of disappointment.

'Very well, Mr. Ackerley; I am going. At what time to-morrow may I bring my *gift*?'

'*Send* it,' I said.

'*Send* it? Not *bring* it?' His eyebrows went up.

'Yes, Abdul, *send* it.'

'Very well, Mr. Ackerley, I will *send* it. Good evening, Mr. Ackerley—and do not say a word to any other person of what we have been talking. You will not?'

'Oh, go away!' I cried angrily.

He fled.

I spoke to His Highness the other day about Narayan.

'Prince, I want to speak in honour of Narayan,' I said.

'Say what you wish.'

'You told me once in Garha that although he is the grandson of your old physician, whom you loved, you didn't know much about him—in fact, that you had never even looked him closely in the face.'

'It is quite true.'

'No doubt. Otherwise you wouldn't listen to discreditable stories about him.'

'Do you want me to give him more salary?'

'No, I want you to give him more respect'—and I went on to say all the nice things I could think of about Narayan, laying particular emphasis upon his loyalty. When I had finished he seemed rather pleased.

Later on, Narayan informed me that His Highness had called him and told him that I had spoken very highly of him, and because of this, and for no other reason, he himself was well disposed to Narayan, would examine him to verify the truth of my belief, and if he was satisfied, would give him employment in the Palace and a good salary.

So Narayan was to come to him for examination every third or fourth evening for a month, and they would converse together. Narayan had inquired, rather suspiciously perhaps, what sort of employment was meant, and had been told that the position he would get would be that once held by a greatly valued servant 'who did all works for me and on whom I very greatly depended.' Beyond that His Highness had not been disposed to commit himself.

271

'What did the Sahib say about me?' Narayan had asked.

'No need to tell,' replied the Maharajah. 'But you may be sure that no one could have spoken more highly of any man.'

So the interview had ended and (shades of Abdul!) produced uneasiness in at least three minds. Narayan himself was a little alarmed at this prospect of employment in the Palace, and neither his father nor Sharma felt quite comfortable about it. Both had recommended him to ask my advice.

'Go and ask the Sahib,' Sharma had said, 'and do whatever he tells you.'

Narayan's father had said:

'Go to your master and talk to him.'

That is what we were all doing here this evening while I had my dinner.

I offered Sharma a sweet, but he shook his head.

'Ask him why he won't take a sweet from me,' I said to Narayan.

'He say me "How can it be? I am an Indian and you are a European," ' interpreted Narayan, laughing.

'Does he know that *we* know that he eats and drinks all manner of sinful things in his house—such as eggs and invalid port?' I asked.

'Yes, he know.'

'Then tell him he is a fool-*buchcha* and I will not give him an ice!'

This produced consternation in Sharma; ices being permissible food and much appreciated; but we all looked very sternly at him, and even the grave, expressionless Hashim joined in the little joke, keeping back the third ice in the kitchen.

Sharma did not quite know what to make of it all; his nervous gaze darted from one face to another, and now he laughed and now he looked very serious, until our gravity broke down and he ran into the kitchen and got his ice himself. When they went I said I would walk with them, and getting a lantern from Hashim—for there was no moon—I strolled out with Sharma, leaving Narayan, who was talking to the cook, to follow. After a moment Sharma took the lantern from me, without a word, and carried it himself, on his far side so that it should not knock against me. His near hand was in his coat pocket. I put my arm through his.

Immediately he took his hand from his pocket, so that for a second I thought myself rebuffed; but instead he seized my hand in his and linked his fingers with mine.

May 8th

'How is Napoleon the Third, Prince? I hope he has quite got over his leprosy?'

'Yes, yes, he is better. But now he has had his *choti* cut off by mistake, and he is quite in-inconsolable.'

'Poor Napoleon!' I said. 'And what is his *choti?*'

'Do you not know?' His Highness shook with husky laughter. 'It is *pigtail!* What is pigtail?'

It appeared that Napoleon had taken a sudden fancy for a European hair-cut, so the court barber was sent for and the operation performed. Naturally his little tail of hair had been snipped off; but Napoleon had not intended this to go, and realising too late what had happened, had burst into lamentations, saying that they had shamed him, they had turned him into a Mohammedan and what would his people say?

'We have all tried to comfort him,' said His Highness, between gasps, 'but he will not speak to any of us. He is very angry indeed.'

'Five days!' said Narayan sadly, as we all three sat on the verandah yesterday evening. Sharma, who was sitting on the other side of me catching fireflies and watching them glow on his dark palm, understood both these words and, suddenly apprehensive, asked Narayan what he meant.

'The Sahib is going away in five days.'

Sharma's face at once took on an expression of the deepest despair. I told him that that did not mean that we should never meet again, and that meanwhile I would send him picture postcards of Piccadilly; but he refused to be comforted; he turned his face away and gazed, with ominously bright eyes, over the dark countryside, responding neither to my smiles nor to the pressure of my hand in his.

'He got much sorrow,' explained Narayan.

They both wept together all the way back to the city; but this morning, when Narayan told me this, the sky was serene again, and each presented me with a jasmine blossom from the garden of Dilkhusha or Heart's Ease.

His Highness said this evening that it was a pity I was not staying on through the rainy season, for the country looked very beautiful during the rains, though he was afraid, for some reason or other, that they were going to be particularly heavy this year, as bad, perhaps, as they had been some years ago, when the rivers had overflowed and flooded the whole countryside. It had been a terrible time, he said; the rains had gone on and on, far beyond their normal period, as though they were never going to stop, and there was much panic, for the people thought it was a judgment upon them and offered sacrifice to Indra, the God of Rain.

His Highness began to shake with suppressed amusement.

At that time, he said, there had been a boy in Chhokrapur named Dhama who came to him one day and told him that he had had a vision. He had dreamed, he said, that if a pair of baskets were attached to the shoulders of a certain other boy named Kanaya, and he were thrown up into the air, he would be enabled to fly to Indra and petition him to turn off his devastating rain.

Dhama, as His Highness very well knew, was always teasing Kanaya, for they were both sons of rival jewellers; but Dhama told his vision so convincingly that Kanaya was immediately sent for and baskets were fastened to his shoulders without loss of time.

These baskets, said His Highness, were shaped rather like elephant's ears and used for sifting grain.

Rather surprised at these proceedings, Kanaya asked for an explanation, and His Highness, amused and excited, informed him that he was going to be sent to heaven, and that when he got there he must find Indra and beg him to stop the rain. And no sooner were the baskets attached than Kanaya was bundled out into the Palace courtyard by Dhama and four or five servants. There, in the pouring rain, he was firmly grasped by the legs and ankles, raised from the ground, and with the impetus of half a dozen preliminary swings, flung high into the air.

'Fly! fly!' cried Dhama, as he heaved.

'Fly! fly!' cried every one.

But Kanaya didn't. He fell, instead, on to his head, and was severely bruised, much to the surprise of the spectators —and to their subsequent delight when Dhama confessed that he had never had a vision at all. His Highness rocked and choked with laughter.

'I expected to see him go up! up! up!—but he fell down on his head! Such a bang!'

The car trickled on over the dusty roads through the shifting, blinding haze, and His Highness said that to-day he was going to take leave of me at the Palace, and the car would then convey me back to the Guest House.

'If I give you land,' he cried, 'will you come with all your family and live here?'

I said at once that I thought it might be arranged, knowing that immediate acquiescence was the most effective way of quenching his singular enthusiasms; and, indeed, it was in a far less eager voice that he asked:

'How much land will you want?'

I gazed out over the stony, unmanageable jungle.

'Just enough to sit on,' I said.

275

He nodded pensively. We reached the Palace at last. Under the pink porch the armed guard, in a dilapidated khaki uniform, with puttees but no boots or socks, was dozing with his back against one of the pillars. Some servants were gossiping on the steps. Through the doorway at the top the hindquarters of the sacred cow protruded.

'Honk!' said the car.

The servants scrambled to their feet and bowed their foreheads to the ground; the guard, his turban over his nose, started upright and executed a shaky presentation of arms; the tail of the sacred cow twitched to and fro.

The car stopped; His Highness descended; leaning on the shoulder of his grey-bearded cousin, he climbed stiffly up the steps, and pushing the cow to one side, disappeared into the Palace.